Baked Products

Baked Products:
Science, Technology and Practice

Stanley P. Cauvain and Linda S. Young

BakeTran, High Wycombe, Bucks, UK

Blackwell
Publishing

© 2006 by Stanley P. Cauvain and Linda S. Young

Blackwell Publishing editorial offices:
Blackwell Publishing Ltd, 9600 Garsington Road, Oxford OX4 2DQ, UK
  Tel: +44 (0)1865 776868
Blackwell Publishing Professional, 2121 State Avenue, Ames, Iowa 50014-8300, USA
  Tel: +1 515 292 0140
Blackwell Publishing Asia Pty Ltd, 550 Swanston Street, Carlton, Victoria 3053, Australia
  Tel: +61 (0)3 8359 1011

First published 2006 by Blackwell Publishing Ltd

ISBN-10: 1-4051-2702-3
ISBN-13: 978-1-4051-2702-8

Library of Congress Cataloging-in-Publication Data

Cauvain, Stanley P.
  Baked products : science, technology and practice / Stanley P. Cauvain and Linda S. Young.
    P. cm.
  Includes bibliographical references and index.
  ISBN-13: 978-1-4051-2702-8 (hardback : alk. paper)
  ISBN-10: 1-4051-2702-3 (hardback : alk. paper)   1. Baked products.   I. Young, Linda S.   II. Title.
  TX552.15.C375   2006
  664'.752–dc22
2006004707

A catalogue record for this title is available from the British Library

Set in 10/13 pt Palatino
by SNP Best-set Typesetter Ltd., Hong Kong
Printed and bound in India
by Replika Press Pvt Ltd

The publisher's policy is to use permanent paper from mills that operate a sustainable forestry policy, and which has been manufactured from pulp processed using acid-free and elementary chlorine-free practices. Furthermore, the publisher ensures that the text paper and cover board used have met acceptable environmental accreditation standards.

For further information on Blackwell Publishing, visit our website:
www.blackwellpublishing.com

We dedicate this book to the memory of our parents
Stanley W. and Theresa P. Cauvain
and
John H. and Doris L. Hughes
and in doing so recognise the importance of their support and encouragement
during our formative years.

Contents

Preface

From the start, we recognised that writing one book to cover the world of baked products was an impossible task; there are so many types of products and variants that to cover all the necessary details would require the production of an encyclopaedia. There are many books and papers that cover the details of the various groups of baked products so why produce another one?

Between us we have spent over 65 years working in and with the baking industry on its technology and production processes. During that time our research experiences alerted us to the value for individual companies and the baking industry as a whole of having the body of baking knowledge assembled in appropriate forms. In some cases the most appropriate form is the written word while in others computer-based solutions can be more relevant. Whatever the final form, gathering and systemising the available knowledge is the first and most critical step in the process.

When studying baking technology, one is immediately struck by the complexity and detail that separate the various sub-groups that comprise the world of bakery products; inevitably 'knowledge products' have to address that level of complexity and detail. In all cases, a knowledge of ingredients, recipes, processing methods and equipment is essential to the successful manufacture of products. While appreciating the complexity that characterises bakery products, it is also the case that there are scientific and technical issues which cross the boundaries between the sub-groups.

The need for detailed scientific and technical information in the development of new bakery products is obvious. However, the rules that are used by the developer tend to be product-based rather than technology-based and it was such observations that provided the impetus for this book. One objective was to deal with the common themes that link the various sub-groups of bakery products, as a means of identifying ways of developing new products and processes. This requires thinking 'outside of the boxes' in which we classically put bakery products. In doing so, some of the low-level detail for many individual products is not discussed in this work; to get that detail we recommend that readers access some of the texts suggested in the Further Reading section.

In attempting this work, we have tried to challenge some of the conventional approaches used in discussing the manufacture of baked products. In doing so we do not wish to denigrate the approaches and work of many individuals who have attempted to discuss this complex subject; we do so more in the spirit of research, to see if, by taking an alternative approach, we can add to the knowledge base that can be applied to the manufacture of baked products. We hope that we have done so and that the approach we have used sparks the creative talents of those working in the baking industry and so bring future benefits to manufacturers and consumers.

Chapter 1

Current Approaches to the Classification of Bakery Products

Introduction

The term 'baked products' is applied to a wide range of food products, including breads, cakes, pastries, cookies and crackers and many other products, and it can be difficult to identify a common thread linking the members of such a diverse group. The most commonly-identified link is that they all use recipes that are based on wheat flour. This definition, though, would need to be expanded to include baked goods such as gluten-free products, used by people with coeliac digestive disorders, or rye bread, which are still considered to be baked products even though they are based on cereals other than wheat. However, the same leniency of definition could hardly be extended to include meringues, which contain no cereal-based material at all, let alone wheat flour, their main components being sugar and egg white. It may be more appropriate to consider that baked products are those products which are manufactured in a bakery, that is the place of manufacture defines the product rather than some ingredient, recipe or process feature.

One view is that baked products should be defined as having undergone heat processing – baking – which causes changes in both form and structure. This is certainly true for the many different base products manufactured in bakeries. Some exceptions to this definition might include Chinese steamed breads, some steamed puddings and doughnuts, which are fried, though all of these products do undergo a heat-conversion process. By using the presence of a heat-processing step to characterise bakery goods we can capture some composite products, such as fruit and meat pies, since the fillings in such products do undergo physical and chemical changes as the result of the input of heat. Not captured in the heat-processed definition of those products made in bakeries would be the fillings and toppings that are applied or used after baking. In this category will fall creams and icings, even though they will become part of the product offered in the shop or store.

The weakness of defining baked products as being those which have undergone a heat-processing step is that the same definition could be applied to any form of cooked product. Physical and chemical structures in all food are changed through heating, albeit in many cases adversely. In many people's minds there is no distinction between the 'baking' of bread and the 'cooking' of bread, though bakers would be loath to accept that bread is 'cooked'. If we are to characterise or define baked products then it will have to be using a composite definition, perhaps something like:

> *Baked products* are foods manufactured from recipes largely based on or containing significant quantities of wheat or other cereal flours which are blended with other ingredients, are formed into distinctive shapes and undergo a heat-processing step which involves the removal of moisture in an oven located in a bakery.

These thoughts illustrate the problems of defining baked products and also show the arbitrariness of the definitions that are commonly applied to the concepts of both a bakery and baked products. They also suggest that, to some extent, definitions of baked products are of limited value since they all involve arbitrary judgments and so will be subject to individual interpretation. The arbitrary nature of these judgements also affects published works on bakery products, and this book will be no exception. However, our aim is to offer alternative ways of defining bakery products and to suggest new rulesets for controlling particular product characteristics. In doing so, we hope to encourage new ways of looking at baking, which will provide a basis for innovation, new product development, quality optimisation and problem solving. We do not propose that we have all of the answers to the questions which may be posed by the reader; we can only provide you with the stimulus and some of the means to improve existing products and develop new ones.

Historical background to the manufacture of baked products

Baked products have a long history of production, though the moment in time when humans first learnt how to bake with cereal grains to improve their palatability and digestibility is not known. A flat, unleavened bread is most likely to have been the first baked product developed in the ancient Middle East, the accepted home of domesticated cereal-grain production. It is likely that the flat breads of antiquity were similar to those made by traditional means in the Middle East to this day. Baking would have been a craft practised in most, if not all, households following its discovery. No doubt not all early bread production was based on wheat, with barley being a common ingredient, even in the peasant breads of the Middle Ages in Europe.

It is said that the Babylonians passed on the art of baking to the ancient Egyptians who in turn developed the first organised bakeries, that is, they made baking a specialist occupation. A painted panel of Rameses III at Thebes, dated c. 1200–1175 BC, depicts the court bakery making breads of different types (Pomeranz and Shellenberger, 1971). It also shows the manufacture of cakes in different forms, including some baked in moulds or pans and others which were fried in hot oil. In many cases the moulds or pans used to manufacture the breads and cakes took the shape of animals (some sacred to the Egyptians) and this suggests that the products were used in religious ceremonies or ritual feasting. No doubt the consumption of elaborate forms of breads, and certainly the more expensive cakes, was mainly restricted to the higher social classes, with bread consumption in the lower classes being confined to coarse, flat breads.

The ceremonial functions of bread are recorded in many ancient texts. Fermentation and its role in bread aeration were known about at this time. The ancient Hebrews distinguished between the leavened and unleavened forms of bread. Even today the unleavened bread is reserved for certain ceremonial occasions. Bread quickly took its place in the psyche of humankind in the ancient world, and the technology spread rapidly wherever wheat and other cereal grains could be grown. Later, as wheat and other grains began to be imported and exported around the ancient world, the art of baking either spread with the grain or was discovered in different locations. No doubt three thousand years ago bakers were developing their own distinctive style of bread based on their cultural beliefs or just for the simple reason of wanting to be different from their competitors.

References to bread and baking begin to appear in Greek literature from the seventh century BC. Wheat became so important that at one time its export from Greece was prohibited, and bread was such a staple and important food that its weight and price were fixed in law. The place of wheat and bread in religion remained pivotal and the Greeks built temples to the goddess Demeter, who has remained associated with agriculture since those ancient times.

The importance of bread was not lost on successive Roman emperors either, and the goddess Ceres was high on the list of important gods. So important was the provision of bread to the Romans, that it is considered that much of the expansion of their empire was driven by the need to acquire control of more wheat-growing areas to feed her armies and growing homeland population. Indeed, it is claimed by some that the Roman invasion of the British Isles was mostly about acquiring control of the large wheat and barley growing areas that existed at that time.

The status of the baker began to change during the years of the Roman Empire. It became a profession for men, and baking acquired a respectable and significant status as a trade. During this period the first guilds, or trade unions, of bakers began to form, reflecting the respectable nature of the trade. Government interference with the trade of baking was never far away. This was because of the political importance of bread and its use to manipulate popular opinion (popularised in the saying 'bread and circuses' when applied to pleasing the masses). Control was ever present, with the weights of bread and its price being fixed on many occasions. Free bread was the Roman form of alms and if the Emperor could not provide everyone with bread he soon lost the Imperial Crown, if not his life!

While the manufacture of bread may largely have disappeared from the historical records of the so-called Dark Ages it certainly still persisted. There are occasional references to baking activities. For example, in England a legend has it that an Anglo-Saxon king, Alfred, burnt the cakes while thinking about the forthcoming struggle with the Vikings for control of England. Whether true or not such stories continue to reinforce the crucial position that bread and baking had in people's minds. Control of the baking industry was ever present throughout history. In the UK, the Assize of Bread was introduced in 1226 to control weight and price, and remained in force for 450 years.

In the Middle Ages baking was well established as a profession throughout Europe and many of today's bread forms were developed. The basis of some of the change and development was the use of sifting to remove branny materials from the ground meal. White flour was used to make products for the richer elements of society with wholemeal and coarse, mixed grain breads being reserved for the lower orders. The diversification of baked products which accelerated in the medieval period in Europe gave us the basis of our modern cakes and pastries. The association with whiteness, purity and status, was a significant theme throughout history and persists today, even though health gurus would now encourage people to eat the 'peasant' breads of history.

The availability, weight and price of bread remain important political issues right up to the present day, and bread remains firmly in place in our psyche. We refer to bread as the 'staff of life', bread as a staple food, the 'breadwinner' of the household and, in common parlance, the term 'bread' is equated with money. Bread still retains its religious significance today with expressions such as 'breaking bread together' and the ceremonies of the Christian religion – for example, 'Give us this day our daily bread'.

Traditional basis for classifying bread and fermented goods, cakes, pastries and biscuits

Given that baking has such a long history and so many traditions associated with it, how have the various groups of baked products come to be defined? Unlike botany or zoology there has never been an attempt to develop a specific taxonomy of baked products. In part this may be because of the long, local traditions associated with the manufacture of baked products and therefore the difficulties associated with translation from one tongue to another of the terms and descriptors used for the products and their associated baking processes.

To some extent, this nomenclature problem has persisted to the present day. For example, in English the term 'biscuit' is commonly used for describing a low moisture, hard-eating, sweetened, thin product with a long shelf-life, that is eaten as a snack. In the USA, however, it commonly refers to a sweetened product of intermediate moisture, commonly eaten at breakfast along with savoury foods. The UK biscuit is closer to the US cookie while the US biscuit is closer to a UK scone. To increase the confusion, the French *biskuit* refers to a low-moisture, dry-eating, long-shelf-life, sponge-type cake with an aerated structure. The closest UK product to the French *biskuit* is indeed a sponge cake, though with higher moisture content.

We cannot blame differences in language and culture entirely, though, for the lack of a baking taxonomy – after all the same problems must have arisen (and probably still exist today) in botany and zoology. However, scientists involved in such subjects did eventually agree a common taxonomy (largely) and a common descriptive language (Latin). One wonders whether the long traditions and more emotive nature of baking have prevented such a development. After all, get a handful of bakers together in a room and they seldom agree on anything to do with baked products. Despite (or because of) its long history, baking still has strong and deep roots in the craft and still struggles to develop its scientific credibility. Until it truly graduates to being a science a common taxonomy remains impossible.

Common English dictionary definitions for groups of baked products include:

- Bread – *n.* food made of flour or meal (and) baked
- Cake – *n.* baked, sweetened bread
- Biscuit – *n.* dry, small, thin variety of cake
- Pastry – *n.* article of food made chiefly of flour, fat and water

All of the above definitions illustrate the difficulties associated with defining the various groups of baked products. These difficulties are further compounded by other imprecise definitions, such as the phrase 'fine bakery wares', which was applied to the display of cakes and pastries illustrated in Figure 1.1. This term has become more universally accepted and used in recent years but remains a relatively uncharacterised grouping.

Why should we be so concerned with baked product groupings and definitions? In one sense we do not need to be concerned at all. We can simply continue to live with the current amorphous lists and texts that exist. Redefining baked-product groupings will not change their existing character and, if a new baked product is developed, does it really matter what it is called or into which category it is placed? The practical answer for many people is clearly 'No!'

While baked-product nomenclature or groupings in themselves do not matter, we cannot take the same *laissez-faire* attitude towards product definitions or groupings when it comes to understanding and using the underpinning science itself. This is because product definitions and groupings become more important in the development of the rulesets which determine the final quality of a baked product and, in turn, its acceptance by consumers. The same rulesets are needed in order to ensure that consistent product quality is achieved and to provide the basis for correcting product deficiencies. Thus, developing the appropriate underpinning scientific knowledge of the raw

Figure 1.1   Display of 'fine bakery wares'.

materials used, the recipe construction and the processing technology applied are all crucial activities in the manufacture of baked products. This requires a systematic approach to knowledge gathering, the structures used to store the information and the methods by which it is applied to the different aspects of baked-product manufacture.

A key factor in the purchase of a particular baked product by consumers is the consistency of the product. Since all baked products are based on natural raw materials, however, there will be variations which inevitably occur in the raw-material inputs. This is especially true for the most common raw material – wheat flour – since environmental and agronomic conditions can have a profound impact on the quality of the grain. This in turn will lead to some quality variation in the flour, despite the best efforts of the flour miller to blend wheat varieties to give a uniform and consistent product quality.

Part of the challenge that faces millers and bakers is that no flour specification or analytical technique captures all of the essential end-performance information that is required. This is not because we do not have suitable testing methods, but because even after much study we simply do not completely understand what determines flour performance in baking. The development of quality rulesets is thus very important for ensuring product consistency and troubleshooting when things go wrong.

The traditional baked products with which we are all familiar have a long history of development through trial and error rather than systematic study. The origins of many baked products can be assigned to the error category. Indeed, the discovery of leavened bread has been ascribed to the error of leaving dough overnight before baking, and the discovery of laminated pastry to the apprentice who forgot to add fat to the bread dough and tried to recover the situation by folding the missing ingredient into the dough after mixing (though there can be no absolute proof of either story). More recently, systematic studies have been applied to the development of new baked products but most commonly the rulesets applied have tended to be limited and confined by the traditional definition of baked products.

The constraining nature of baked-product groupings can best be illustrated by asking the question: 'In UK terminology, what is the difference between a cake and a sponge?' There will be many answers based on:

- Size (weight and specific volume)
- Shape (sponges tend to be round while cakes assume many shapes – but what about the Swiss roll?)
- Recipe (sponges tend to have lower fat levels – but what about a Victoria sponge?)

- Processing methods (sponges tend to be aerated by whisking and cakes tend to be beaten with a paddle – but with continuous mixing is there a difference?)
- Cell structure (sponges tend to be more open and cellular in structure while cakes have less obvious cellular structure and a denser character)
- Eating qualities (sponges tend to be drier-eating while many cakes are considered moist-eating)
- Organoleptic shelf-life

However, one could argue that popular differences are based purely on the artificial constraints that we have imposed on them using traditional terms and definitions. Further one could argue that by constraining our thinking with traditional rulesets we have created barriers to innovation and the development of new baked products.

The concept of recipe balance in the development of baked products

An illustration of how conventional thinking may constrain baked-product development can be given based on the development of a knowledge-based computer program known as *BALANCE* (Young *et al.*, 1998). The program was part of a suite of programs comprising a *Cake Expert System* (Campden & Chorleywood Food Research Association [CCFRA], undated). The development of the *BALANCE* module in the *Cake Expert System* was based on the premise that it was possible to identify a series of technological rules which could be used to define particular types of cakes and sponges and to identify the limits which might be applicable to the ratios of ingredients used in the recipe. The rules that were available, though derived from the systematic study of the effects of changing ingredient ratios by a number of workers (e.g. Devlin, 1954), were largely empirical in nature and based on traditional forms of a limited range of cake types. The most common cakes studied were the round sponge cake, the round Madeira-type cake and the loaf-shaped, unit cake commonly baked in a bread pan.

In the 1950s and 1960s the quality of ingredients available for the manufacture of cake products changed, so that along with chlorine treatment of flours intended for cake making it became possible to manufacture what have become known as 'high-ratio' cakes, that is cakes in which the weights of sugar and liquid (largely the sum of water, egg and milk) individually exceed the weight of the flour used in the recipe. If the levels of sugar and liquids are lower than that of the flour then the products are commonly considered as low ratio and the use of treated flour was not essential. A comparison of the same form of high- and low-ratio cakes is illustrated in Figure 1.2.

There are two important points to be made here. First, it is common to express baker's recipes on the basis of the flour weight used in the recipe. Further, it has become common practice to develop bakery-product recipes based on 100 parts of flour, expressed in various units, such as kilograms, grams, pounds or ounces. This method was developed by bakers so that the functional effects of ingredients in a given recipe could be readily identified. For example, for a given high-ratio cake the sugar level should be between 105 and 135 parts of flour because, if lower, the cake volume will be restricted and, if higher, collapse of the structure may occur. Such a 'rule' is developed based on the fact that the level of sugar in the recipe (or the sucrose concentration) has a direct impact on the temperature at which starch will gelatinise and thus, in turn, the setting of the structure of the cake.

Second, chlorine treatment of flour is no longer permitted in the UK and many other countries of the world. It has been replaced by the treatment of flour with heat. The heat-treatment process largely confers the same technological benefits as chlorine treatment, but without the

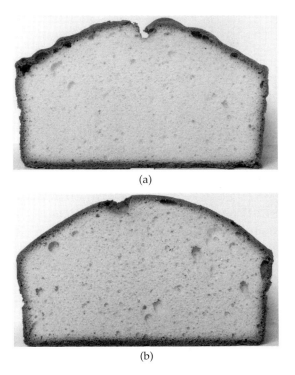

(a)

(b)

Figure 1.2 Comparison of (a) high- and (b) low-ratio slab cakes.

bleaching effect (though this was never a significant reason for chlorine treatment).

Following the development in the USA of the high-ratio cake, and its subsequent introduction into the UK in the 1950s, new rules for cake-recipe balance were evolved. This evolution can be followed in a number of (sadly now unavailable) ingredient-company publications (Thomas Headley & Co. Ltd., undated) and relevant textbooks (Street, 1991). Similar, though perhaps less elaborate, rules have been developed for other baked products.

In the development of the *BALANCE* program, the acceptable ranges for a number of different cake ingredients, with respect to flour weight, could be defined. The initial approach taken had been to break the recipes down according to whether they were cakes and sponges and to define the recipes as high- or low-ratio. A further sub-division, based on a shape and/or size criterion, was proposed. This represented a conventional way to define the world of cakes. However, closer scrutiny suggested that a division based on high- or low-ratio was not required since the rules which would be applied would differentiate between the product types and define the type of flour required without having to be specified by the user.

The subsequent approach suggested defining rulesets on the basis of whether products were:

- A cake or a sponge
- Plain (based on whole egg), white (using egg white only), chocolate (containing cocoa solids) and fruited (containing fruit or particulate materials)
- Baked as a unit (loaf-shaped), slab, layer, cup, Swiss roll, sandwich (round) or drop (small flat shape, often baked directly on the oven sole)

The above classifications allowed for a theoretical $2 \times 4 \times 7 = 56$ recipe combinations. However, when it came to defining the individual rulesets that would be required for each of the 56 combinations it was clear that quite a number did not exist in a completeness that would be required with the knowledge-based system.

In some cases there was doubt as to whether it was possible to make particular combinations. To some extent this view was formed because of the traditional classification of products. For example, sponge cakes were commonly associated with the shape/size classifications Swiss roll, sandwich and drop yet there appeared to be no practical reason why some sponge recipes could not be baked in other shapes, for example loaf-shaped or large slab. A few simple experiments showed that a number of combinations initially thought not to be possible in fact were possible. This led to the realisation that new rulesets could be defined by populating them with information derived from the more conventional views of sponge and cake making.

In the development of the *Cake Expert System*, some 1200 experiments were performed to study the quality impacts of changing the levels of the major ingredients used in the manufacture of sponges and cakes. The changes in external and internal features were recorded. These photographic records were then combined with the rulesets which had been evolved so that in *BALANCE* it was possible to show the user the likely consequences of increasing or decreasing a range of ingredients in a given recipe by comparison with a standard or control product.

The combination of image and knowledge base presented new opportunities for product development, since it was possible to visualise changes in key physical properties of individual products and to link those features with a particular recipe structure. The use of the *BALANCE* module did not restrict recipe formulation to a limited range of products; rather it allowed users to concentrate on developing particular features in new products without having to worry about remembering all of the rules by which recipes were structured. And, most importantly, it provided a rapid and inexpensive way to try out ideas before undertaking the more expensive and time-consuming test baking for new product development.

Reconsidering the basis for baked-product classification

As stated earlier, one of the purposes of the approaches that will be taken to considering the family of baked products is to provide the opportunity for greater innovation using underpinning knowledge of how baked products are characterised. In Chapter 2 we will consider in more detail the influence of ingredients and recipe variation on the final quality of baked products, along with the factors that link and separate the various categories of baked goods. However, at this time we would like to introduce briefly a concept of characterising baked products which has been around for some time but has yet to be fully exploited for innovation.

In Figure 1.3 the positions of examples of baked products are plotted using a 2-dimensional diagram in which the two axes are based on the ratio of sugar to flour in the recipe (X axis) and the ratio of fat to flour in the recipe (Y axis).

The world of bakery products does not consist of discretely-defined groups clearly separated from one another by rigid rules. In fact many successful new products are successful because they break the conventional rulesets that have evolved to define particular product areas. In

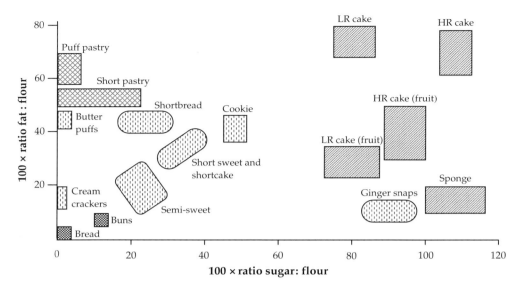

Figure 1.3 A two-dimensional representation of bakery products based on ratios of sugar and fat to flour in the recipe.

view of the lack of clearly-defined boundaries between groups of bakery products there is a strong argument for viewing the world of bakery products as one continuous spectrum, with one product merging into another.

This view invokes comparison with the world of colour, where the boundaries between particular colours with defined wavelengths are most certainly blurred by the intermediate wavelengths. Two-dimensional colour models based on wavelength and three-dimensional models exist to define the colour space. In the case of the three-dimensional model, the shifts from one defined colour segment to the next are very small. An analogy for the bakery world is to consider each of the colour segments as representing a particular bakery product and in doing so the close relationship between products may be observed (the coloured segments are illustrated as shades of grey in Figure 1.4). However, three dimensions are inadequate to represent the differences and similarities between bakery products, and so better means of visualising how bakery products are related or differ are required. One possible way is through the use of the spider diagram, so often used in sensory science (Jones, 1994). An example is given for selected parameters based on a subjective scoring system for each of the five identified parameters (Fig. 1.5). The properties used could readily be augmented or replaced with objectively measured data.

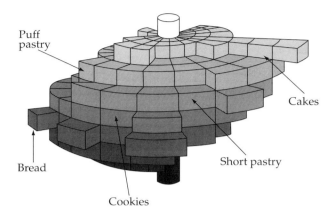

Figure 1.4 Diagrammatic representation of the relationship between bakery products based on the colour solid.

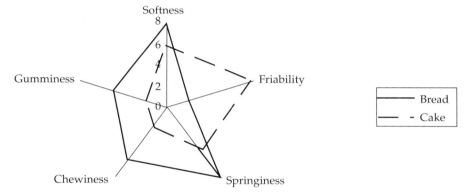

Figure 1.5 A visual representation of key characteristics for bread and cake based on spider or radar plots.

These few examples illustrate that by being able more readily to visualise relationships between bakery products and groups of bakery products it may be possible to identify new product and process opportunities. A further benefit of this approach will be the improved capability to optimise the quality of existing and new products. In order to gain best value from such visualisations it is important that a sound and extensive knowledge base is available on which to base innovation. In the next few chapters this knowledge base will be explored and provided.

Chapter 2

Key Characteristics of Existing Bakery-Product Groups and Typical Variations within Such Groups

What makes baked products different from other processed foods?

Those involved in the manufacture of any processed food will always make the same claim: namely that their particular food is unique and that special rules, which make their own food sector different from all other food sectors, apply. It is true that in defining any processed food there will be factors that are unique to that particular sector and are not shared to any significant degree by other manufactured foods. However, there may be one factor which characterises all processed food: the raw materials used undergo some changes in physical and/or chemical form as they make the transition to a processed food. Usually, the key step in the process is some form of heat process – boiling, frying, roasting, steaming or baking.

The fundamental nature of the heat-induced changes can be appreciated by considering the processing of potatoes. As a raw material, potatoes can be eaten raw, though their palatability is considerably improved by some form of heat processing. In this respect baking, boiling or roasting potatoes may be compared to the conversion of raw dough to a baked product. The dough could be eaten raw, though its lack of palatability would be evident and would contrast greatly with the vastly improved palatability of the baked product. A similar discussion could be applied to the preparation of baked products such as biscuit dough, sweet and savoury pastes and batters, all of which undergo major changes in palatability during baking.

Clearly, the presence of a heat-setting process is not unique to baked products but applies to many other raw materials that are included in processed foods. The difference between baked products and other processed foods may then lie with the definition of the 'raw material'. In the example of potatoes discussed above, the raw and processed forms can remain very similar. The same cannot be said for the manufacture of bread and other baked products. This is because the basic raw material in these cases is wheat or wheat flour. In the case of wheat, the flour-milling process is required to provide wheat flour, which is the starting point of most bakery processes, and the wheat flour itself needs further conversion to a dough/paste/batter before it becomes a 'raw material' for the heat-setting process – baking.

With baked products, again unlike the potato, wheat flour has to have another raw material added to it before baking. The other ingredients combined with wheat flour in the baked products recipe impart considerable changes to the functionality of wheat flour. For example, while the addition of sugar to bread, cake and biscuit recipes provides sweetness, the functionality that the sugar imparts to structure formation is an equally important aspect of its use in baking. The multifunctional properties of sugar include the restriction of available water and therefore the reduction in the gluten-forming potential of wheat proteins and the modification of the gelatinisation properties of wheat starch, both during and after baking. While there may be interactions between ingredients used in other processed foods, few tend to be as complex or comprehensive as the ingredient interactions which characterise bakery products.

An introduction to the methods used to characterise baked products

Take any baked product and you will observe that it has a number of different textural and sensory attributes. Even the matrix of a loaf of bread is not as homogenous as it first appears. Starting from the outside, we would see a light- to dark-brown surface which, when fresh, is hard to the touch and has a dry and crisp eating character. The inside of the loaf, however, has a sharply-contrasting appearance. It is white or light brown (depending on whether white, brown or wholemeal flour has been used in its preparation) and has an expanded and cellular structure. By comparison with the crust, the crumb is soft to the touch and may well spring back after compressive forces are removed. The sensory properties in the mouth will be dominated by softness and chewiness. The degree of variation depends very much on the bread recipe and the process employed, especially in the dough making, but there will almost always be a contrast between the surface and interior properties of the loaf. A range of texture and sensory variations is also experienced when base cakes, pastries and biscuits are examined. When the base product is combined with other foods, for example as in a jam- and cream-filled sponge cake with a sugar-icing topping, the contrast of textures and sensory sensations is greatly enlarged.

The assessment of the characteristics of all baked products (and indeed most food) starts with the visual observation of physical appearance, then aroma/odour, texture, mouth-feel and flavour. In making any subjective assessment of baked-product character, individuals are primarily affected by their cultural background, which is then modified in the light of their personal experiences and preferences. None of the influences on product quality remain unchanging, so that overall assessment of product quality by an individual will change with time. The impact of aging of the product on the assessment of product quality has been discussed in detail elsewhere (Man and Jones, 1994).

It is inevitable that the subjective judgment of product quality begins with its exterior – after all we see the product, touch and smell it before it finally reaches our mouths. As the saying goes 'The first bite of a baked product is with the eyes.' This has become very important to baked products and has contributed considerably to the variation that one sees with products that are nominally the same. For example, changing the size, shape or surface cutting on breads can distinguish a particular baker's product from that of the competition, and if associated with particular pleasurable sensory experiences will considerably enhance the prospect of repeat purchases by consumers.

While the ultimate assessment of baked-product quality lies with the consumer, in the manufacture and optimisation of existing baked products and the development of new ones, objective assessment of particular product characters is important. This is not to say that subjective sensory evaluations should not be carried out, but one of the problems of relying on sensory characterisation lies with the difficulties of calibrating the individual assessment or panel. There have been numerous attempts to make sensory assessment of foods more objective and readers are referred elsewhere for detailed discussions of this topic (Kilcast, 2004).

Assessing baked-product quality starts with a consideration of the external features and moves to the internal features. The main features that are likely to be considered are listed in Table 2.1.

As will be discussed in later chapters, there are many factors contributing to variation in baked-product qualities. Some of the main ones may be summarised as follows:

- Size
  - Dough or batter piece weight
  - Product volume

Table 2.1   Main features considered in making an evaluation of baked-product qualities.

	External	Internal
Size	Y	N
Shape	Y	N
Crust character	Y	N
Colour	Y	Y
Crumb cellular structure	N	Y
Softness	N	Y
Mouth-feel	Y	Y
Taste	Y	Y
Aroma	Y	Y

- Shape
  - Moulding, shaping, forming or depositing
  - Using pans, trays or processing as a free-standing item
- External colour
  - Ingredients and their qualities
  - Formulation, ingredient ratios
  - Baking and other processing technologies
- Crust character
  - Baking temperatures, times and control of oven atmosphere, e.g. the use of steam or oven damper
- Crumb cellular structure
  - Ingredient qualities
  - Formulation, ingredient ratios
  - Mixing and other processing technologies
  - Heat transfer during baking
- Internal colour
  - Ingredient qualities
  - Formulation, ingredient ratios
  - Crumb cellular structure
- Crumb softness
  - Final product moisture content
  - Ingredient qualities
  - Formulation, ingredient ratios
  - Crumb cellular structure
  - Baking temperatures, times and control of oven atmosphere
  - Post-baking treatment, for example packaging and staling
- Mouth-feel
  - Moisture
  - Crumb cellular structure

- ○ Formulation, ingredient ratios
- ○ Post-baking treatment
- • Taste
  - ○ Specialist processing, such as prolonged fermentation of bread dough
  - ○ Ingredient qualities
  - ○ Formulation, ingredient ratios
  - ○ Crumb cellular structure
  - ○ Baking temperatures, times and control of oven atmosphere
  - ○ Post-baking treatment
- • Aroma
  - ○ Specialist processing
  - ○ Ingredient qualities
  - ○ Formulation, ingredient ratios
  - ○ Crumb cellular structure
  - ○ Baking temperatures and times
  - ○ Post-baking treatment

Methods for evaluating the character of baked products

Brief descriptions of methods that might be used in the evaluation of baked products, with some appropriate references, are given below.

Subjective scoring sheets

This approach goes beyond the simple recording of product attributes and tries to provide a framework for making more objective comparisons of baked-product qualities. Among the main problems with subjective evaluations are the inevitable variations in scoring between individuals and drift with time for any given individual. Thus, in order to make effective use of scoring sheets it is necessary to have trained individuals making the assessment. It is also helpful to have some fixed reference points that any assessor may use. These usually comprise templates of size or shape, photographs (especially for internal appearance), colour prints or 'chips' and standard descriptors. Examples of scoring sheets for bread, cake and pastry are given in Figures 2.1 to 2.3.

Measurement of size

In many cases it is possible to carry out a simple measurement of product dimensions with an appropriately graduated rule. The most useful measure for fermented products and cakes baked in pans tends

External	Score		Quality descriptors
	Number	Descriptor	
Volume score (10)			A. Small B. Large
Average volume, cc			
Specific volume, cc/g			
Uniformity of shape (10)			A. Lack of boldness B. Uneven top C. Shrunken sides D. Low side E. Low middle F. Flat top G. Small end
Crust characteristic (10)			A. Light B. Dark C. Uneven D. Dull E. Thick F. Tough G. Brittle
Break and shred (10)			A. Wild B. None C. Shelled D. Insufficient
Subtotal 40			
Internal			
Cell structure (20)			A. Open coarse B. Thick cell walls C. Holes D. Non-uniform
Crumb colour (10)			A. Dull grey B. Creamy
Crumb strength (10)			A. Tough B. Weak
Texture (10)			A. Rough B. Core C. Crumbly D. Firm E. Gummy
Flavour and aroma (10)			A. Satisfactory B. Unsatisfactory
Subtotal 60			
Total score 100			

Numbers in brackets refer to proportion of score for the characteristic being assessed

Figure 2.1 Bread quality score sheet.

to be height. This follows because of the physical constraining effect of the pan. The pan has fixed dimensions and so any variation of dough or batter expansion mostly occurs upwards (provided the baking dough or batter does not overflow the sides of the pans before they are set in the oven). Thus, variations in dough gas retention and batter expansion, which are both directly related to product volume, can be assessed quickly in terms of height.

External	Score		Quality descriptors
	Number	Descriptor	
Volume score (20)			A. Small B. Large
Average volume, cc			
Specific volume, cc/g			
Uniformity of shape (10)			A. Uneven top B. Shrunken sides C. Low side D. Low middle F. Sunken top
Crust characteristic (10)			A. Light B. Dark C. Uneven D. Dull E. Thick
Subtotal 40			
Internal			
Cell structure (20)			A. Open coarse B. Thick cell walls C. Holes D. Non-uniform
Crumb colour (10)			A. Dull grey B. Dark C. Streaks/cores
Crumb strength (10)			A. Tough B. Weak
Texture (10)			A. Rough B. Streaks/cores C. Crumbly D. Firm E. Gummy
Flavour and aroma (10)			A. Satisfactory B. Unsatisfactory
Subtotal 60			
Total score 100			

Numbers in brackets refer to proportion of score for the characteristic being assessed

Figure 2.2   Cake quality score sheet.

Many pan breads and cakes have a domed shape after baking, that is the highest point is in the approximate middle of the product and the ends of the product are lower. It is usually desirable that the overall shape should be uniform. A more realistic assessment of product height would therefore be to take the measurement at selected points along the (usually longitudinal) product cross-section – typically 2–4 measurements would be used. If the product dome is not uniform then multiple height measurements become more valuable as they can provide useful ingredient- and process-related information.

Dimensional data can be obtained from individual slices, using image-analysis systems such as C-Cell (Calibre Control International, Warrington, UK). Measurements include slice height, width and area.

External	Score		Quality descriptors
	Number	Descriptor	
Volume/lift score (10)			A. Low B. High
Height/thickness (mm)			
Uniformity of shape/lift (10)			A. Irregular B. Sunken
Crust characteristic (10)			A. Pale B. Dark C. Uneven
Surface appearance (10)			A. Blistered
Subtotal 40			
Internal			
Cell structure (20) (laminated pastry)			A. Open coarse B. Thick cell walls C. Non-uniform
Texture (20)			A. Fragile B. Pasty C. Gummy
Flavour and aroma (20)			A. Satisfactory B. Unsatisfactory
Subtotal 60			
Total score 100			

Numbers in brackets refer to proportion of score for the characteristic being assessed

Figure 2.3 Pastry quality score sheet.

Estimates of the degree of concavity associated with a slice may also be obtained (Whitworth *et al.*, 2005). C-Cell may be used for measuring the external dimensions of bread, fermented products and cake slices. Its use for the assessment of crumb structure is discussed below.

In the case of pastries, biscuits, cookies and other free-standing products, height data may be supplemented using length and width data. Product eccentricity may be calculated by comparing product dimensions with those of the cutter which may have been used in the product preparation.

Measurement of volume and density

The measurement of product volume provides valuable information about product quality and is an invaluable tool with which to make comparisons of ingredient and process effects. Unfortunately, baked products cannot be measured by the basic method of liquid displacement so we have to use other modifications on the displacement principle. The most commonly encountered method for measuring product volume is using seed displacement (Street, 1991). In this case seeds, usually rape or canola seeds or pearled barley, take the place of a liquid. The process is quite straightforward. A box of known volume will be filled with seed and the weight of seed required to just fill the box is noted. The sample is introduced and the seed poured back into the box. The volume of seed displaced is equal to the volume of the product. The more seed that is displaced the larger the product volume.

More recently, an instrument has come onto the market which uses a laser sensor to measure product volume (TexVol instruments, BVM-L series, www.Texvol.com) (Fig. 2.4). This technique has specific advantages over the traditional seed-displacement techniques, such as no compression of the sample, but provides the same information on product volume.

Figure 2.4   TexVol instrument for volume measurement. Reproduced with permission of TexVol Instruments AB, Viken, Sweden.

After volume data have been obtained it is common practice to consider product density. This is simply described as the mass of the product divided by its volume, $d = m/v$. An alternative form of expressing such information is as specific volume (SV) which is simply the reciprocal of density, that is sample volume divided by sample mass, $SV = v/m$. Both density and SV terms are encountered in discussions of baked-product quality, the lower the product density, the higher its specific volume and vice versa.

Measurement of colour

Product colour may be determined using comparisons with standard colour charts, such as the Munsell chip system (Munsell, undated), or by using Tristimulus colorimeters (Anderson, 1995). Such techniques for the measurement of crust colour are relatively straightforward, since the surface texture of a loaf or roll has only a limited impact on the measurement. The basic concept for Tristimulus readings is to be able to express a given colour using three attributes: one comes from a scale of 0–100 that represents black to white; one covers red to green hues; the third covers yellow to blue. In baking, our interests lie mainly in the red-yellow part of the colour spectrum for **crust colour**.

Crumb colour on the other hand presents a greater problem. The cellular structure of the product will have a direct impact on the measurements because of the shadows which are cast by the individual cells. The Tristimulus colorimeters are able to provide a reading on the intrinsic colour of the crumb. For crumb colour we will be mostly interested in the yellow to white regions of the colour spectrum.

The measurement of **crumb brightness** is of particular importance, because, in the case of white-flour products, the brightness of the product crumb is one of the factors which consumers use to make their judgement of product quality. In the case of Tristimulus data, this would be covered by concepts such as the Y and Whiteness Index values. Crumb brightness may be measured using C-Cell (Calibre Control International, Warrington, UK) and is directly related to the perception of sample brightness as perceived by human observers. In addition to the measurement of slice brightness, C-Cell provides data on the contrast between the shadow cast by the cells and the brightness of the cell-wall material. Both measurements provide useful data on how consumers will view crumb quality.

Texture properties

Measurements of product texture properties fall into two broad groups: sensory and mechanical. The latter category includes compression testing, Texture Profile Analysis (TPA) and crispness testing. One of the most common methods used by consumers to make an assessment of product quality is the 'squeeze test'. This is particularly the case with wrapped bread. They do this to try and get an impression of the freshness of the product. On the store shelf the bread is most often cold, but consumers have learned that fresh bread is easy to squeeze and will spring back to its original shape when the compressing force is removed. A similar test method is applied by experts when they assess bread texture. You will see them gently compress the surface of the loaf with their finger tips and watch the spring-back of the crumb (Fig. 2.5). This is a classic example of a sensory test of the subjective kind because the methodology used and the interpretation of the results depend on the individual carrying out the test.

It should be recognised that sensory science is not an exact science and the data provided in many cases are only indicators and not guarantees of commercial success. Sensory tests can also be an expensive business, because of the large numbers of people and time involved in such activities. It is not surprising, therefore, that objective instrumental methods for the routine testing of product softness and texture have been developed. It is important that appropriate and strong links are

Figure 2.5 Compression of bread crumb.

established between objective and sensory tests so that results from one type of testing may be related to other forms of testing.

The use of sensory, or taste, panels provides a disciplined approach to subjective texture analysis. Sensory panels may be untrained or trained in sensory science. In the case of the latter, assessments are carried out by individuals who have received training to help them deliver greater objectivity in the context of the texture or taste questions which need to be answered. Commonly, sensory panels are called upon to identify differences between samples with different formulations or to evaluate changes in product quality. It should be noted that sensory analysis need not be confined to the testing or eating of products – appearance can also be assessed in this way. The subject of sensory science is too extensive to be covered in this book and so readers are referred elsewhere for more detailed information (Kilcast, 2004).

Many of the tests which are used to assess product softness or texture are designed to mimic the approach that consumers and experts use and so commonly use some form of controlled compression of the sample. Various forms of compressimeter have been evolved over the years (Bourne, 1990), but all operate using similar features and provide similar data. There are two main ways in which tests are carried out: one is based on compressing the whole slice and the other on compressing a core taken from the product.

A typical compression test will either subject the product to a standard force applied for a fixed time or compress the sample through a given distance and measure the force required to achieve a given percentage thickness compression (Cauvain, 2004a). Both techniques provide useful information on the softness of the sample. Resilience data or sample springiness can be determined by removing the compressing force and measuring the degree to which the sample recovers, usually after a fixed time. To some degree, the ability of the sample to recover depends on the level of compressing force that was first applied. The greater the compressing force the less likely the sample is to show significant resilience.

A wide range of tests can be designed to provide texture information on baked products. The form of the test depends on the information being sought and can encompass composite bakery products. For example, a puncture method may be used to evaluate the crispness of apple pie pastry (Fig. 2.6). A needle-shaped probe is driven at a fixed speed through the lid pastry, filling and base pastry in one continuous movement and the forces encountered recorded. This technique has been used to follow the migration of moisture from the apple filling to the base pastry during the storage of apple pies (Cauvain, 1991) and to

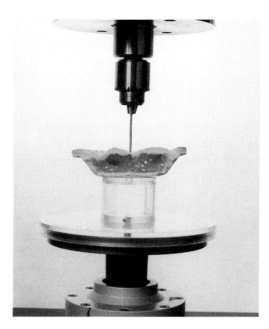

Figure 2.6   Puncture testing of composite apple pies.

evaluate the effects of stabilisers added to the filling to restrict this moisture migration.

It is important to recognise that the sample moisture content and density will have an effect on both the perception of softness and its objective measurement. Since both vary between samples, test comparisons between different products are best made on a basis of standardised moisture content. It is fair to say that this does not reflect the situation that will be observed by consumers who perceive breads and cakes of different moisture content as being different, even if they were made on the same day. They will also tend to assess products with different densities as being different, even if they have the same moisture content. In general terms, consumers perceive bread and cake products with higher moisture contents and lower densities as being fresher, provided that they also show the required resilience.

The value of being able to correct sample data for differences in moisture content and density is that the underlying contributions, positive or negative, of ingredient, recipe or process changes can be identified. A knowledge of which changes make positive contributions to the textural properties of baked products is invaluable for countering the negative impacts. One of the ways correction for sample moisture and density may be made involves sub-sampling a whole product slice. One technique for this involves the removal of a cylindrical core from a bread or cake slice (Cauvain, 1991). The location of the core is fixed relative to the product base, since the density and moisture content will vary according to the location of the core in the slice cross-section. However, the exact location may be varied depending on the type of product being assessed (but not between test samples). The core has fixed dimension (radius and height) so that a simple weighing can be used to obtain the sample density (from density = mass/volume) and the moisture content of the sample can be measured (see below).

Measurement of cellular structure

The cellular structure of the crumb of the product may be assessed by eye or by using objective image analysis. A more detailed description of the techniques that may be used and their importance in understanding the nature of baked-product structure is given in Chapter 5.

Measurement of moisture content

The techniques most commonly used to assess moisture content are based on driving off water with heat (Cauvain and Young, 2000). Relatively little equipment is required: an oven fitted with fan and thermostat, a desiccator to hold the samples, some lidded sample pans and an accurate balance. Sample moisture is based on the loss of weight that occurs when a known weight of sample is heated. Standard methods are readily available (AACC, 1995; ICC, 1995). Oven-drying methods are usually favoured because they are not directly affected by product formulation, structure or density. Alternative methods are available including nuclear magnetic resonance, near infrared, direct heating with infrared and the use of an electrical current passed through the sample to measure its electrical conductance or capacitance (Cauvain and Young, 2000).

Water activity and its relevance

The water activity of a product (a_w), or its equilibrium relative humidity (ERH), is an important property that is related to many aspects of product shelf-life. Water activity and ERH are related by the relationship $ERH = a_w \times 100$. ERH is expressed on a scale of 0–100 and expressed as a percentage, while a_w is expressed on a scale of 0–1. Thus, an ERH of 80% equals an a_w of 0.8. The ERH of a product may be defined as:

> The ERH is that unique humidity at which moisture is neither gained nor lost from a product, or at which the rate of evaporation of moisture

from a product equals the rate at which moisture is absorbed by the product

In other words, the humidity within the product is in equilibrium with that of the atmosphere surrounding it. If the product ERH is higher than the relative humidity of the surrounding atmosphere then it will lose moisture and dry out, but if the product ERH is lower than the relative humidity of the surrounding atmosphere it will gain moisture.

The loss or gain of water during storage can have a profound impact on the eating qualities of the bakery products. ERH is also important for understanding the potential for moisture migration within products or between different components in a composite product. The ERH of a product is a critical factor in its spoilage-free shelf-life. Its impact on microbial activity has been discussed in detail in many other publications (Cauvain and Young, 2000). It is sufficient at this point to recognise that the lower the product ERH the longer its spoilage-free shelf-life.

Product ERH may be measured directly or may be calculated from ingredients and recipe data (Cauvain and Young, 2000). The latter technique is useful in the context of product development because it is not necessary to make up samples for testing. However, in order to ensure that the ERH calculations are relevant it is necessary to have appropriate data on the ingredients.

The data required depend on the calculation method being used. There are two main methods, known as the **sucrose equivalence** and **sucrose concentration** methods. In the former, the assumption is that there is sufficient water in the recipe to solubilise all of the ingredients. If there is not, then the sucrose-concentration method gives more relevant results. There are inaccuracies associated with both the direct measurement of ERH and its calculation. The relationship between product ERH and spoilage-free shelf-life is not an absolute one and any prediction should be made with care. For a more detailed discussion of the issues surrounding the ERH of bakery products the reader is referred elsewhere (Cauvain and Young, 2000).

Key physical characteristics of bread and fermented goods

Bread is characterised by a **crust**, a dry thin layer that encloses a soft, sponge-like cellular structure. The crust will usually have a light golden-brown colour. In some bread products the colour may be darker, as when wholemeal (wholewheat), brown or non-wheat flours are used in its production. Rye breads, which are especially popular in Scandinavia, eastern and northern Europe, tend to produce darker crust colours.

Many different factors affect crust colour, which appears during baking because of the Maillard reaction (Manley, 2000) and is based on a reaction between proteins and sugars present in the dough. The reaction starts when the product surface temperature exceeds 115°C. This can only happen when sufficient water has evaporated from the crust surface. It takes a few minutes of exposure to heat in the oven before this happens. The depth of bread-crust colour achieved during baking is influenced by the pH of the dough, with lower pHs (i.e. more acid conditions) yielding darker crust colour. This effect of lower dough pH accounts, in part, for the darker crust often seen with sponge-and-dough or sour-dough breads.

Bread crust has considerably lower moisture content than that of the crumb. On leaving the oven, and for some while after cooling, the crust moisture content will remain lower than that of the crumb. Typically, crust moisture contents are in the range 12–17%, while for bread crumb they will be in the range 35–40%, depending on bread type.

Variations in crust character may be significant. In general, bread crusts will have a hard and brittle eating character. Two major factors contributing to that character are the low moisture content and the thickness of the crust. Typically the latter is 1–3 mm, though only the first mm or so will be coloured brown. Regional and product variations in crust character are significant and major contributors to differences in bread quality between the regions of the world. The variations in crust character extend to surface decoration though in many cases the marking or cutting of the dough surface actually has a process control function and contributes to product quality, as will be discussed later.

All bread types are characterised by having an open, cellular crumb structure and (by comparison with other foods) an intermediate moisture content. A key contribution to the cellular structure of breads comes from the release of carbon dioxide gas from baker's yeast fermentation. As has already been described, key characteristics of bread crumb are a relative softness combined with a degree of resilience or springiness and a degree of chewiness. Moisture plays a significant contributory role to these eating characteristics, with lower moisture contents resulting in an increase in firmness and losses in springiness and chewiness. Such changes in eating quality are commonly associated with bread staling, though moisture losses are not the sole reason for bread staling (Pateras, 1998; Chinachoti, 2003).

An equally important contributor to the character of bread crumb is the nature of the cellular structure. Bread crumb cell structure is comprised of two components, the small holes or 'cells' and the cell walls (i.e. the material surrounding the cells), the crumb itself. The size of the cells and their spatial distribution within a loaf have a significant impact on the thickness of the cell-wall material. The formation of the cells and wall material are determined by the qualities of the ingredients used (primarily wheat flour, which is the contributor of gluten-forming proteins), the formulation used and many aspects of dough processing (most importantly dough mixing).

The variations in the cellular structures in bread products are significant and are major contributors to variations in eating qualities. The tendency is for bread-cell structures with small cell sizes uniformly distributed within the slice, commonly referred to as fine, to be soft-eating and slightly chewy in character. Bread crumb characterised by larger cell sizes, thicker cells walls and a more random distribution of cell size within the slice, commonly referred to as open or coarse, tend to yield bread with firmer and more chewy eating characteristics.

There are major differences between the densities of different breads (Table 2.2). Product density is directly related to the expansion of the dough during proving and baking and the retention of gases within the gluten structure, up to the point of foam-to-sponge conversion. Many ingredient, formulation and processing factors input to final product density. These are mainly manifest through changes in product volume and cell structure.

Bread products are not highly flavoured by comparison with other baked products and many other foods. In part this is because bread formulations do not contain highly-flavoured ingredients or, if they do, they are present at very low levels. The exception is salt, and this is perhaps the greatest contributor to bread flavour.

A significant contribution to bread flavour comes from the crust and is developed during the Maillard reactions which occur during baking. There are significant variations in the ratio of crust to crumb among bread products. These variations occur as the results of differences in the size and shape of the dough pieces used, and they are accentuated by the baking conditions. Baked products that are very long and thin, that is with a narrow diameter and relatively large surface area (such

Table 2.2 Densities of bread products.

Product	Density (g/ml)
UK sandwich bread	0.22–0.25
Baguette	0.15–0.18
US pan bread	0.17–0.20
Hamburger buns	0.17–0.20
Rolls	0.20–0.25
Hearth breads	0.21–0.25

as baguette), tend to be perceived as having more flavour than those which are short and fat, that is have a large diameter relative to their surface area (such as a pan loaf).

The crumb of bread and other fermented products does contribute to the flavour of the baked product. Not only are there significant contributions from the ingredients, but also from the fermentation process itself or, more correctly, from the by-products of that fermentation. The development of bread flavours from fermentation is a complex and specialist subject largely outside the scope of this book. However, since the fermentation process not only modifies flavour but also other important dough characteristics it will be considered in Chapter 7. At this time it is sufficient to recognise that fermentation conditions, especially temperature, influence flavour development by the baker's yeast that is added, and by the various micro-organisms present in the flour itself. Briefly, lower temperatures, such as are used in retarding (Cauvain, 1998a), favour the activities of lactic acid bacteria in the dough, while the warmer conditions of proof favour the activities of baker's yeast (*Saccharomyces cerevisiae*). The reader is referred elsewhere for a detailed discussion of flavour development in fermented products.

Key physical characteristics of sponges and cakes

Sponges and cakes represent a more diverse group of products than bread and other fermented products. They do, however, have some unifying characteristics which distinguish them from other baked products. They may be classified as intermediate-moisture foods though the total moisture content is lower by some 10–20% of that of bread. Some typical moisture contents for cakes are given in Table 2.3.

Cakes do have a crust though it is somewhat thinner than the average crust on breads. Cake crust does have a lower moisture content than cake crumb but equilibration of crust and crumb tends to be

Table 2.3 Typical moisture contents and densities for cake products.

Products	Moisture content (%)	Density (g/ml)
Plain	22–30	0.30–0.40
Chocolate	18–28	0.35–0.45
White	26–34	0.25–0.35
Fruited	18–26	0.40–0.55
Plain sponge	25–32	0.18–0.25
Chocolate sponge	24–28	0.21–0.24

more rapid than may be seen with breads. A hard, dry, crisp crust is not normally considered to be a desirable characteristic of cakes. The crust colour tends to be more variable than that of bread because of the ingredient influences, but commonly it falls in the yellow-brown regions of the colour spectrum.

The cellular structure of cakes tends to be less well defined than that of bread. However, there is considerable variation, with sponge cakes having a comparatively well-defined cell structure. There is also a wide variation in the density of cake products, as shown in Table 2.3, though, in the main, densities of cake products are greater than that of breads. The aeration of sponges and cakes comes from the use of baking powder rather than through the yeast-based aeration which is used in bread production.

The lack of any significant gluten development in cake batters (for reasons which will be discussed in later chapters) and the major impact of ingredients such as sugar determine that cakes have soft and friable eating qualities. There is little resilience in cake crumb and so they are not considered to have a chewy character. Both moisture and product density have major impacts on cake eating quality. Lower moisture contents yield firm, dry-eating products while more dense cake products tend towards pasty eating characteristics.

The flavours of sponges and cakes are determined entirely by the choice of ingredients and the recipe used. Dominant flavours tend to come from the sugars in plain cakes, through the addition of fruit and nuts in fruit cakes, the addition of cocoa solids in chocolate cakes, the addition of ground almonds in almond cakes and so on. Sponges and cakes are expected to be more highly flavoured than breads and may have low levels of intensely-flavoured ingredients (e.g. spices and liquid flavours) to augment those contributed by the main ingredients.

A key attribute of cakes is the relatively longer shelf-life that they enjoy compared with that of bread. Both organoleptic and mould-free shelf-life are lengthened, mostly because of the lowering of water activity (see above), which restricts moisture losses from the product and growth of micro-organisms (Cauvain and Young, 2000).

Key physical characteristics of biscuits, crackers and cookies

There are many significant differences between biscuits, cookies and crackers and other classes of baked products. First, and perhaps most obvious, is their size and weight. Most products in this group will weigh considerably less than 100 g and typically the unit weight is only 15–16 g. Biscuits and cookies are thin, usually less than 10 mm thick, and commonly round (Fig. 2.7) or rectangular in shape. The moisture content of biscuit products is very low, typically under 5%. The low moisture content, coupled with the thinness of the products, gives them a crisp, hard eating character. In more recent years the eating character of cookies has been extended to include a softer eating character – the so-called soft-eating or chewy cookies. In part this comes from having higher moisture contents and in part from changes in recipe.

The low moisture content and low water activity of products in this group mean that they have long mould-free shelf-lives, typically many months. Organoleptic shelf-life is also very long since the product staling and moisture loss are not usually a problem. However, there are potential problem areas. One problem is the potential to absorb moisture from the surrounding atmosphere, which can lead to softening of products and loss of crisp eating characteristics (**staling**). The second is the risk of fat rancidity arising from the combination of long storage time with low water activity (Manley, 2000).

As is the case with cakes, the flavouring of biscuits is dominated by the ingredients and the recipe used. There is some contribution from the baking process. There is no significant crust formation, though there may still be a small moisture gradient within the thickness of the products. Biscuits and cookies are much denser than breads or cakes, mainly because there is limited gluten development and no significant foam formation during mixing and, in turn, limited development of a sponge structure during baking of the products.

The range of products encompassed in this group is considerable, at both local and regional levels. Indeed so wide is the product variation that it is sometimes difficult to consider this to be a single group.

Figure 2.7 Biscuit dough units leaving the moulder and entering the oven.

However, it can be argued that the products are unified by the characteristics described above and only separated by the technologies and engineering used in their manufacture. For example, while mixing is common to all biscuit types, the methods of forming the individual units vary from sheeting (semi-sweet), to moulding (short dough), extrusion (rout pressing), sheeting and lamination (crackers) and even depositing (wafers). There are strong ingredient–formulation–process interactions in the manufacture of all biscuits.

Key physical characteristics of pastry

Few pastry products are eaten alone, that is without some filling or topping, or both. Pastries are a versatile medium which could be considered 'edible packaging', as in meat pies. While the fillings may have a wide range of textures, moisture contents and water activities, the pastry employed tends to be relatively uniform in character, with a moisture content above that of biscuits but below that of cake. The typical moisture content of pastries tends to confer a firm and relatively crisp eating character to the product when freshly baked. Since the water activities of pastries are commonly below that of the fillings used in them, water readily moves from the filling to the pastry with the result that the pastry softens and loses its crispness (Cauvain and Young, 2000). The shelf-life of the pastry can be quite long but the migration of moisture from filling to paste reduces this considerably so that typical shelf-lives will range from a few days for meat-containing pastries to a few weeks for pastries with sweet fillings.

There is a very wide range to the shapes and uses of pastry products with many local and regional variations. However, in general pastry products are relatively thin, ranging from a few mm up to 20 mm. Pastry flavours tend to be relatively subtle, since the fillings are more highly flavoured. A light, golden brown characterises the colour of most pastry products. There is no significant foam creation in the paste during mixing or processing, which means that the paste is relatively dense. There are similarities between biscuits and pastries in that both sheeting and blocking/forming/moulding are employed in order to achieve the desired end results.

Chapter 3

Characterisation of Bakery Products by Formulation and the Key Functional Roles of the Main Ingredients Used In Baking

Introduction

The functional properties of the ingredients used in the manufacture of baked products are many and varied. Individual ingredients may have more than one function in a given baked product or group of baked products. A broad classification of the functionality of ingredients commonly used in baking is as follows:

Structure forming

Ingredients in this category make **major** contributions to the structural properties of the intermediate (dough, batter, paste) or final baked product (bread, etc.).

Aeration

This heading encompasses ingredients which make **major** contributions to the entrapment and stabilisation of air in the intermediate (e.g. fat and emulsifiers in cake batters) or provide additional gases during processing of the product (e.g. yeast in proof and the early stages of the baking of bread dough, baking powder in cake).

Eating quality

While all ingredients make some contribution to the eating quality of baked products, this category applies to those which make **major** contributions to eating quality directly, because of their level of addition (e.g. fat in biscuits and cookies). It may also include those which have an indirect impact because of their significant effect on product structure formation or moisture content.

Flavour

Ingredients which make a **major** contribution to flavour are encompassed by this heading (e.g. cocoa powder in chocolate products). The addition of intense liquid or powdered flavours, often used at low levels in baked-product formulations, is not included.

Colour

Included under this heading are ingredients which make **major** contributions to baked product colour, either because they themselves are coloured (e.g. cocoa powder) or because of interactions with other ingredients as part of colour-forming mechanisms during baking (e.g. Maillard reactions).

Shelf-life

This heading covers both organoleptic and microbial shelf-life and includes all ingredients that make **major** contributions to these characteristics. Preservatives clearly play a major role in this context.

Key functional roles of individual ingredients

The contributions of the main bakery ingredients to the characters of the four main groups of baked products are summarised in Tables 3.1–3.7. The information given collectively in the tables shows that many ingredients used in the manufacture of baked products have multi-functional roles, while others have more relatively-confined roles and may only appear on a single table. Some ingredients have not been included though they do make significant contributions to one or more of the individual characters. For example, preservatives, such as potassium sorbate and calcium propionate, are important in the control of

Table 3.1 Direct contributions to the character of intermediates, i.e. dough, batter, paste.

	Bread and fermented products	Sponges and cakes	Biscuits, cookies and crackers	Pastries
Wheat flour	M	M	M	M
Fibres	L	N	L	N
Soya flour	L	N	N	N
Cocoa powder	N	M in chocolate products	N	N
Sucrose	N	M	L	L
Dextrose/glucose syrups	N	L	L	N
Honey/invert sugar	N	L	L	N
Glycerol/polyols	N	N	N	N
Whole liquid egg	N	M	N	N
Liquid albumen	N	M	N	N
Dried whole egg	N	M	N	N
Dried albumen	N	M	N	N
Baking powder	N	N	N	N
Baking acids	N	N	N	N
Sodium bicarbonate	N	N	N	N
Dried vine fruit	N	N	N	N
Chocolate chips	N	N	N	N
Candied fruits	N	N	N	N
Fat/butter/margarine	N	L	M	M
Emulsifiers	N	M	N	N
Salt	M	N	N	L
Yeast	M	N	N	M in croissant
Ascorbic acid	M	N	N	M in croissant
Enzymes	M	N	N	M in croissant
Water	M	M	M	M
Milk	L	M	L	L
Milk/whey powders	N	N	N	N

Key for Tables 3.1–3.7.
Product names are used in the tables where appropriate to qualify the ingredient contribution.
M = a major contribution and will usually be level dependent
L = a limited contribution and absence or presence will be detectable
N = no significant contribution

microbial activity in bread and cakes but can have negative effects on yeasted products (i.e. inhibit yeast activity). The reader is referred elsewhere for a more detailed discussion of the use of such ingredients (Cauvain and Young, 1998; Cauvain and Young, 2000).

Table 3.2 Direct contributions to product baked structure.

	Bread and fermented products	Sponges and cakes	Biscuits, cookies and crackers	Pastries
Wheat flour	M	M	M	M
Fibres	M	L	L	L
Soya flour	L	N	N	N
Cocoa powder	N	L in chocolate products	N	N
Sucrose	L	M	M	L
Dextrose/glucose syrups	L	M	L	L
Honey/invert sugar	N	L	N	N
Glycerol/polyols	N	N	N	N
Whole liquid egg	N	M	N	L
Liquid albumen	N	M in white cakes	N	N
Dried whole egg	N	L	N	N
Dried albumen	N	M in white cakes	N	N
Baking powder	N	M	L	L
Baking acids	N	M	L	L
Sodium bicarbonate	N	M	L	L
Dried vine fruit	N	N	N	N
Chocolate chips	N	N	N	N
Candied fruits	N	N	N	N
Fat/butter/margarine	M	M	M	M
Emulsifiers	L	M	L	L
Salt	M	N	L	L
Yeast	M	N	L in crackers	M in croissant
Ascorbic acid	M	N	N	L in croissant
Enzymes	M	N	M for proteolytic forms	M
Water	M	M	M	M
Milk	L	L	L	L
Milk/whey powders	L	L	L	L

How baked-product formulations are expressed

For centuries, bakers have developed recipes and expressed them in different forms. Before scales and measuring devices became standardised, bakers would use whatever unit of measurement was most

Table 3.3   Direct contributions to product aeration.

	Bread and fermented products	Sponges and cakes	Biscuits, cookies and crackers	Pastries
Wheat flour	M	L	L	M in laminated pastes
Fibres	M with a negative impact	N	L	L
Soya flour	N	N	N	N
Cocoa powder	N	M with a negative impact	N	N
Sucrose	N	M	L	N
Dextrose/glucose syrups	N	L	L	N
Honey/invert sugar	N	L	N	N
Glycerol/polyols	N	L	N	N
Whole liquid egg	N	L / M in no-fat sponges	N	N
Liquid albumen	N	M in white cakes	N	N
Dried whole egg	N	L	N	N
Dried albumen	N	L	N	N
Baking powder	N	M	M	M
Baking acids	N	M	N	L in laminated pastes
Sodium bicarbonate	N	M	M	N
Dried vine fruit	N	N	N	N
Chocolate chips	N	N	N	N
Candied fruits	N	N	N	N
Fat/butter/margarine	M	M	M	M
Emulsifiers	M	M	L	L
Salt	L	N	N	N
Yeast	M	N	N	M in croissant
Ascorbic acid	N	N	N	N
Enzymes	N	N	N	N
Water	N	N	N	N
Milk	N	N	N	N
Milk/whey powders	N	N	N	N

practical, and much use was made of volume measurement, for example pints and quarts. In fact it is still the case that bakers use the volume term to describe some mixer types, e.g. a 10- or 20-quart planetary mixer. In some software, such as *Cake Expert System* (CCFRA, 2002), the

Table 3.4   Direct contributions to product eating quality.

	Bread and fermented products	Sponges and cakes	Biscuits, cookies and crackers	Pastries
Wheat flour	M	M	M	M
Fibres	M	N	L	N
Soya flour	N	N	N	N
Cocoa powder	N	M in chocolate products	L	N
Sucrose	M	M	M	M
Dextrose/glucose syrups	L	M	L	L
Honey/invert sugar	N	M	L	N
Glycerol/polyols	N	L	N	N
Whole liquid egg	N	M	N	L
Liquid albumen	N	M	N	N
Dried whole egg	N	L	N	N
Dried albumen	N	L	N	N
Baking powder	N	L	L	L
Baking acids	N	N	N	N
Sodium bicarbonate	N	N	N	N
Dried vine fruit	L	M in fruited products	L	L
Chocolate chips	N	M in fruited products	L	L
Candied fruits	L	M	L	L
Fat/butter/margarine	L	M	M	M
Emulsifiers	L	M	L	L
Salt	L	N	N	L in laminated products
Yeast	N	N	N	N
Ascorbic acid	N	N	N	N
Enzymes	N	N	N	N
Water	M	M	M	M
Milk	L	M	M	M
Milk/whey powders	N	N	N	N

ingredients can be displayed by category, for example flour category, fat category, etc. This method helps technologists determine whether the ingredient proportion ratios are in line with the requirements for the product type.

Three different methods of expressing baked-product formulations have evolved over time: these are **Baker's percent** (Baker's %), **Total percent** and **Ingredient weight**. Each method has its own advantages

Table 3.5   Direct contributions to product flavour.

	Bread and fermented products	Sponges and cakes	Biscuits, cookies and crackers	Pastries
Wheat flour	L	N	N	N
Fibres	L	N	N	N
Soya flour	N	N	N	N
Cocoa powder	N	M in chocolate products	M in chocolate products	N
Sucrose	L	M	M	M
Dextrose/glucose syrups	L	M	L	L
Honey/invert sugar	L	M	M	M
Glycerol/polyols	N	N	N	N
Whole liquid egg	N	L	N	N
Liquid albumen	N	N	N	N
Dried whole egg	N	L	N	N
Dried albumen	N	N	N	N
Baking powder	N	M	L	N
Baking acids	N	M	L	N
Sodium bicarbonate	N	M	M	M
Dried vine fruit	L	M	L	L
Chocolate chips	N	M	L	L
Candied fruits	L	M	M	M
Fat/butter/margarine	L	M	M	M
Emulsifiers	N	N	N	N
Salt	M	M	M	M
Yeast	L	N	N	L
Ascorbic acid	N	N	N	N
Enzymes	N	N	N	N
Water	N	N	N	N
Milk	L	L	L	L
Milk/whey powders	L	L	L	L

and disadvantages. The three methods of expressing baked-product formulations are compared in Table 3.8, using the example of a plain unit cake.

Baker's percent (Baker's %)

The Baker's % method gives each ingredient as a proportion of the flour used in the formulation. The close relationship between the baker and the miller may have led to this approach or, more likely, the importance of flour to the baker's products made it a natural choice as the yardstick ingredient. After all, many bakery formulations comprised flour and few other ingredients. Flour was delivered in sacks, and so bakers

Table 3.6   Direct contributions to product colour.

	Bread and fermented products	Sponges and cakes	Biscuits, cookies and crackers	Pastries
Wheat flour	N except wholemeal etc.	N	N	N
Fibres	L	N	N	N
Soya flour	L	N	N	N
Cocoa powder	N	M	M	N
Sucrose	M	M	M	M
Dextrose/glucose syrups	M	M	M	M
Honey/invert sugar	M	M	M	M
Glycerol/polyols	M	M	M	M
Whole liquid egg	N	L	L	L
Liquid albumen	N	N	N	N
Dried whole egg	N	L	L	L
Dried albumen	N	N	N	N
Baking powder	N	N	N	N
Baking acids	N	M	M	M
Sodium bicarbonate	N	M	M	M
Dried vine fruit	N	N	N	N
Chocolate chips	N	N	N	N
Candied fruits	N	N	N	N
Fat/butter/margarine	N	L	L	L
Emulsifiers	N	N	N	N
Salt	N	N	N	N
Yeast	N	N	N	N
Ascorbic acid	N	N	N	N
Enzymes	N	N	N	N
Water	N	N	N	N
Milk	L	L	L	L
Milk/whey powders	L	L	L	L

developed an easy way of measuring their ingredients in relation to the flour. It has the advantage of being unit-less and so whatever units the baker chooses, be it grams, kilograms, pounds or cups, the recipe can be converted to them. It prevents calculation errors, which often creep in when conversion tables are used. Flour is therefore the first item in the formulation, but thereafter there is no standard order for the other ingredients.

Total weight percent (Total weight %)

This method expresses each ingredient as a percentage of the total weight of the ingredients. This method is used for comparison of one

Table 3.7   Direct contributions to product shelf-life.

	Bread and fermented products	Sponges and cakes	Biscuits, cookies and crackers	Pastries
Wheat flour	N	N	N	N
Fibres	M	M	M	M
Soya flour	N	N	N	N
Cocoa powder	N	N	N	N
Sucrose	M	M	M	M
Dextrose/glucose syrups	M	M	M	M
Honey/invert sugar	M	M	M	M
Glycerol/polyols	M	M	M	M
Whole liquid egg	M	M	M	M
Liquid albumen	M	M	M	M
Dried whole egg	N	N	N	N
Dried albumen	N	N	N	N
Baking powder	N	L	N	N
Baking acids	N	L	N	N
Sodium bicarbonate	N	L	N	N
Dried vine fruit	L	L	L	L
Chocolate chips	N	N	N	N
Candied fruits	L	L	L	L
Fat/butter/margarine	N	N	N	N
Emulsifiers	L	L	N	N
Salt	L	M	L	L
Yeast	N	N	N	N
Ascorbic acid	N	N	N	N
Enzymes	M	N	N	N
Water	M	M	M	M
Milk	M	M	M	M
Milk/whey powders	N	N	N	N

Table 3.8   A comparison of the methods used for expressing baked-product formulations.

Ingredient	% flour weight	% total weight	kg
Flour	100.0	25.706	38.56
Sucrose	117.5	30.205	45.30
Fat	35.3	9.074	13.61
Egg (whole liquid)	30.7	7.894	11.84
Baking powder	4.5	1.157	1.74
Salt	1.0	0.257	0.39
Water	100.0	25.706	38.56
Totals	*	100.00	150.00

recipe with another. It is also used for determining the costs of the recipe and for defining the nutritional values required for product labelling.

This method has the advantage that it can be based on a single unit weight, which can readily be scaled up to a batch weight. Thus, if it is known that a 10 kg batch of dough made using given amounts of ingredients yields 10 cakes, then if 15 cakes are required each of the ingredients can be multiplied by 1.5 (i.e. 15/10) to give the required quantity of each of the ingredients.

Ingredient weight

This method of expressing a recipe is used most popularly in non-commercial bakery publications, e.g. home cookery books. It is also found in technical bakery publications where the flour is expressed as 1 kg. In these cases the remaining ingredients are, in fact, also expressed as a percentage of flour weight based on 1 kg being equal to 100%.

Other methods

With the advent of nutritional labelling of ingredients on product packaging, companies will often convert their recipes to ones in which the ingredients are listed in descending order by ingredient level. This makes the transfer of information for the statutory labelling of products easier to manage. It also facilitates the energy calculations needed for nutritional purposes (calories, KJ or Kcal).

Conversion factors

In many older books on baking technology, the formulations are expressed using the 'sack' as a measure of flour while the remaining solid ingredients are expressed in lb and oz and liquids expressed in pints or gills – all very confusing. Table 3.9 gives the conversion factors for Imperial to metric measurements.

Typical recipes used in the manufacture of baked products

Relationships between product groups

The relationships between the different product sub-groups that are part of the family of baked products have been discussed in Chapter 1. The relationships are complex and difficult to understand from recipes such as those given below. One way of illustrating the relationships was shown in Figure 1.3, using three common ingredi-

Table 3.9   Conversion factors for Imperial to metric measurements.

Imperial	Metric
1 lb (16 ounces)	0.453 kg
2.205 lb	1.0 kg
1 oz	28.35 g
0.035 oz	1 g
1 cwt	50.802 kg
1 pint	575 ml
1 gallon	4.55 l
1 gallon (US)	3.79 l
1 cup	250 ml
1 tablespoon	15 ml
1 dessertspoon	10 ml
1 teaspoon	5 ml
1 sack (280 lb)	127 kg

ents – flour, fat and sugar – as the basis for recipe comparison, but this is only one of many comparisons that might be represented in this way.

A key part of any comparison between sub-groups of baked products is their moisture content and shelf-lives as determined by water activity (a_w and ERH). There is a strong relationship between moisture and product a_w as has been discussed in Chapter 2 and in greater detail elsewhere (Cauvain and Young, 2000). Final-product moisture content is partly determined by the recipe water level (in general, the higher the starting level the higher the finishing level), in part by processing conditions (in general a higher heat input leads to lower product moisture content) and in part by product type (generally speaking thin products tend to have lower moisture contents).

Water activity is significantly affected by ingredient choice, level and recipe and through the direct relationship between a_w and moisture content (in general, the lower the moisture content the lower the a_w). This close relationship between product water activity and moisture content is illustrated in Figure 3.1 for a small number of sub-groups of baked products. Products that are high in moisture and low in soluble ingredients (e.g. sugar) are placed in the top right-hand corner of the graph while those that are low in moisture and soluble solids (e.g. extruded products) fall in the bottom left-hand corner. Between these two extremes lie many other baked products, their precise position depending on a combination of soluble ingredients (recipe) and final moisture content.

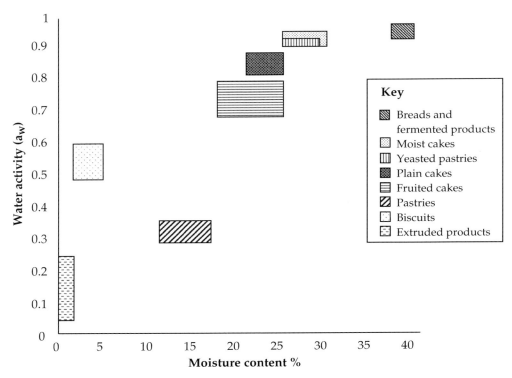

Figure 3.1   Relationship between product water activity and moisture content.

Flour types

The description of flour types required for baked products varies and can be confusing. Table 3.10 gives the flour descriptors used in the recipes below and shows their typical protein contents and any relevant special features.

Sample recipes

Formulations for baked products will vary from country to country and from company to company. Many companies guard their formulations assiduously. However a book of this nature on baked products would not be complete without some reference formulations for generic products. These recipes can be used as a starting point for developing products with characteristics similar to those of the chosen product. The recipes are given in baker's percent to facilitate comparisons.

Table 3.10 Flour types used in the manufacture of baked products.

Flour type	Protein content range (%) (based on 14% moisture)	Special features and other specified properties
CBP	10.0–12.0	Starch damage, Hagberg Falling Number, colour
Bakers' grade	11.5–12.5	Starch damage, Hagberg Falling Number, colour, gluten strength
Bread	12.0–13.5	Starch damage, Hagberg Falling Number, colour, gluten strength
Strong	12.5–13.5	Starch damage, Hagberg Falling Number, colour, gluten strength
Medium	11.0–12.0	Limited gluten strength
Soft	10.0–11.0	Made from softer milling wheats
Weak	9.0–10.0	Made from softer milling wheats with poor gluten-forming properties
Biscuit	9.5–10.5	Low resistance high extensibility gluten often specified
Wholemeal	12.0–14.0	Bran particle size may be specified
Cake	8.0–10.0	Particle size often specified. May be treated with chlorine gas.
Cake – heat treated	8.0–10.0	Particle size often specified

Bread and fermented products

UK white breads		
	Tinned	Oven bottom /freestanding/crusty
Ingredient	*Baker's %*	*Baker's %*
Flour (CBP or baker's grade)[+]	100	100
Yeast	2.1	2.3
Salt	1.7–2.1	1.9–2.1
Water	60.0–62.0	55.0–58.0
Improver*	1.0–1.5	1.0–1.5

Figures 3.2 and 7.4 (p. 157) show UK pan breads and Figures 3.3 and 7.5 (p. 157) show UK bloomers.
[+] Depending on bread-making process employed.
* A typical improver may contain ascorbic acid, soya flour, emulsifier and enzyme-active materials (Cauvain and Young, 2006).

Figure 3.2   UK farmhouse pan breads.

Figure 3.3   Bloomers.

French baguette/sticks

Ingredient	Baker's %
Flour (baker's grade)	100
Yeast	3
Salt	1.7–2
Water	64.0–66.0
Improver*	1.0–2.0

The manufacture of traditional baguettes is highly regulated in France (Fig. 3.4). They cannot be made with an improver and must be based on a fermentation process. The recipe given above is for products more commonly referred to as baguettes or French sticks in the UK (Fig. 3.5). These products are characterised by the cutting pattern on the surface.
* In addition to ascorbic acid, soya flour and enzyme-active materials, improver may contain lecithin.

Figure 3.4 Traditional French baguettes.

Figure 3.5   UK baguettes or French sticks.

Irish soda bread (with yeast)

Ingredient	Baker's %
Flour (CBP or baker's grade)	100
Yeast	3.6
Salt	1.6
Water	59–61.0
Fat	3.6
Improver*	1.0–2.0
Baking powder	3.1
Milk powder	1.6

Soda bread is a traditional regional product which may also be made by replacing the yeast with baking powder.
* Typical improver will contain ascorbic acid and malt flour.

Soft rolls (Fig. 3.6)

Ingredient	Baker's %
Flour (baker's grade)	100
Yeast	3.1
Salt	1.8
Water	61.0–63.0
Fat	2.2
Improver	2.0
Milk powder	2.0–2.5
Sugar	1.6

Figure 3.6   Soft rolls.

Currant buns

Ingredient	Baker's %
Flour (baker's grade)	100
Yeast	5.4
Salt	0.7
Water	41.1
Fat	10.7
Milk powder	2.9
Sugar	10.7
Frozen egg	17.9
Improver	2.0–2.5
Currants	28.6
Sultanas	28.6
Peel	5.4

Hamburger rolls

Ingredient	UK-style Baker's %	US-style Baker's %
Flour (CBP or baker's grade)	100	100
Yeast	4	3
Salt	1.8	1.8
Water	55.4–62.2	55.4
Fat	5.0–5.4	3–5
Milk powder	1.6–2.0	1.6
Sugar	3.0–3.6	5–10
Improver	1.5–2.0	1.5–2.0

Wholemeal or wholewheat bread (Figs 2.5, p. 24, and 3.7)

Ingredient	Baker's %
Wholemeal flour	100
Yeast	2.7
Salt	1.8
Water	62.5
Improver	1.0–2.0

These products may have legally-restricted ingredients lists.

Figure 3.7   Wholemeal bread.

Mixed-grain bread (Fig. 3.8)

Ingredient	Baker's %
Mixed-grain flour	100
Yeast	2.1–2.3
Salt	1.8–2.1
Water	58.0–62.0
Improver	1.0–2.0

Figure 3.8   Mixed-grain breads.

Malt bread

Ingredient	Baker's %
Flour (CBP or baker's grade)	100
Malt flour (low diastatic)	7.7
Yeast	2.3
Salt	1.1
Water	61.1
Fat	1.1
Improver	1.0
Treacle	5.0

Rye bread

Ingredient	Straight dough Baker's %	Sour dough Baker's %
Sour dough	n/a	80
Flour (rye)	100	60
Yeast	3	1
Salt	1.6	1.2*
Water	60.7	25
Fat	0.71	
AA	0.02	

* 60% of the salt is contained in the sour dough.

Sponge-and-dough, including North American pan breads

Breads made by the 'sponge and dough' or 'flour brew' methods involve a two-stage process. The sponge containing a proportion of the flour, yeast and water is mixed and held in a tank for a fixed period of time (depending on the flavour required). This sponge is then added to the recipe as an additional ingredient and the dough is mixed as in normal processing.

Sponge recipe for 16-hour sponge

Ingredient	Baker's %
Flour (CBP or baker's grade)	100
Yeast	0.8
Salt	1
Water	56

Recipe for final dough

Ingredient	Baker's %
Flour (CBP or baker's grade)	100
Yeast	2.4
Salt	2.4
Water	61.3
Improver	1.5
Sponge	52.6

Sponge and dough recipe (ingredients given as % of total weight of flour)

Ingredient	Sponge	Dough
Flour	25.0	75.0
Yeast	0.2	1.8
Salt	0.25	1.8
Water	14.0	46.00
Improver	0	1.1
		+sponge

Pizza bases

Ingredient	Baker's %
Flour (CBP or baker's grade)	100
Yeast	6.5–7.0
Salt	2.0
Water	56–58
Oil	0–8.0
Sugar	0–1.5
Skimmed-milk powder	0–2.5
Improver	1.0

Brioche

Ingredient	Baker's %
Flour (baker's grade)	100
Yeast	7.0
Salt	3.0
Caster sugar	11
Skimmed milk powder	1.5
Water	11
Liquid whole egg	55.5
Butter	28.0

Brioche is a traditional French speciality product made from a rich dough containing a high level of butter and eggs. They are made in many shapes and sizes but the most typical brioches are similar in shape to an English cottage loaf (Cauvain and Young, 2001).

Bagels (Fig. 3.9)

Ingredient	Baker's %
Flour (baker's grade)	100
Yeast	1.2
Salt	2.0
Sugar	7.0
Water	42.0
Liquid whole egg	6.2
Vegetable oil	3.1

Bagels are characteristically ring-shaped and are distinguished from other roll-type products by a preliminary boiling step, when the bagels are immersed in a boiling water/sugar solution for up to 10–15 seconds, then taken out and baked.

Figure 3.9 Bagels.

Doughnuts

Doughnuts (yeasted)

Ingredient	Baker's %
Flour (CBP or baker's grade)	100
Yeast	8.9
Salt	0.8
Water	46.4
Fat	8.9
Milk powder	3.1
Sugar	10.7
Whole egg	8
Improver	1.0–2.0

Yeasted doughnuts are usually made in a ball or finger shape.

Doughnuts (chemically leavened) (cake doughnut)	
Ingredient	*Baker's %*
Flour (baker's grade)	25.0
Flour (cake)	75.0
Sucrose	39.3
Whole eggs	31.3
Salt	1.7
Mace	0.4
Shortening	10.7
Skimmed-milk powder	12.5
Baking powder	4.1
Vanilla	0.2
Water	14.4

Cake doughnuts are usually made in a ring shape.

Cakes

Cake recipes are often classified as high ratio or low ratio. A high-ratio cake is one in which the level of sugar and liquids (largely the sum of water, egg and milk) individually exceed the level of the flour used in the formulation. If the levels of sugar and liquids are lower than that of the flour then the products are commonly considered as low ratio.

Plain high-ratio cakes				
	Unit[#]	Slab*	Layer	Cup
Ingredient	*Baker's %*	*Baker's %*	*Baker's %*	*Baker's %*
Flour – heat treated	100.00	100.00	100.00	100.00
Sucrose	117.50	117.50	117.50	117.50
Fat (solid)	35.30	35.30	35.30	35.30
Egg (whole liquid)	30.71	30.71	30.71	30.71
Baking powder	4.50	2.00	4.50	5.50
Emulsifier – paste	–	0.50	1.00	–
Salt	1.00	1.00	1.00	1.00
Water	100.00	100.00	100.00	100.00

[#] Figure 7.3 (p. 155).
* Figure 3.10.

Figure 3.10 Layer cake made from three different coloured portions of slab cake.

Chocolate high-ratio cakes				
	Unit	Slab	Layer	Cup
Ingredient	*Baker's %*	*Baker's %*	*Baker's %*	*Baker's %*
Flour – heat treated	100.00	100.00	100.00	100.00
Cocoa*	21.00	21.00	21.00	21.00
Sucrose	130.00	130.00	130.00	130.00
Fat (solid)	52.50	52.50	52.50	52.50
Egg (whole liquid)	30.71	30.71	30.71	30.71
Baking powder	4.50	2.25	4.50	5.50
Emulsifier – paste	1.00	1.00	0.50	1.00
Salt	1.00	1.00	1.00	1.00
Water	120.00	120.00	120.00	120.00

* Cocoa solids level may be subject to legislation.

White high-ratio cakes				
	Unit	Slab	Layer	Cup
Ingredient	*Baker's %*	*Baker's %*	*Baker's %*	*Baker's %*
Flour – heat treated	100.00	100.00	100.00	100.00
Sucrose	130.00	130.00	130.00	130.00
Fat (solid)	30.00	50.00	50.25	50.25
Egg (albumen liquid)	25.44	45.00	42.61	42.61
Baking powder	4.50	2.25	4.50	4.50
Tartaric acid	–	0.10	0.10	0.10
Emulsifier – paste	–	1.00	–	0.5
Salt	1.00	1.00	1.00	1.00
Water	126.40	80.26	80.01	80.12

Fruited high-ratio unit cake (Fig. 7.3, p. 155)

Ingredient	Baker's %
Flour – heat treated	100.00
Sucrose	120.00
Fat (solid)	50.00
Egg (whole liquid)	46.00
Baking powder	3.00
Tartaric acid	0.20
Currants	140.00
Salt	2.00
Water	68.00

Sponge cake products

Plain		Low fat
Ingredient	Baker's %	Baker's %
Flour – heat treated	100.00	100.00
Sucrose	105.00	105.00
Oil	17.50	2.50
Egg (whole liquid)	35.00	35.00
Baking powder	3.50	2.50
Emulsifier – paste	1.52	1.52
Salt	1.00	1.00
Water	84.00	84.00

The above may be made into Swiss roll, sandwich sponge (Figs 3.11a and b) or sponge drops.

Chocolate		Low fat
Ingredient	Baker's %	Baker's %
Flour – heat treated	100.00	100.00
Cocoa	15.03	14.35
Sucrose	115.00	115.00
Oil	17.50	2.50
Egg (whole liquid)	35.00	35.00
Baking powder	3.50	2.50
Emulsifier – paste	1.75	1.73
Salt	1.00	1.00
Water	84.00	84.00

The above may be made into Swiss roll, sandwich sponge or sponge drops.

(a)

(b)

Figure 3.11   Sponge cake (a) and internal crumb (b).

Cookies, biscuits and crackers

Biscuits (crackers, cookies, hard-sweet, semi-sweet, wafers) are characterised by low moisture in the finished product and high fat and/or sugar levels. Each biscuit product is made with a particular dough-forming process which is very much part of the product itself. Generally speaking, during baking, a biscuit dough is not contained within a pan/tin (as is required for cakes and some breads) and is baked on a band or a flat tray. Their crisp eating character typifies the product (with the exception of soft cookies). They are a convenience food because of their long shelf-life and their compact individual sizes (Manley, 2000). Table 3.11 compares the most common types of biscuit.

Table 3.11 Comparison of biscuit types.

| | Crackers | Semi-sweet | Short dough | | Soft | Wafer |
			High fat	High sugar		
Added water in dough	33%	21%	2–3%	2–3%	15%	140%
Moisture in biscuit	3–4%	1–2%	2–3%	2–3%	3+%	1–2%
Critical ingredients	Flour	Flour	Fat	Fat and sugar particle size	Fat and sugar particle size	Flour and batter
Dough piece forming	A	A	B,C,D,A	B,C,D,A	C,B,D,A	E
Baking time (minutes)	3	5–6	15–25	7	12+	1.5–3

Key: A Sheet, gauge, cut
    B Rotary mould
    C Wire cut
    D Extrude
    E Deposit

The recipes included here are a representative sample of the different types.

Short dough biscuits (rotary moulded)

Ingredient	Baker's %
Flour	100.0
Fat	32.1
Sucrose	29.5
Skimmed-milk powder	1.8
Sodium bicarbonate	0.4
Ammonium bicarbonate	0.2
Salt	1.1
Water	8.0–14.0
Flavours	As required

Digestive biscuit (rotary moulded) (Fig. 3.12)

Ingredient	Baker's %
Biscuit flour	78.0
Wholemeal flour	22.0
Vegetable shortening	31.0
Caster sugar	8.3
Demerara sugar	16.0
Golden syrup	7.1
Malt extract	1.2
Sodium bicarbonate	1.56
Ammonium bicarbonate	0.38
Tartaric acid	1.67
Salt	1.1
Water	14.3

Figure 3.12   Digestive biscuits.

Shortbread biscuit (rotary moulded)

Ingredient	Baker's %
Biscuit flour	100.0
Butter	44.0
Shortening	6.0
Caster sugar	28.0
Salt	0.5
Water	2.0

Semi-sweet biscuits (sheet and cut)

Ingredient	Baker's %
Flour	100.0
Fat	13.0–20.0
Sucrose	19.0–25.0
Syrup and/or malt extract	2.0–4.0
Skimmed-milk powder	1.4–1.7
Sodium bicarbonate	0.4–0.6
Ammonium bicarbonate	0.4–1.5
SMS	0.030–0.035
Salt	1.0
Lecithin	0.26–0.4
Water (approx)	19.0–24.0

Cream crackers (sheet and cut)

Ingredient	Baker's %
Flour – strong	50.0
Flour – weak	50.0
Fat	12.5
Yeast	1.83
Sodium bicarbonate	0.25
Salt	1.42
Water (approx)	32.1

Water biscuits (fermented) (sheet and cut)

Ingredient	Baker's %
Flour	100.0
Malt extract	0.7
Fat	8.9
Syrup	5.4
Yeast	0.54
Salt	1.6
Water (approx)	26.0

Wafers (deposited)

Ingredient	Baker's % (range)
Flour	100.00
Sucrose	1.7–3.5
Oil or fat	2.4–5.3
Skimmed-milk powder	1.7–2.5
Dried egg powder	0.3–2.9
Soda	0.25–0.32
Ammonium bicarbonate	0.83–0.89
Lecithin powder	0.95–2.05
Salt	0.18
Water	133–145

Rye crispbread

Ingredient	Baker's %
Rye flour	100.0
Salt	1.2
Water – iced	129.0

Pastries

Pastry recipes are classified as:

- Cold water pastes – short, sweet and savoury
- Puff or flaky pastry (also known as laminated pastry)
- Suet pastry
- Hot water paste – semi-boiled and full-boiled
- Choux pastry

Generic recipes for such products are as follows.

Short pastry (Fig. 3.13)

Ingredient	Sweet Baker's %	Savoury Baker's %
Flour – medium	50.0	50.0
Flour – soft	50.0	50.0
Fat	50.0	43.0
Sugar	12.5	–
Egg/milk/water	12.5	–
Salt	–	1.5
Water	–	26.5
Soya flour	–	6.0

Figure 3.13   Short pastry fruit pies.

Puff pastry

Ingredient	Baker's %
Flour	100.0
Total fat	50.0–100.0
– of which dough fat proportion	12.5% of flour weight
– of which laminating fat	Total fat – dough fat
Salt	1.0
Water (approx)	44.0–56.0
Rework	12–44% of base dough

Points to note:
- The higher the % laminating fat, the greater the lift
- The higher the % dough fat, the lower the lift and the shorter the eating quality
- Increasing the % dough fat softens the dough and it may be necessary to reduce the water content to compensate

Suet pastry

Ingredient	Baker's %
Flour – medium	100.0
Fat – suet	50.0
Baking powder	5.0
Salt	1.5
Water	62.5

Hot water paste (semi-boiled) (Fig. 3.14)

Ingredient	Baker's %
Flour – medium to strong	100.0
Fat	44.0
Salt	1.5
Water	37.5

Note: Fat is rubbed into flour, hot water (boiling) is added, paste is mixed until cooler and used when cold.

Hot water paste (full-boiled)

Ingredient	Baker's %
Flour – medium to strong	100.0
Fat	37.5
Salt	1.5
Water	37.5

Note: Water, fat and salt are boiled and flour is added; paste is mixed until smooth and used hot.

Figure 3.14   Savoury paste pork pie.

Choux pastry

Ingredient	Baker's %
Flour – strong	100.0
Fat	50.0–66.5
Water	125.0–167.0
Eggs	161.0–172.5
Ammonium bicarbonate (Volume)	0–0.7

Water and fat are boiled, flour is stirred in and mixture is cooked, then cooled.
Eggs are beaten in gradually.
Paste is piped into products and baked.

Fermented pastries

Croissant (Fig. 3.15)

Ingredient	Baker's %
Flour	100
Shortening	9.7
Sugar	6.1
Egg	2.6
Skimmed-milk powder	6.5
Salt	1.8
Yeast (compressed)	5.5
Water	52.2
Laminating margarine/butter	50–57

Danish pastry

Ingredient	Baker's %
Flour	100
Shortening	9.6
Sugar	9.2
Egg	12.4
Skimmed-milk powder	5.4
Salt	1.3
Yeast (compressed)	7.6
Water	43.6
Laminating margarine/butter	62–64

Figure 3.15   Croissants.

Unleavened breads

There are many types of flat breads found throughout the world. They commonly use an unleavened recipe.

Chapattis	
Ingredient	*Baker's %*
Flour	100
Water	70
Salt	Optional
Oil	Optional

Naan (Fig. 5.8, p. 117)

Ingredient	Baker's %
Flour	100
Yeast	3.8
Salt	0.6
Baking powder	1.3
Caster sugar	2.5
Egg	15.0
Oil	7.5
Natural yoghurt	15.0
Milk	43.8

Papadams

Ingredient	Baker's %
Blackgram flour	100
Water	45
Salt	8
Sodium bicarbonate	1

Tortillas (flour)

Ingredient	Baker's %
Flour	100
Water	33
Lime (calcium hydroxide)	0.1

Other products

Crumpets (Fig. 5.9, p. 119)

Ingredient	Baker's %
Flour – medium	100
Yeast	1.0
Salt	3.6
Baking powder	3.0
Sugar – granulated	5.2
Glucono-delta-lactone	2.0
Water	103
Stabiliser	0.3
Vinegar (12%)	1.54
Potassium sorbate	0.3

A similar product is the pikelet, which is thinner and wider and has the same surface appearance (Fig. 3.16).

Figure 3.16   Pikelets.

Scones

Ingredient	Baker's %
Flour – medium	100
Baking powder	5
Sugar	22
Butter/margarine/fat/oil	25
Milk	61
Eggs	6
Salt	0.7

Note: Fruit may be added at 20–30% flour weight (Fig. 3.17).

Figure 3.17   Fruited scones.

Chapter 4

Ingredients and Their Influences

Wheat flour

There are two principal types of wheat flour: wholemeal and white. In the case of wholemeal flour, the whole of the wheat grain is crushed to yield flour. There are two main processes for its manufacture: the first is **stone grinding**, in which the grain passes through two pairs of stones during the crushing process; the second is more complicated and consists of a series of crushing and sieving steps – a process known as **roller milling**. In the latter case, the separation of the bran and endosperm of the grain is optimised, with the different fractions being recombined at the end of the process to yield the wholemeal flour. In fact, the roller-milling process was developed to optimise the removal of the grain endosperm, which is the white flour commonly used in the manufacture of baked products. The reader is referred elsewhere for a detailed explanation of the modern flour-milling process (Sugden and Osborne, 2001; Webb and Owens, 2003).

The unique properties of wheat flour have been commented on above and in many other texts in the literature (see Further Reading). As discussed earlier (see Chapter 3), baked-product formulations tend to be expressed on a flour-weight basis, so the level of flour does not vary in typical recipes. This means that the influence of wheat flour on baked-product character is more commonly expressed on the basis of its composition, protein, starch, fibre content and other important physicochemical properties, such as particle size and protein quality. It is therefore possible to consider the influence of flour on structure formation using such properties.

The key role of wheat-flour protein in the formation of the gluten structures essential for breadmaking has already been introduced. In general, an increase in the protein content leads to an increase in the gas-retention properties of the dough and therefore an increase in bread volume. The extent to which the product volume will increase depends on a number of recipe and process factors. It also depends on the ability of the wheat proteins to form a gluten network with the appropriate rheological properties. Such properties are strongly influenced by protein-quality attributes, which are notoriously difficult to define, measure and, to some extent, standardise. As a general rule, wheat flours with higher protein contents have more appropriate protein qualities than those with lower protein contents and are therefore better suited to breadmaking.

Wheat proteins were clearly defined by Osborne (1924) and his broad classification still remains in use today. Of the four main types of protein defined by Osborne, two have attracted greatest interest – the prolamins (gliadins) and the glutelins (glutenins) – because they comprise the gluten-forming proteins so essential in baking. The other proteins that are present are the albumins and the globulins. The main wheat proteins of interest in baking are classically divided into two fractions, referred to as gliadins and glutenins and both contribute to flour quality and dough rheological properties. Variations in the ratio of gliadins to glutenins arise largely from wheat genetics and are therefore quite specific to an individual wheat variety. Inevitably, such differences are carried through to the flour milled from the wheat and thus contribute greatly to the breadmaking potential of the material. The glutenins are largely responsible for the elastic properties of gluten once it is formed in wheat flour. The molecular basis of wheat proteins and the formation of gluten in dough are complex. Recent work has shown that the glutenin may be divided into high-molecular-weight (HMW) and low-molecular-weight (LMW) sub-units (Shrewry and Miflin, 1985), with ratios of the two forms playing major roles in determining their potential uses in the manufacture of baked products.

Not all of the input to the protein content of wheat and therefore flour comes from the genetic background of the variety – agronomic and environmental factors also play a part. The agronomic practice of applying nitrogen and sulphur-based fertilisers to crops has a significant effect on the final protein content of the wheat grain. The timing of the application of nitrogen-based fertilisers is critical. Sufficient time needs to be given for the growing plant to take in the nitrogen so that it can play a part in determining the functional properties of the gluten-forming proteins. The use of sulphur as part of modern agronomic practices arises because of increasing sulphur deficiencies of soils in many parts of the world. It has been suggested that in the UK increasing sulphur deficiency has arisen because of the reduction in pollution of the atmosphere from the 1950s to the present day.

The protein content of the flour assumes a lesser importance in many baked products other than bread that do not rely on gluten formation, and so the choice of wheats for the milling grist may be based on lower and less functional (i.e. less gluten-forming) protein. The levels of protein typically present in white wheat flours for various baking applications are summarised in Table 4.1.

The study of wheat proteins has dominated the underpinning science associated with baked products. In part this is because of the importance of wheat-based products in human nutrition and the requirement for the development of a gluten structure in products such as bread. However, the composition of wheat flour is dominated by the carbohydrate known as starch (Table 4.2). The starch is contained within the cells of the endosperm, which is located inside the outer bran skins of the grain. The individual starch granules are enveloped in a protein matrix and provide a food source for the grains when germination starts.

In the manufacture of bread, the function of starch is mostly concerned with the absorption of water, which leads to swelling as the temperature rises, particularly during baking. The ability of the starch granules to absorb water is limited, but is increased during the milling process that converts the wheat grains to flour. During the milling process, a proportion of the starch granules are physically damaged and this increases their ability to absorb water five-fold.

The absorption of water by the starch, and the input of heat, encourages a process referred to as **gelatinisation**. Starch comprises two polymers – amylase and amylopectin. The former is essentially a linear

Table 4.1   Protein contents (14% moisture basis) for bakery applications.

Application	Typical protein content ranges (%)
Pan breads	10.5–13.0
Crusty breads	11.5–13.0
Baguette	10.5–12.0
Rolls	12.0–13.0
Laminated products	11.5–13.0
Cakes and sponges	7.0–10.5
Fruited cakes	10.0–12.0
Biscuits and cookies	9.0–11.0
Pastries	9.0–11.0

Table 4.2   General composition of wholemeal and white flour.

Flour component (%)	Wholemeal	White
Moisture	13.0–14.0	13.0–14.5
Starch and other carbohydrates	67.0–73.0	71.0–78.0
Protein	10.0–15.0	8.0–13.0
Lipid	~2.0	1.0–1.5
Crude fibre	~2.0	~0.2

polymer, apparently amorphous, while the latter has a branched structure. Together these polymers are held in a rigid network characterised by crystalline junction points. During the absorption of water, the starch granules swell and the bonds holding the polymers together begin to weaken. Further disruption is encouraged by heat and at gelatinisation, which commonly occurs at 60–90°C depending on the product, disruption of the granules is complete. Thus, the process of gelatinisation of starch granules may be seen as the progression from a relatively ordered structure to a totally amorphous one.

However, gelatinisation does not occur in all baked products, and the degree to which it occurs depends on the availability of water. In low-moisture recipes, such as for biscuits and pastes, the water level is generally too low and the competition for that water too high for significant gelatinisation to occur. Gelatinisation during baking plays a significant role in the formation of the product structure and the changes that subsequently occur as the product is cooled and stored.

The firming of bread crumb during storage owes much to the of a more crystalline structure in the product. This process, commonly referred to as **retrogradation**, can occur even when no moisture is lost from the product. Both gelatinisation in the dough during baking and staling in the bread on cooling and storage involve the movement of water on a micro-scale – that is between the protein and the starch. There is no consensus as to whether the water moves from the protein to the starch or vice versa. Wilhoft (1973) proposed loss of water from protein to starch while Cluskey *et al.* (1959) proposed the reverse. Whichever is the appropriate mechanism it is clear that water movement is critical and that starch plays a key role in deciding baked-product quality.

The impact of damage to the starch granules extends beyond increasing the water-absorption capacity of the flour. High levels of starch damage in white flours can lead to the loss of bread volume. Cauvain and Young (2006) discussed the effect of excessive damaged starch in the context of the Chorleywood Bread Process (CBP), where it lead to a more open cell structure and greying of bread crumb. Farrand (1964) observed such quality losses and considered that they arose because the level of damaged starch exceeded the protein[2] divided by 6. This precise relationship has little relevance today because of changes in breadmaking methods, but the basic principle remains relevant, namely that the higher the damaged starch level in the flour the higher should be its protein content.

Damaged starch is susceptible to enzymatic hydrolysis by *alpha*-amylase. The enzyme concerned is naturally present in wheat flour and the level of activity in flour is commonly assessed by measuring the Hagberg Falling Number (Cauvain and Young, 2001): the greater the level of *alpha*-amylase activity the lower the Falling Number. This relationship between starch damage and *alpha*-amylase activity has profound implications for baked-product quality, especially for bread and fermented goods. Naturally present in the flour is another form of amylase, *beta*-amylase. Together the *alpha*- and *beta*-amylases act on the starch granules and break them down, first to **dextrins** and then to **maltose**. In the process, the water that was previously held in the starch granules is released into the dough matrix where it may, or may not, be picked up by the gluten proteins.

The release of water from the starch leads to softening of the dough which may cause processing problems, while the presence of high levels of dextrins can lead to problems when slicing bread (Cauvain and Young, 2006). The maltose released by the action of the amylases can be used as a substrate by the yeast in the dough, though this is more important in dough that is based on a period of fermentation in bulk before dividing than in no-time dough systems. If the Falling Number of the flour is too low this can lead to collapse of the sidewall crusts in bread, a phenomenon referred to by bakers as **concavity** (Fig. 4.1).

As supplied to the baker, wheat flour will contain a small level of moisture, in the range of 10–14%. The majority of this water comes from the grain, but the level is usually increased as the result of

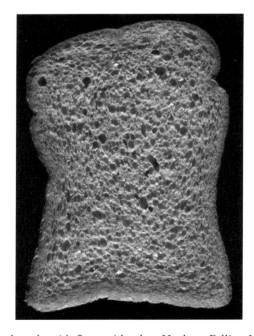

Figure 4.1   Bread made with flour with a low Hagberg Falling Number.

flour-milling practices. In particular, the miller will add extra water to facilitate the separation of the outer bran layers of the grain from the inner endosperm in the production of white flours (Sugden and Osborne, 2001). The greater the amount of water in the flour as supplied, the less must be added in the bakery in order to achieve a consistent dough rheology or batter viscosity, and vice versa.

Low levels, 1–2% of soluble proteins, or **pentosans**, are present in wheat flours. Once again the major influence on the level present is varietal. Pentosans absorb high levels of water (Stauffer, 1998) and so have an impact on the flour water-absorption capacity (that is the measure used by millers and bakers when adjusting water levels in baked-goods recipes).

The contribution of the branny layers, or fibre, depends on whether the flour is white, brown or wholemeal. There are legal definitions that are applied to brown and wholemeal flours. In the case of wholemeal flour, 100% of the wheat grain should be present, so that fibre levels will commonly be around 13%. The physics and chemistry of bran are complicated, not least because each of the seven bran layers varies in its form and composition. Commonly they are grouped together when it comes to a discussion of functionality. The presence of bran particles will reduce the ability of the flour to retain gas in breadmaking. It interferes with the formation of gluten and impinges on gas-bubble surfaces. The higher the level of bran present in the flour the greater the adverse effect on the gas-retention properties of the dough and the greater the loss of bread volume. The bran-particle size also has an impact, with fine particles having a greater adverse effect on gas retention than coarse ones.

The use of wholemeal or bran-supplemented flours is largely confined to the manufacture of bread and fermented goods and some forms of crackers. They are seldom used in cake-making, though they may find limited and specialist uses in the manufacture of biscuits (e.g. Digestives) and occasionally in pastry items.

In the past, it has been common practice to treat flour in the mill in order to modify its baking potential. This practice has largely been abandoned for bread flours in Europe and many other parts of the world, though it remains in use for some forms of cake and speciality flours. Cake flours are treated in one of two main ways: either through the application of chlorine gas (Street, 1991) or by the application of dry-heat treatment (Cauvain and Young, 2001). In both cases, the treatment aims to permit the cake recipe to be adjusted by adding higher levels of sugar and liquids than might otherwise be possible. The high-ratio cakes that result from using flour so treated have a different eating quality and longer shelf-life than low-ratio cakes. The concept of high- and low-ratio cakes has been discussed further in Chapter 3.

Fibre

Fibrous materials from sources other than wheat may be added to baked-product recipes in order to confer particular nutritional or sensory properties. Fortification of bread and similar products with such fibres is more common than the fortification of other groups of baked products. The fibres may come from many sources including barley, oats, rice, soya, apple, sugar beet and pea (Katina, 2003). Their chemical and physical properties have some similarities with those of wheat fibre and they all tend to have high water-absorption capacities, so that additional water will be required in the recipes in which they are used, if the batter and dough viscosities are to remain constant.

One problem with the addition of fibre to bread dough is that the uptake of water or hydration of the fibre is slower than that of the flour (endosperm) particles. This often results in significant changes in dough viscosity with increasing processing time. Initially, many fibre-containing bread doughs, including wholemeal, have a slightly sticky feel when they leave the mixer, but begin to lose that stickiness gradually as the water is absorbed by the fibre and become increasingly firm. In breadmaking this change is most often seen in the transition of dough from mixer to final moulder. In the moulding stage, increased dough viscosity (a **tight dough** in baker's terminology) can contribute to damage of the relatively delicate bubble structure in the dough and subsequent loss of bread quality, commonly manifest as dark streaks and firm patches in the bread crumb (Cauvain and Young, 2000).

A significant impact of fibre is to reduce dough gas retention and thus bread volume. As the level of fibre increases so does the adverse effect on bread volume. The volume loss may be overcome with recipe adjustment to augment the gas retention properties of the dough. The impact of particle size is similar to that discussed above for wheat bran, namely that fine particles tend to have a greater impact on the loss of bread volume than coarse ones. The addition of fibres also has an impact on the mouth-feel and, to a lesser extent, the flavour of baked products, but such changes are usually considered more acceptable.

The fibre source may sometimes be added as whole grains. Again such uses are almost exclusive to bread and fermented products. The grains may be subjected to some form of additional processing, such as malting or softening, in order to confer special flavour and mouth-feel characteristics. The whole grains contribute nothing to the development of the product structure but their addition may reduce dough gas retention: the higher the level of whole grains the greater the loss of bread volume.

Soya flour

Interest in the soya bean most commonly centres on its oil content and its nutritional value for animal and human feed. In the context of baked goods it is the flour that can be produced by milling the soya beans that is of greatest interest. Soya-bean flour is available de-fatted, enzyme inactivated or with full enzyme activity.

Enzyme-active soya flour has commonly been used in breadmaking as a bread improver or as the base material for bread improvers. It absorbs a greater mass of water than the same quantity of wheat flour. It makes a small contribution to the gas-retention properties of the dough but its main use is for whitening the bread crumb through the effect of its naturally-occurring **lipoxygenase** (Williams and Pullen, 1998). It has been suggested as a moisture-retention aid in cake making, though it is doubtful that it plays a significant role in this respect by comparison with other cake-making ingredients.

Cocoa powder

There are two basic types of cocoa powder available for baking – natural and Dutched. The latter form comes from a process in which the roasted, shelled and nibbed beans are treated with alkali. In addition to the two basic forms, the fat content of cocoa powders may vary from around 8–32%. Cocoa powders are most commonly used in the manufacture of chocolate-coloured and -flavoured cake, biscuit and cookie products. In some parts of the world legislation requires a minimum quantity of cocoa solids to be included in the formulation for a product to be given the description of chocolate.

Cocoa powder provides colour and flavour to baked products. The powders are dry, so if they are added to recipes the level of water should be increased in order to adjust dough, paste or batter rheology. The addition of cocoa powders tends to raise the normally slightly acidic pH products so that it is closer to 7.0 or slightly above. In the case of cake products the alkalinity of the product may be enhanced through an addition of a small excess of sodium bicarbonate in the recipe. This intensifies the chocolate colour and the resultant increase in pH to just above 7.0 and has special benefits in increasing the spoilage-free shelf-life of the product (because the growth of many moulds is restricted by alkaline pH).

Sugars and sweeteners

Sucrose

The main sources of sucrose are sugar cane and sugar beet (Jones *et al.*, 1997). Available in a number of different crystalline forms, it is widely used in the manufacture of baked products. The different forms of sucrose, granulated, caster, pulverised and icing, are distinguished by their particle size, with the largest being the granulated form. The main effect of particle size is to influence the rate at which the sucrose crystals will dissolve in water. The most common form encountered in the manufacture of baked products is the one described as **caster**. It is chosen because of its relatively rapid solubility and is used in bread, fermented goods and cakes. Where the recipe water content is lower, for example in biscuits and cookies, a finer form, **pulverised**, is more commonly used.

Sucrose confers sweetness and colour to baked products, but also has a key function in structure formation. In particular, the concentration of sucrose solution in a recipe has a significant effect on the gelatinisation characteristics of wheat and other starches – the higher the sucrose concentration, the more significant the delay in the gelatinisation temperature of the starch. For example, in the presence of a 50% sucrose concentration (similar to that seen in cake batters) the gelatinisation temperature of wheat starch may rise from around 60°C to 80°C. By contrast, the sucrose concentration has relatively little effect on the coagulation temperature of the proteins in the system. The impact of sucrose on starch gelatinisation and the implications for structure formation are discussed in more detail in later chapters.

The main effect of sucrose on a baked product is most commonly observed in cakes and similar products. A typical example, using a loaf-shaped cake, is shown in Figure 4.2. As the level of sugar in the recipe is increased, the top of the cake gradually becomes flatter in shape and eventually the product sinks. Accompanying the changes

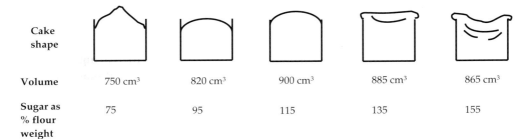

Cake shape					
Volume	750 cm³	820 cm³	900 cm³	885 cm³	865 cm³
Sugar as % flour weight	75	95	115	135	155

Figure 4.2 Impact of level of sugar on volume and shape of cake.

in shape are changes in product volume. As the sucrose level increases, the cake-crust colour becomes progressively darker, but, with very high levels of sugar, re-crystallisation leads to a lightening of the crust appearance.

Sucrose levels are generally low in bread and fermented goods, though in some parts of the world (e.g. southern India) the addition of sucrose may reach as high as 30% of the flour weight. Increasing levels of sucrose affect the gas-producing ability of baker's yeast. The addition of 15% sugar based on flour weight more than doubles the time that it would take for a piece of dough to reach a given height in the prover (Fig. 4.3). Because of this effect it is common practice to increase the yeast level in sweetened, fermented-product recipes.

The considerable impact of sucrose in baking arises from its affinity for water and the bonds that are formed between it and water when a solution is created. The impact is immediate when the ingredients are brought together during mixing and exerts a limiting effect on gluten formation. The sucrose effect is not as great as would be seen with ionic substances like salt, but is nevertheless considerably greater than might be seen with wheat-flour components. The restriction of water availability is partly responsible for the effect on starch gelatinisation.

An important role for sucrose is the effect on the water activity of the baked product (Cauvain and Young, 2000). Increasing levels of sucrose lower product water activity and have a significant effect on product spoilage-free shelf-life. The impact is similar to that on baker's yeast, discussed above. High levels of sucrose restrict the ability of the micro-organisms to grow, and increase the time that it takes for mould colonies to become large enough to be visible to the naked eye (the

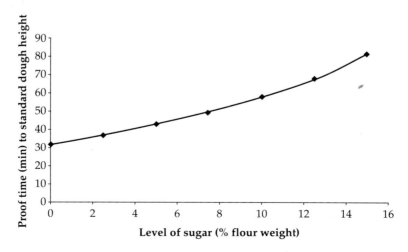

Figure 4.3   Effect of sugar on yeast fermentation.

point at which most consumers consider that the product has reached the end of its shelf-life).

Dextrose/glucose syrups

Glucose and other non-sucrose syrups are derived from a number of sources, including wheat and maize starch (Jones *et al.*, 1997). Dextrose monohydrate is the powdered form of glucose. Glucose syrups are commonly defined by their dextrose equivalent (DE), which relates to the dry solids present in the glucose syrup – the higher the DE the greater the quantity of the dextrose solids present. The behaviour in reducing terms of 100 g of a 42 DE glucose syrup indicates it would be equivalent to 42 g dextrose.

Dextrose and glucose syrups play a similar role to that of sucrose in conferring sweetness and colour to baked products. They are commonly less sweet than sucrose and they are more active in the Maillard reactions which occur during baking. This often leads to excessive browning of products and so their levels of use in many baked products are much lower than those commonly seen with sucrose. A typical example of this problem may be seen in cake baking, where higher levels of dextrose cause a light brown discolouration of the cake crumb rising from the product base for some way up the product cross-section. The degree to which this problem may be seen depends to a large extent on the size and shape of the product, with slab cakes being more susceptible than thin layer cakes. They have a similar impact on starch gelatinisation to sucrose and so contribute to structure formation in a number of products.

Invert sugar/honey

Invert sugar syrups and honey comprise a mixture of sugars, usually glucose and fructose, with low levels of sucrose. In addition to providing sweetness they confer some benefit by extending the mould-free shelf-life of baked products because they lower product water activity to a greater extent than an equivalent level of sucrose (Cauvain and Young, 2000). Their impact on product structure is similar to that of dextrose and glucose syrups.

Glycerol and sorbitol

Polyhydric alcohols such as glycerol and sorbitol are mainly used in baked products for their water-activity-lowering effect (Cauvain and Young, 2000) and their impact on glass transition temperatures. They tend to make no contribution to product flavour but, at higher levels, are associated with unacceptable browning of the product crumb and loss of product volume.

Fats

Oils and fats occur in abundance in nature and have been added to modify the mouth-feel of baked products since prehistoric times. In more recent times, an understanding of the chemistry of fats has lead to the development of the compound fats that are commonly used in the manufacture of almost all baked products today. Fats are esters of fatty acids and glycerol, which commonly form triglycerides in which three fatty acids are attached to the glycerol molecule. The basic building block of oils and fats is the fatty acid and it is the chaining together of carbon atoms in the fatty acids that characterises the particular oil or fat (Podmore and Rajah, 1997).

Fats may be **saturated** or **unsaturated**, depending on the way in which the four available carbon atoms are used. In the saturated form, all of the available carbon bonds are linked with hydrogen atoms, while in the unsaturated form a double bond between carbon atoms reduces the number of potential bonds for the hydrogen atoms. In addition, some fatty acids can exist in two or more forms, which are referred to as **isomers**. In this case the chemical bonds are the same but the spatial arrangement of the molecule (the fatty acid) differs.

The variation in fat chemistry has a profound effect on its physical form. In particular, the variations account for the difference in temperature at which a pure oil will make the transition to a solid. It is more common to describe the reverse process – that is the transition from solid to liquid – and this is often referred to as the melting point of the fat. The process by which fats solidify is not simple, because fats can exist in different polymorphic forms. On cooling, the triglyceride molecules can pack together into different crystalline arrangements, commonly designated as the *alpha*, *beta* **prime** and *beta* forms. The size of the crystals varies with the form, with the *alpha* form having the smallest crystal size (typically <2 μm) and the *beta* form the largest (typically with sizes in the range of 5–30 μm). In the *alpha* form the packing is relatively random, in the *beta* prime the order is more structured and the ends of the triglyceride crystals may sit at right angles with one another while in the *beta* form the end of the triglycerides run in more or less parallel rows. Stauffer (1999) provides photomicrographs of the different triglyceride crystal forms. It is worth noting that most fats comprise a mixture of the three forms though the nature of the solidification process may favour one form more than the other two. The particular form which is created during solidification depends on the manner in which the liquid oil is cooled. Though the chemical composition of the fat remains unchanged, the different physical forms have very different properties.

In the context of baked products, differences in fat crystalline form may show themselves as variations in the potential of the fat to incorporate air in the manufacture of cakes. In Figure 4.4, the abilities of the three fat polymorphs to incorporate air into the batter are compared, and the data clearly show that the beta prime form has the best air-retaining properties because, when used at the same level of addition, batter density is lower than seen with either of the other two polymorphs.

The crystal form and size of the fat also has an impact on the gas retention properties of the dough, with smaller crystal sizes allowing more gas retention. The role of fat in improving gas retention in modern breadmaking has been illustrated many times (Williams and Pullen, 1998). Although the effect of increasing the level of fat in the recipe is to increase the gas-retention properties of the dough, a maximum point is reached eventually, beyond which there appears to be little effect of increasing the level.

This maximum point has been hard to define, in part because it appears that the improving effect of fat is linked with flour properties in some way that has yet to be explained. The relationship with flour explains why the impact of a given level of added fat is less with whole-meal flour than with white flours. It has also been observed that the gas-retention properties of flours that have been stored for a long period of time can be restored by adding fat over and above that normally used in the breadmaking recipe.

In view of the complications and uncertainties over the interaction of fat and flour in the breadmaking process it has become common

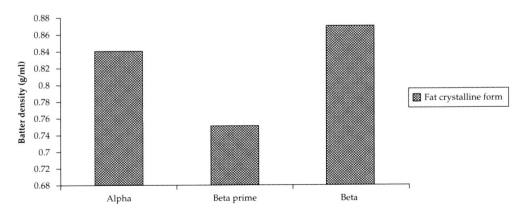

Figure 4.4   Effect of fat crystal form on cake batter aeration.

practice to set a blanket level of addition to avoid any failure of gas retention. When the Chorleywood Bread Process was first introduced, a level equivalent to 0.7% flour weight of a bakery shortening with specified characteristics was recommended (Cauvain and Young, 2006). Since its introduction, added fat levels in UK bread recipes have fallen, but this is in part because of the increased use of emulsifiers (see below) and more appropriate blends of fats.

The key role of fats in a number of baking processes requires a more detailed explanation of the composition of bakery fats. They are in fact a mixture of solid fat and liquid oil of different types. Today vegetable fat sources dominate the blends, whereas in the past marine and animal sources were commonly used as part of the composite fat.

As the temperature of a composite bakery fat is raised, more of the solid components turn to liquid oil until eventually a temperature is reached at which all of the material is in the liquid form. This is referred to as the **melting point** of the fat – that is, the temperature at which all of the material will reach the liquid form. The melting point of fats varies and in a composite fat there are in effect a series of melting points, each related to a different component. This means that to assess the baking potential of a composite fat effectively it is necessary to measure the proportion of fat which exists in the solid form over a range of temperatures. The solid fat content, or solid fat index, of three fats commonly used in baking are illustrated in Figure 4.5.

The oil component of a bakery fat at typical bakery temperatures (15–30°C) is an important part of the mechanism by which the solid

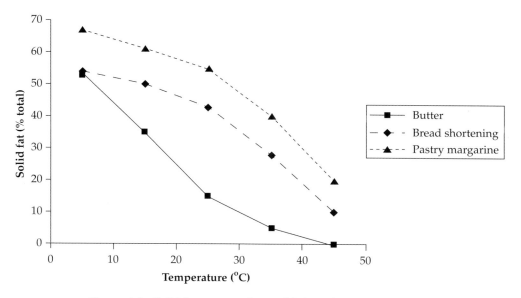

Figure 4.5   Solid fat content of typical bakery fats.

fat crystals are dispersed through the particular matrix while the solid fat component plays the major role in determining the functional and sensory properties in baked products.

The main roles of solid fat in bakery products may be summarised as follows:

- Bread and fermented goods
  - Stabilisation of gas bubbles incorporated into the dough, which leads to improvement to the gas-retention properties of the dough, which is usually manifested as improved oven spring (the difference in height between the dough entering the oven and the baked bread leaving it)
  - Inhibition of gas-bubble coalescence, which leads to finer (smaller cell size) crumb structure in the baked product
  - A contribution to crumb softness at higher levels of addition
- Cakes
  - Enhancement of air incorporation during batter preparation
  - Inhibition of gas-bubble coalescence, which leads to finer (smaller cell size) crumb structure in the baked product
  - A contribution to crumb softness at higher levels of addition
- Laminated products
  - Improvements to product lift by slowing down the diffusion of steam between dough layers. Laminated pastry lift increases with both the quantity and quality of the laminated fat. In the latter case, the higher the melting point or the greater the proportion of solid fat at a given temperature the greater the pastry lift (Fig. 4.6).
  - Significant contribution to the sensory properties of the product, with higher-melting-point fats conferring unacceptable palate-cling and waxy mouth feel
- Biscuits and cookies
  - Contribution to biscuit aeration
  - Significant contribution to the sensory properties of the product, with higher-melting-point fats conferring unacceptable palate-cling and waxy mouth feel
- Pastries
  - Significant contribution to the sensory properties of the product with higher-melting-point fats conferring unacceptable palate-cling and waxy mouth feel
  - A reduction in moisture migration in composite pastry products (Cauvain and Young, 2000)

Some composite bakery fats may contain one or more emulsifiers. The presence of the emulsifier reduces the tendency of the fat to change

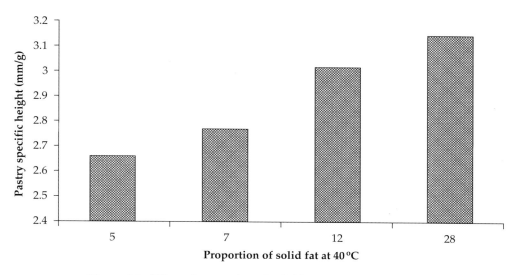

Figure 4.6   Effect of proportion of solid fat at 40°C on pastry lift.

crystal form during storage, especially if the fat is to be subjected to any warming or cooling (for example during transfer to and from refrigerated storage). Composite bakery shortening may also contain water to aid dispersion of the solid fat crystals during preparation. In this case the emulsifiers aid the dispersion of the water throughout the fat during manufacture, and help maintain stability of the blend during subsequent storage. The presence of the emulsifier also aids the incorporation of small air bubbles into the fat and so increases the direct contribution that the fat makes. The water phase of blended fats may be acidified and contain a microbial inhibitor to prevent mould growth during prolonged storage.

Butter

Butter is an animal fat that remains in favour despite the general move towards the use of vegetable-based fats. It retains its popularity because of its sensory properties and the perception of added value and naturalness in consumers' minds. There are legal definitions of butter and its composition is strictly controlled in many countries. In addition to the butterfat it will contain milk solids (2%), water (16%) and may contain salt. Anhydrous butters are available (Podmore and Rajah, 1997) but this can present problems with the use of the descriptor 'butter' in relation to the product and its labelling.

In view of its popularity with consumers it is ironic that it is technically one of the hardest fats for the baker to use. There are two main reasons for this: one is that, being a natural material, butter is subject to natural variability; the second is that the crystal form and solid-fat content profile of butter are not entirely compatible with the functional roles of fat required in the manufacture of baked products. The effect of the natural variability of butter is best illustrated by the seasonal variability which may occur in solid fat (Bent, 1998). These variations come from changes in the feeding patterns of cows, especially when they make the transition to winter feed in the autumn or to grass feeding in the spring. The effects tend to be short-lived – perhaps a few weeks.

The natural melting point of butter is relatively low (25–28°C) and it readily turns to oil even under normal bakery conditions. When butter is used in the manufacture of laminated products, careful control of the processing temperatures is required. In cakes, the creaming properties of butter are relatively poor and its use may require that the recipe is supplemented with an emulsifier (see below) in order to get the best results. Certainly, when butter is used in baking, careful storage and tempering of the material is required in order to reduce variability in its performance. Tempering is used to improve the mixture of crystal forms in the butter, but repeated warming and cooling should be avoided (Podmore and Rajah, 1997).

Margarines

The composition of margarines is often regulated to be similar to that of butter, but the mixture of oils, and therefore the functionality, of different margarines will be different. In addition to milk solids, water and salt, margarines may contain an emulsifier to aid the dispersion and stability of the water phase in a manner similar to that discussed above for high-ratio fats.

Emulsifiers

Emulsions are two-phased systems in which one phase (**disperse**) is suspended as small droplets in the second phase (**continuous**). Substances that promote stability in emulsions are known as emulsifiers and they work by providing a bridge between the two phases. The two common types of emulsion are oil in water (salad dressings) and water in oil (margarines). Batters and doughs are complex emulsions and a number of different emulsifiers are used successfully to aid oil and, more critically, air dispersion and their stability during all stages of baking processes. In addition to potential interactions with oils, liquids and gases, emulsifiers may play a role in starch-complexing (anti-staling) and interact with proteins (Kamel and Ponte, 1993). Natural surfactants (emulsifiers) do occur in nature but many are the result of manufacturing technologies available today.

Some of the emulsifiers commonly encountered and their typical functions in baking are discussed below. All of them (and others not discussed) may also be particularly useful when fat-reduced recipes are being prepared for the manufacture of all baked-product groups. In such cases the emulsifier is more powerful than the fat on a weight-for-weight basis at promoting many of the required properties, for example batter aeration and gas-bubble stability.

Mono- and diglycerides

The most commonly encountered form is glycerol monostearate (GMS), sometimes used in its more refined distilled form, GMS (DGMS). This emulsifier has a long history of use as a softening (anti-staling) agent in the manufacture of bread and fermented products. It is able to form complexes with the starch, which slows down the retrogradation process in the baked product during storage (Pateras, 1998). Its effect initially increases with additional quantities, but levels off with higher volumes. Typical amounts added to a mixture are less than 1% of the flour weight. GMS may be used as a micro-bead powder, but its effectiveness is increased if it is prepared as a dispersion in water – a **gel**. In water the GMS may exist in a number of crystalline forms depending on the concentration and the manner of preparation.

For baking it is generally considered that the most effective form for GMS is the alpha-crystalline form. This is especially true in the manufacture of cake batters, where the GMS makes significant contributions to air-bubble incorporation and gas-bubble stability during processing. Cauvain and Cyster (1996) reviewed the critical role that GMS plays in sponge-cake quality. They showed that an optimised level of GMS contributed to sponge-cake volume, structure and softness. The effect of GMS was not linear. Low levels of addition could lead to poorer quality products than recipes which contained no GMS (loss of volume and crumb structure) and high levels of GMS could also lead to quality losses (loss of volume, closeness of structure and crust defects).

In the manufacture of cake products containing relatively high levels of solid fat or an unsuitable fat (e.g. butter), GMS can be used to ensure adequate aeration of the batter.

Diacetyl tartaric acid esters of mono- and diglycerides (DATEM)

Sometimes referred to as DATA esters or simply DATA, these emulsifiers are commonly used in baking. They are often seen in bread and fermented-product recipes where they aid the stability of gas bubbles and prevent their coalescence during processing. In practical terms this leads to an improvement in the gas retention of the dough (increased oven spring) and cell structure (finer).

Sodium and calcium stearoyl lactylate (SSL and CSL)

These emulsifiers are often seen in bread and fermented-product recipes where they aid the stability of gas bubbles and prevent their coalescence during processing. In practical terms this leads to an improvement in the gas retention of the dough (increased oven spring) and cell structure (finer).

Egg products

Traditionally, **whole liquid egg**, which is about 75% water, was the ingredient used to deliver water in the manufacture of baked products. It also conveys flavour and colour. The proteins of the egg albumen can contribute to cake-batter aeration and structure formation but only in a limited range of products: an example is in the manufacture of non-fatted sponges, since the presence of fat negates the foam-promoting properties of the egg albumen. Even if the egg proteins do not directly contribute to batter aeration, they do contribute to the physical strength of the baked crumb and therefore to eating quality. The egg yolk is rich in fat and lecithin (an emulsifying agent).

Liquid egg is most commonly used as a chilled or frozen liquid in order to avoid microbial problems. The liquid form may be supplied combined with sugar, which also helps limit microbial activity.

Liquid albumen (egg white) is used in a number of baked products, where the yellowness conferred by the egg yolk is unacceptable, for example in white layer cakes. The liquid egg albumen is mainly a mixture of water (around 80%) and globular proteins (albumen). Egg albumen proteins make a contribution to the eating quality of cakes by improving their physical strength.

In its most common form, **dried whole egg** is de-sugared and spray dried. The solids in the dried form have similar functional properties to those in the liquid form. The dried product may be rehydrated before use.

In its most common form, **dried albumen** has been de-sugared and spray dried. The solids in the dried form have similar functional properties to those in the liquid form. The dried product may be rehydrated before use.

Baking powders and their components

Baking powder comprises a mixture of (usually) sodium bicarbonate and a food-grade acid used to provide a source of carbon dioxide gas. The total quantity of carbon dioxide released from a baking powder depends on the quantity of sodium bicarbonate that is present in the mixture, but only to the extent that the baking acid is able to react with it. Usually the level of baking acid is balanced to achieve a complete reaction with the sodium bicarbonate. This is commonly referred to as the **neutralisation value** of the acid: the quantity of the baking acid required to release all of the available carbon dioxide from the sodium bicarbonate. This may readily be calculated from the chemical composition of the particular baking acid (Thacker, 1997). In some cases, the active ingredients in baking powder may be diluted with an inert carrier, starch for example.

The level of baking powder used in the manufacture of cakes has a significant effect on product volume and quality. Cake products that do not contain baking powder tend to be low in volume and have a dense, close structure. Initially, as the level of baking powder in the recipe increases, cake volume increases and the crumb structure increases. Eventually, a maximum volume is achieved and thereafter as the level of baking powder continues to increase the product collapses, volume falls and the crumb structure becomes coarse and open in nature (Fig. 4.7).

The rate at which carbon dioxide is released is a key factor in the use of baking powder. The rate of carbon dioxide release depends on a number of factors, including the temperature of the batter. A significant factor in controlling the rate is the particle size of the acid and bicarbonate components and the choice of acidulant. It is important to ensure that the components of the baking powder are able to go to complete reaction. If the particle size of any of the components is too coarse then not only will there be a loss of carbon dioxide through an incomplete reaction but there may also be spots of unreacted material that lead to quality losses associated with product appearance and taste.

The nature of the acidulant is probably the most important factor in controlling the rate of carbon-dioxide evolution. In broad terms, baking powders may be classed as slow- or fast-acting, or, if a mixture of slow- and fast-acting acids is used, as double-acting. The choice of which type of baking powder to use in a given mix will be based on when gas evolution is required. The contribution of the different types of baking powder to final product quality is discussed in subsequent chapters.

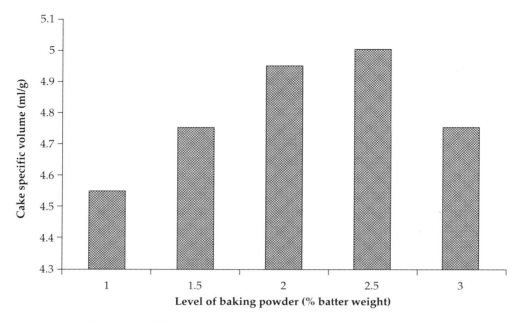

Figure 4.7   Effect of level of baking powder on cake volume.

Baking powders are mainly used in the manufacture of cakes, biscuits and cookies, though they may also be used in pastries and in specialist yeast-raised products.

A number of different **acidulants** (organic acids) may be used in the manufacture of baked products. Their uses range from reacting with sodium bicarbonate to yield carbon dioxide and aiding structure formation in the manufacture of white cakes, to lowering product pH to assist with the extension of mould-free shelf-life (Cauvain and Young, 2000).

Acids commonly used in baking include:

- *Acid calcium phosphate monohydrate (ACP)* – a fast-acting acid used in the ratio of 1.25 to 1 part sodium bicarbonate
- *Tartaric acid* – a moderately fast-acting acid used in the ratio of 0.9 to 1 part sodium bicarbonate
- *Sodium acid pyrophosphate (SAPP)* – a slow-acting acid used in the ratio of 1.33 to 1 part sodium bicarbonate
- *Sodium aluminium phosphate (SALP)* – a slow-acting acid used in the ratio of 1 to 1 part sodium bicarbonate
- *Potassium hydrogen tartrate* (cream of tartar) – a slow-acting acid used in the ratio of 2.2 to 1 part sodium bicarbonate
- *Glucono-delta-lactone (GDL)* – a slow-acting acidulant used in the ratio of 2.12 to 1 part sodium bicarbonate

Sodium bicarbonate is an inorganic compound used to generate carbon dioxide through its reaction with an acid. Carbon dioxide can only be driven off by heating sodium bicarbonate alone once the temperature has reached 90°C, but the residual carbonate is alkaline and the flavour largely unacceptable. In most cases, neutral reactions between the sodium bicarbonate and an acid are favoured; however, in the manufacture of chocolate cake, a small excess of sodium bicarbonate may be used to enhance the colour of the product.

Potassium bicarbonate may be used as an alternative to sodium bicarbonate but the level of neutralising acid needs to be increased and the residual flavour is distinctly different from that of the sodium salts. In order to yield the same quantity of carbon dioxide, the level of potassium bicarbonate is increased.

Ammonium bicarbonate (traditionally known as **vol**) is used in the manufacture of some biscuits and specialist choux pastries (Cauvain and Young, 2001). It decomposes rapidly at around 60°C to release carbon dioxide, water vapour and ammonia. It may be used to provide a rapid expansion of the product in the very early stages of the baking process.

Dried and candied fruits

Raisins, sultanas and currants are added to flavour many products. Dried vine fruits have relatively high levels of sugar present and so contribute to product sweetness, and their particulate nature has an impact on dough and batter processing as well as on the final product eating qualities. They have a relatively low moisture content and high sugar concentration, which can lead to moisture migration from the product crumb to the fruit, making the former dry eating (Marston, 1983; Cauvain and Young, 2001).

Dried fruits are used in many bakery products, with the possible exception of pastries. The amount added depends as much on cost as it does on personal preference. However, it should be remembered that dried fruits will contribute little or nothing to structure formation in the product and are effectively an inert material which must be carried by the other structure-forming components in the recipe.

Cherries and citrus peel may be used to confer flavour and modify product eating quality, mainly in cakes and fruited fermented products. The high levels of sugars which are part of the product also contribute to the extension of mould-free shelf-life. As with dried fruits, candied fruits make no contribution to structure formation.

Chocolate chips

The main contributions of chocolate chips are those associated with flavour and eating quality and they are mainly used in cakes and cookies. They can come in many forms and need to withstand exposure to the high temperatures associated with baking.

Salt (sodium chloride)

Salt is used for a variety of purposes in the manufacture of baked products. First and foremost it makes a major contribution to product flavour. It is also important, because of its ionic nature, in the control of product water activity and therefore mould-free shelf-life (Cauvain and Young, 2000).

In the manufacture of fermented products, salt limits the activity of yeast in dough and so recipes should be balanced to take this into account. The lower the level of salt in the dough the lower the yeast level will be to maintain a given proof time (Williams and Pullen, 1998). There is also some impact of salt on gluten formation in the dough-making stage.

Yeast

Baker's yeast, *Saccharomyces cerevisiae*, is used to produce carbon dioxide in the manufacture of bread, rolls and other fermented products. It acts on simple sugars to produce both carbon dioxide and alcohol (Williams and Pullen, 1998). The alcohol is driven off during baking and so is of limited relevance to baked products. The carbon dioxide is an important part of the expansion of baked products and contributes significantly to changes in texture and eating quality.

The higher the level of yeast present in the recipe, the faster the rate at which carbon dioxide will be produced. The reaction is very temperature sensitive and increases as the temperature rises to 40–43°C. Thereafter, the rate of evolution of carbon dioxide falls until the yeast is inactivated at 55°C. This temperature profile is critical in the manufacture of bread and fermented products and is discussed in subsequent chapters.

Ascorbic acid and other improvers

Ascorbic acid has a number of uses in the manufacture of baked products, but by far its main use is as an oxidising agent in the production of bread and fermented products. In the strict chemical sense, ascorbic acid is a reducing agent and sometimes described as an anti-oxidant, for example it may be used to prevent discolouration of potatoes. In the breadmaking process, the availability of oxygen allows for its conversion to dehydroascorbic acid, which then acts as an oxidising agent and plays an essential part in the development of gluten in modern breadmaking processes (Williams and Pullen, 1998).

As the level of ascorbic acid added increases, bread volume increases and the cell structure of the product becomes finer. At some stage, increasing levels of ascorbic acid no longer result in increases in bread volume. This is because the effectiveness of the ascorbic acid as an oxidising agent is limited by the level of oxygen that is available for conversion to dehydroascorbic acid. Within the dough, competition for oxygen is significant, especially from the yeast, and by the end of dough mixing, or very soon after, the oxygen in the dough has disappeared and the effect of ascorbic acid is restricted. As will be discussed later, the availability of oxygen during mixing depends on the type of mixer and the mixing conditions employed. The greater the quantity of available oxygen, the greater is the potential for ascorbic-acid-assisted oxidation of the dough. Thus, the limiting level of ascorbic acid will vary according to that oxygen availability – typically levels of addition ascorbic acid are 100–200 ppm flour weight.

Ascorbic acid may be used at low levels of addition (<50 ppm flour weight) in the manufacture of laminated products to increase their lift. However, in such circumstances it is common for shrinkage of such products to occur and this may limit the level of ascorbic acid which may be used.

The list of other oxidising agents permitted for breadmaking is quite small. Commonly, in many parts of the world, ascorbic acid is the only one, but the use of **potassium bromate**, **azodicarbonamide** and **calcium peroxide** as bread improvers is retained in the USA and some other countries. As is the case with ascorbic acid, the function of these oxidants is to improve dough gas retention and therefore bread volume.

L-cysteine hydrochloride may be added as a reducing agent in the manufacture of bread dough and laminated pastries in some circumstances. It reduces the elasticity of the dough or paste and reduces the shrinkage that might otherwise occur after moulding, sheeting and forming.

Enzymes

Enzymes are proteins with very specific functions that are found widespread in nature. They have always been present in baking, since they are found in flour and yeast. More recently they have assumed greater importance in baking, with the new restrictions on ingredients which may be used as improvers, especially in the manufacture of bread and fermented products. The enzymes used in baking come from a number of sources. In many cases the enzymes that are used are not normal components of the flour and yeast but come from other microbial sources, that have been used as the manufacturing environment for their production.

In baking, the addition of enzymes is commonly used to modify dough rheology, gas retention and crumb softness in bread manufacture (Williams and Pullen, 1998), to modify dough rheology in the manufacture of pastry and biscuits (Manley, 2000), to change product softness in cake making (Sahi and Guy, 2005) and for the reduction of acrylamide formation in bakery products (de Boer *et al.*, 2005). The levels of addition for enzymes in baked products are very low. They are often described as processing aids and in many countries they do not need to be listed on product labels.

The choice of enzyme is specific to the function to be fulfilled and a full discussion of each of the possible enzymes is outside the scope of this book. The more commonly encountered enzymes and their effects on baked-product quality are discussed below.

Alpha-**amylases** are an important enzyme group that is encountered in one of four main forms, cereal, fungal, bacterial and modified bacterial, all of which act on the damaged starch in flour. They are used to improve the gas-retention properties of fermented dough, which leads to improvements in product volume and softness. In the case of the modified bacterial form of *alpha*-amylase, there is also an anti-staling effect.

The main differences between the various forms are their thermal stability profiles, especially the temperature at which they are inactivated during the baking process, and their relationship with gelatinising starch (see Chapter 7) – the lower the temperature of inactivation the less the effect on the gelatinising starch.

The fungal form of *alpha*-amylase has a long history of use and has found favour because, while giving the benefit of increased bread volume (Cauvain and Chamberlain, 1988), there is no negative effect associated with dextrin formation, which is likely to occur when using either the cereal or bacterial forms. The modified bacterial *alpha*-amylase has a similar heat-stability profile to that of the fungal form (Williams and Pullen, 1998). Bread volume increases as the level of added *alpha*-amylase increases. Actual levels of addition depend on the activity of the enzyme preparation that is used and the effects required in the final product.

The function of **hemicellulases (zylanases)** in the grain is to break down the cell-wall material, commonly referred to as pentosans or soluble proteins. These soluble proteins are present in low concentrations in the subsequent wheat flour but are important because they have very high water-binding properties (Stauffer, 1998). It is with these pentosans that the hemicellulases react to bring about improvements in bread volume. Once again, the actual levels of addition depend on the activity of the enzyme preparation that is used and the effect required in the final product.

The addition of **lipases** has become more popular in recent times. They act on the flour lipids and other fatty materials that might be present in the recipe and may give improvements in bread volume. In addition to improving bread softness, which naturally occurs when bread volume increases, the addition of lipases can retard the rate of staling in the baked product. This effect comes about because the breakdown products of lipase activity form complexes with wheat starch.

Proteolytic enzymes are not commonly used in the manufacture of bread and fermented products, but have some use in the manufacture of pastries, biscuits and cookies. Their action is on the proteins of wheat flour: they reduce gluten elasticity and thereby reduce dough or paste shrinkage after moulding and sheeting.

Water

Chemically, water is the simplest ingredient used in baking (two atoms of hydrogen and one of oxygen), but because of its special properties it plays many significant roles in baking, final product quality and product shelf-life (Cauvain and Young, 2000). Water is present in many ingredients that are used in baking, such as liquid egg, or it may be added as a separate ingredient. It has key roles associated with the solubilising and dispersion of ingredients during the mixing process and in the formation of complexes such as gluten in bread and fermented doughs. In the final product, the water (moisture) content makes major contributions to eating quality and shelf-life as has been discussed previously.

The level of water used in a given product recipe needs to be optimised in order to achieve the required handling properties of the intermediate (dough, batter, paste) and final product character. In the case of bread dough, optimum water levels are associated with the ability to handle the dough during processing and the actual levels used should be as high as possible while remaining consistent with processing requirements. The temptation to reduce added water levels in bread dough should be avoided, because of the contribution it makes to dough development. Often, the stickiness that bakers associate with too much water comes instead from under-development of the dough: that is, the dough has not achieved its full potential. Improvements in the underlying dough development often allow an increase in added water levels.

The amount of water used in the manufacture of cake batters is closely associated with the level of sugar in the recipe. Typically, the levels of these two ingredients are optimised at a sucrose concentration of around 50%.

Water plays a significant role in batter fluidity and affects many aspects of batter handling and baking. Water levels are usually lowest in the manufacture of biscuits, cookies and many pastries, because of the need to bake out the water later.

Milk products

Liquid milk is a mixture of water, fats and proteins. It contributes to the hydration of doughs and batters and confers colour and flavour. It is preferable that the milk be heat-treated before being used in bread-making as it can otherwise cause loss of bread volume in bread doughs (Cauvain and Young, 20001).

Milk/whey powders are two forms of dried solids derived from milk and are used to confer colour and flavour to baked products. The powders should be fully heat-treated to avoid problems associated with loss of product volume (Cauvain and Young, 2001).

Chapter 5
The Nature of Baked Product Structure

Introduction

The degree to which the structures of the various sub-groups of baked products vary has already been introduced. However, at the macroscopic level such structures have two common features in that they are composed of air spaces and solid materials fused together in a more or less ordered structure (Fig. 5.1). At the microscopic level there are many more physical and chemical differences between baked-product sub-groups.

Broadly speaking, baked-product structures may be described as being sponges: that is, they have a cellular structure composed of solid material – the cell walls – through which are interspersed air spaces – the cells. The comparison with natural or synthetic sponges is clear. A key property of sponge structures is that, because there are holes in the cell walls, each cell is interconnected with all of the other cells in the matrix. This means that fluids – gaseous and liquid – can move through the matrix readily and that gas pressures and temperatures in all of the cells are in equilibrium. It also means that the structure is capable of trapping and holding fluids. However, in many cases the liquid, for example water, is not necessarily bound to the cell-wall material and the sponge would release that liquid when subjected to pressure (for example squeezing) or gravity might cause the fluid to drain from the matrix. This principle is best observed using a synthetic sponge in the bath, but would be more difficult (and messy) to observe with a baked product. The synthetic sponge will not dissolve in the bath water nor form chemical bonds with it, in contrast with baked-product sponges.

The link between baked-product structures and the eating quality of baked products has also been introduced. In this respect the structural architecture of the baked product has a profound influence because of the forces required to break it down in the mouth and to masticate it ready for swallowing.

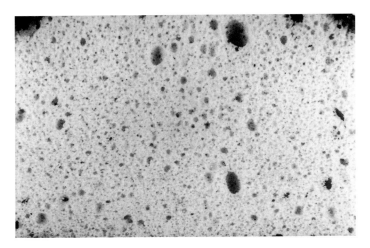

Figure 5.1   Close-up of baked cake-crumb structure.

The importance of the contribution of air cells to baked-product texture should not be underestimated. The numbers, sizes and spatial distribution of the cells within a product all have an impact on texture. Increasing the numbers and sizes physically moves the cell-wall material further apart and so weakens its influence on textural characteristics. Thinner cell walls will inevitably require less force to fracture and will allow the food to break down more readily into small pieces in the mouth. In many bakery foods this conveys the impression of friability when first bitten into. This is not always a sensation that consumers expect from bakery products. Equally, excessive friability presents problems for the manufacturer, because the compression and shearing forces that occur when baked products are sliced, wrapped and bagged can have negative impacts on production capabilities, for example in the formation of crumb waste in the slicing of cake and bread.

The contribution of the spatial distribution of air is less obvious. In this context subjective descriptors such as 'uneven' and 'irregular' are commonly used. They refer to the fact that the air cells are not of uniform size and therefore that the spatial distribution in a given cross-section of the baked product is not uniform. In fact, in most baked products the spatial distribution of cells is seldom uniform, and in many cases it is an integral part of the product characteristic. For example, measurement of the density of bread crumb across a given slice will show that regions under the crust tend to be denser than those within the body of the crumb.

Such variations are illustrated for sandwich-style bread in Figure 5.2. This product is baked in a lidded pan, and compression of the crumb on all four sides provides a contrast to the more cellular structure at

Figure 5.2   Close-up of sandwich bread crumb cell structure.

the centre. The dense layers at the four edges contribute to the hardness of the crust while the lower density at the centre contributes to bread softness (that is lower hardness). As will be discussed in a later chapter, the manufacturing processes have a profound impact on the spatial distribution of cells in the final baked product.

Techniques used to evaluate baked-product structure

Because baked-product structure is of such importance, one might be forgiven for assuming that its measurement was commonplace and carried out in an objective manner. In fact, until relatively recently, the latter has not been the case. For most of the time that baked products have been subjected to scientific scrutiny the evaluation of baked-product structure has been carried out subjectively, albeit in many cases using expert human observers.

The traditional evaluation technique is commonly based on a series of descriptive terms that generally apply to baked products or to one or more of the sub-groups of baked products (Figures 2.1–2.3, pp. 19–21). The main problem with such descriptors is that they tend to have little meaning unless a common terminology is used. This is seldom the case so that the application of terms tends to be product and author specific. At best the descriptors are generic and comparative. Extensions of the descriptors will include the use of adjectives such as 'slightly' as in 'slightly open' but these add little to the objectivity.

Attempts to standardise terms have been tried. One method is to link a scoring system with the attribute or combination of attributes in question. For example, the fineness or openness of a cellular structure may be rated on a scale of 1–5, 1–10, 1–20 and so on. This approach still relies on the expertise of the user and the ability of the reader to understand the meaning of the numbers, but it does supply a series of numbers which may be used in statistical analysis.

Further refinements of the scoring system include the use of standard photographs to which can be assigned a standard score for comparison when the human observer is scoring an unknown product sample. In practice, the photographs provide a useful training tool and cross-check for existing experts. An underlying weakness of scoring systems is that human scorers vary, not just between individuals but for a given individual. There will be drifting with time and even inconsistency of scoring results from one occasion to the next.

Objective methods for assessing crumb cell structure are commonly based on image analysis. The principles are based on the identification of cell-wall material, individual cells and their spatial arrangement within a slice cross-section. Such approaches allow for greater precision in the quantification of the cellular nature of baked products, especially bread, fermented goods, cakes and sponges. The technique can be extended to include some biscuit and pastry products, most noticeably laminated forms.

One of the earliest recorded attempts to quantify cellular structure was by Hodge and Cauvain (1973). They used a method which transferred printer's ink, under carefully controlled conditions, to the cut surface of a sponge cake and then carefully transferred its imprint to a glass slide. The ink marks on the slide were counted using a light microscope fitted with a motorised transverse mechanism to ensure repeatability of measurements. The eye-piece was focussed on a glass screen to which were attached four light-sensitive diodes that registered the presence or absence of ink marks. From the data gathered it was possible to make estimates of the cell size on the basis that more counts for a given scanned distance indicated a finer structure. Hodge and Cauvain used the data so gathered to illustrate the impact of changing levels of carbon dioxide in the sponge-cake batters mixed on a planetary mixer (Fig. 5.3) and were able to show that loss of carbon dioxide during mixing led to a dense, apparently un-aerated, cake structure, even when the batter density remained relatively unchanged.

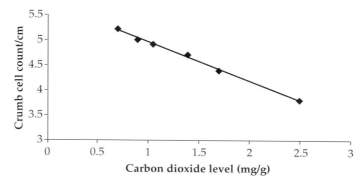

Figure 5.3   Effect of cake-batter carbon dioxide levels on crumb structure.

Figure 5.4   C-Cell instrument for assessing crumb cell structure. Reproduced with permission of Calibre Control International.

In recent years the combination of increased computing power and more advanced scanning and imaging techniques has delivered more powerful and objective cell-structure assessment techniques. Among the many attempts to deliver objective imaging, two have been fully commercialised: the AIB Crumb Scan (Rogers *et al.*, 1995) and C-Cell from Calibre Control International (www.C-Cell.info) (Fig. 5.4). With both pieces of equipment individual cells and their spatial distribution within a slice are identified. Cell structure images in Crumb Scan are captured using a document scanner while those within C-Cell are captured using a video camera (Whitworth *et al.*, 2005).

One difference between Crumb Scan and C-Cell is that the former uses the captured data to convert to a 'baker's score' related to the different products which might be assessed. By contrast, data captured using C-Cell is presented as raw information with respect to cell sizes, distributions, etc. Quality scores for particular products can be derived from C-Cell data if that is what is required by the users, but only after determining which parameters should be included in its determination. C-Cell retains flexibility in determining which parameters to use with particular products and their relative importance which is not available with Crumb Scan.

The formation of cellular structures

The initial formation of a foam and its conversion to a sponge underpins the structure formation of many baked products, but is most relevant in the manufacture of bread, fermented goods, cakes and sponges. There are two main mechanisms that contribute to the initial formation of the foam: one is based on the formation of a protein network while the other relies on the presence of fats and emulsifiers. In both cases the foam is created through the incorporation of small bubbles of air which must remain trapped and stable within the dough or batter. Instability of the gas-bubble structures leads to their coalescence and subsequent loss from the dough or batter, resulting in an inability to form a product structure or its collapse.

In both types of foam, expansion of the gas bubbles can occur before the structure becomes set in the oven. This expansion arises in part from the natural expansion of gases that occurs when their temperature rises – Charles's or Gay-Lussac's Law states that: 'The volume of a given mass of any gas, at constant pressure, increases by 1/273 of its value at 0°C for every degree Celsius rise in temperature'. The thermal expansion of the air bubbles trapped in the dough or batter is supplemented by vapour which is evolved as the water present begins to boil.

In baking it is common to supplement air expansion using other gases. The gas used most often is carbon dioxide, which, in bread and fermented goods, comes from the addition of baker's yeast and in the case of cakes and sponges from the addition of baking powder composed of sodium bicarbonate and a suitable food acid. The volumes of carbon dioxide make the most significant contribution to dough or batter expansion in the manufacture of baked products but the balance between the air incorporated during mixing and the gases retained in processing and baking is a delicate one.

To understand the mechanisms by which baked-product cell structures are formed we must first appreciate the relationship between the gases that are encountered in the dough or batter. The air bubbles that are mixed into the dough or batter are comprised of a mixture of nitrogen and oxygen. The nitrogen remains chemically inert but plays a major physical role in breadmaking. The oxygen in the air bubble is involved in a number of processes in the manufacture of bread but plays a lesser role in the production of cakes.

The third gas that enters the dough system is carbon dioxide, as mentioned above. In baking, carbon dioxide cannot form a gas bubble of its own and would normally escape to the surrounding atmosphere. However, the air bubbles that are trapped in the dough or batter provide nucleating sites for the carbon dioxide and the diffusion of the gas into the bubbles provides the basis for expansion that is seen in fermentation and baking. The expansion mechanism differs between bread and cake products but before considering the details it is necessary to examine the mechanisms by which bubbles are incorporated and stabilised in bread and cakes.

The formation and properties of gluten

The unique properties of wheat proteins have been referred to above and in many other publications relevant to baking. The material that cereal scientists and bakers have come to refer to as **gluten** does not exist as such in the wheat grain or the flour milled from it. The two key factors that contribute to the formation of a gluten structure from wheat flour are hydration of the proteins with water and the input of energy to the flour–water mixture. The former is well appreciated but the role of energy is less well understood. Once formed, the visco-elastic nature of gluten plays a critical role in the development of the cellular structures that characterise bread and fermented products. Whether the formation of gluten structures plays a role in the characterisation of the other classes of baked products will be discussed below.

In reviewing the principles of bread-dough formation, Stauffer (1998) discussed the chemical and physical changes that occurred from when wheat flour was hydrated through to the development of a gluten structure capable of trapping gas in the dough matrix. Following the contact of water with the flour there is an 'explosion' of strands of protein out of the flour agglomerates into the surrounding aqueous phase (Bernardin and Kasarda, 1973). Thereafter the physical movement of the flour–water mixture imparts energy which results in some cross-linking of flour proteins through the formation of S–S bonds at the terminal ends of the protein chains (Wieser, 2003). The result of the cross-linking is an increase in the resistance of dough to further mixing, that is, more energy is required in order to continue the mixing process. Eventually the point is reached at which the mixture is fully hydrated and later a smooth, developed dough is obtained. Continuing mixing beyond this point leads to the breakdown of the gluten structure and considerable changes in the rheological characteristics of the dough.

The formation of gluten structures in flour–water mixtures has been extensively studied. Common techniques have included the Brabender Farinograph®, the Mixograph, the Rheomixer and, more recently, the application of near-infrared spectroscopy (NIR) (Millar, 2003). In most studies it has become common to follow the changes in dough rheology that occur during mixing and to relate these in some way to the properties of a bread or fermented product. If dough resistance using the different measurement techniques is plotted against increasing mixing time then there is an interesting similarity between the curves which are so derived.

A 'representative' curve, in which dough resistance/mixer torque are plotted against increasing mixing time is illustrated in Figure 5.5. The representation shows that there is a hydration period, during which the flour and water are brought together to form a homogeneous mass, followed by a gradual increase in dough resistance with continued mixing. The latter is commonly equated with the development of the gluten matrix in the dough. The end point of the development process is not, as might be expected, when the point of maximum dough

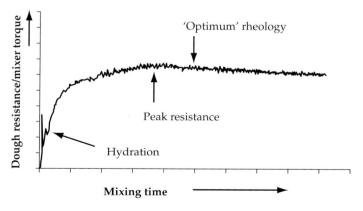

Figure 5.5   Representative dough-mixing curve.

resistance is achieved, but shortly after the maximum, commonly 10–20% 'beyond peak' (Millar, 2003). The precise shape of a specific curve will depend on the type of flour being tested. In some cases, the break-down can be very rapid while in others it may occur over a longer period of time.

Precisely why the point of optimum dough development is a little beyond the point of maximum dough resistance is not clear, though the comparison of NIR traces with bread volume and crumb cell struc-ture (Millar, 2003) shows that the finest cell structure (smallest cell size) obtained with the Chorleywood Bread Process (CBP) occurs before the point of maximum dough resistance to mixing, while the maximum bread volume is obtained sometime after the point of maximum resistance. Coincidentally the NIR minimum defined by Millar falls roughly midway between the time related to finest cell structure and maximum bread volume. One possible conclusion to be drawn from these observations is that a degree of breakdown of the gluten network is required in order to confer the required rheological properties to the dough (most likely its resistance to deformation) to allow it to expand to maximum height.

The description of gluten as a visco-elastic substance is common-place. The contribution of the elastic component of the network is less clearly defined and understood. It is common to read of the require-ment of the gluten network to be elastic and the need to improve gluten elasticity in order to improve bread quality. In practical terms, elasticity alone is not a property bakers require in bread and fermented doughs. This is because elasticity results in a degree of elastic recovery follow-ing moulding and shaping operations. To compensate for this, bakers may increase the force applied to dough during shaping. However, this may lead to problems associated with damage to the relatively delicate gas-bubble structures present in the dough. Cauvain and Young (2000, 2001) have provided examples of typical product-quality defects which may arise when excessive moulding pressures are applied to bread dough.

In practice, the extensibility of the dough is a property of significant interest to the baker because of its link with the ability of the dough to expand during proof and the early stages of baking. The rheological properties of dough have been compared to those of an elastic band (Cauvain, 1998b) with the property of extensibility being defined as how far the elastic band (gluten network) can be stretched before it snaps. In the case of the gluten network, its ability to expand during fermentation is directly related to the gas-retention properties of the dough – the better the dough extensibility the greater the gas-retention properties. Extensibility of the gluten network is a property commonly measured with empirical dough testing equipment, such as the

Brabender Extensograph® and Chopin Alveograph (Hajselova and Alldrick, 2003).

While the case for a developed gluten network is well established in bread and fermented doughs, its presence in other forms of baked products is less certain and in some cases it is considered to be absent. There are, however, circumstances when the development of a gluten network is an integral part of the product character of non-bread products. This is the case in the production of Danish-type pastries and croissants, and, to a lesser extent, in crackers. In such cases, the characteristic layered and flaky structures come from the formation of alternate and discrete layers of dough and laminating fat. Without the development of an extensible gluten structure in the dough layers the characteristic layered structure would not form under the influence of the sheeting rolls (see Chapter 6).

Elasticity in the dough is even less desirable in laminated products than in bread and fermented dough, while extensibility is even more desirable. Highly-elastic dough requires large deformation forces in order to create thin dough sheets. The high forces used, however, often lead to rupturing of the dough layers and the ready loss of steam from between the dough layers, thereby restricting pastry lift. The mechanisms by which laminated pastry products are expanded are further discussed below.

It is not generally considered that a developed gluten structure forms in cake batters. In part this is because the presence of sugar in the recipe restricts the water availability for hydration of the gluten-forming proteins. High levels of water are added to cake recipes (to balance the sugar) and it might be considered that there would be enough water to both dissolve the sugar and start the gluten-development process. However, the high level of water in the recipe also lowers the viscosity of the mixture of ingredients to such an extent that it becomes impossible to deliver sufficient energy to develop a gluten structure, even when mixing times are considerably extended.

To some extent this lack of gluten development in low viscosity systems is not unexpected. It has long been known that the water added to bread dough prior to mixing has a significant effect on the rate at which energy is transferred to the dough. In baker's parlance, 'stiff' (low added water) doughs will develop to a given energy level faster than ones which are 'slack' (high added water) (Cauvain and Young, 2000). Whether any linking together of strands of wheat-flour protein occurs in cake and other batters remains an open question. It should be noted that, even in low-viscosity wafer batters, shearing forces that are exerted when the batter is re-circulated on the plant often lead to the formation of gluten balls and to production problems such as incomplete depositing on the wafer plates before baking (Cauvain and Young, 2001).

While high added water levels will limit the formation of a gluten structure, so too will very low ones. In the manufacture of biscuits, cookies and pastries, levels of added water are much lower than would be seen in bread dough or cake batters. In part this is because it is necessary to bake out much of the added water in order to have the hard eating properties which characterise such products after baking. The principle which has been developed over the years has been to limit the initial addition of water and thereby reduce the amount of heat required to bake it out again.

Cauvain and Young (2000) illustrated the impact of added water level on the resistance of a short paste to penetration under standard conditions. The results revealed that paste resistance fell as the added water level increased from 10–15% of the flour weight but thereafter increased to such an extent that the level of paste resistance with 20% water was similar to that of 10%. This pattern of change in paste rheology can be seen in similar low-water systems. 'Toughening', or increasing development, of gluten structures can occur in pastes when typical mixing times are extended, showing that the transfer of energy is possible, but the level of added water remains a key factor in determining whether a gluten network is developed or not.

In summary, it can be seen that gluten development is most readily observed in bread dough and less readily so in other baked products. Thus, we can reinterpret the data presented in Figure 1.3 (p. 12) and now superimpose surfaces which represent degrees of gluten formation for the various baked-product sub-groups (Fig. 5.6). The further one moves from the origin in both x and y directions the less gluten formation will be observed but this is still only a small part of the picture. A series of four arcs have also been drawn on Figure 5.6 which crudely segregate various products from one another. The negative impact of fat on gluten formation is less than that of sugars because of the latter's significant effect on water activity in doughs, batters and pastes.

The role of fat in the formation of baked-product structures

As discussed above, there is limited, if any, gluten formation in cake batters, yet they have a similar cellular structure to that of bread. Clearly a different mechanism is required to create a foam of gas bubbles in the batter and to stabilise that foam until it reaches the oven. In the traditional sponge cake, based on a recipe of whole egg, sugar and flour, the incorporation of air bubbles is promoted by the action of a wire whisk passing through the egg–sugar mix. Once incorporated, the bubbles are stabilised by the egg lipoproteins, which align themselves at the interface of the gas bubbles and the surrounding aqueous phase. Traditional recipe books refer to the need to scald the mixing

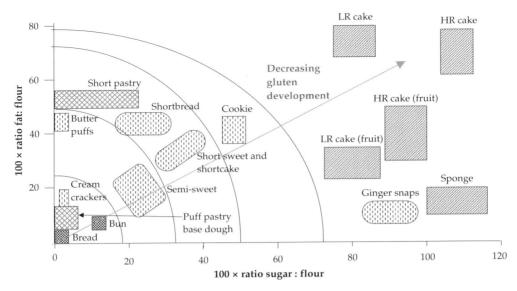

Figure 5.6 Representation of the degree of gluten development in baked products.

bowl and all equipment with hot water before the start of mixing, otherwise the egg–sugar mix will not form a stable foam. This is because the presence of even a small quantity of oil or fat coming into contact with the egg–sugar mix will prevent the egg lipoproteins carrying out their gas-bubble stabilising function. In traditional sponge-cake making, oil or fat are incorporated after the batter has been formed and great care is needed to ensure that the batter does not become de-aerated during their addition.

While low levels of fat inhibit the foam-promotion role of the egg lipoproteins, increasing the level of solid fat can promote air incorporation and gas-bubble stability. In bakery shortenings, which are mixture of oil and solid fat at a given temperature (Fig. 4.5, p. 85), the oil fraction aids the dispersion of the solid fat crystals, which align themselves at the interface of the air bubbles and the aqueous phase of the batter. They displace the egg lipoproteins, which accounts for the traditional concerns over traces of fat being present in sponge batters, but can take over the bubble-stabilising role for themselves.

The role of oil or fat in cake making is commonly supplemented by the addition of suitable emulsifiers. The one that is used most commonly is a distilled monoglyceride – glycerol monostearate (GMS or DGMS) – and it plays a similar role to that of solid fat crystals in that it aids air-bubble incorporation and promotes gas-bubble stability.

While the development of a gluten network dominates structure formation in the manufacture of bread and fermented products, fats and emulsifiers do have a role to play in the formation of structure. It does not appear that the addition of fat or emulsifiers directly aids the incorporation of air bubbles into the dough, or if they do then their contribution is small by comparison with that of the gluten network. However, fats and emulsifiers certainly do play a role in the stabilisation of the air bubbles once they have been incorporated into bread dough and during subsequent processing. This is particularly true of no-time dough-making processes, that is, processes in which the dough proceeds from the mixer to the divider without significant rest (Cauvain, 1998b).

As early as 1942, Baker and Mize showed that the addition of fat improved the structure of bread products (Baker and Mize, 1942). In particular the presence of fat has been shown to improve the gas-retention properties of the dough and its effect is most often seen as an improvement in oven spring (the difference in the height of a dough piece entering the oven and the height of the bread leaving it) (Williams and Pullen, 1998). Chamberlain *et al.* (1965) confirmed the importance of fat in the Chorleywood Bread Process, and fats and emulsifiers have now become a common part of the bread-improver formulations used in no-time dough-making processes.

Fat plays a role in the formation of structure in biscuits and cookies, but not as a promoter of air incorporation or gas-bubble stabilisation. A key role for fat in such products is in limiting the ability of the wheat flour proteins to form a gluten network. One view is that it does this by being smeared over the proteins during mixing and limiting the uptake of water in a kind of waterproofing effect. A similar argument has been put forward for the role of fat in the manufacture of pastry products and has resulted in the development of multi-stage methods in which fat and flour may be creamed together. It is possible that this is the mechanism for the oil portion of a compound fat, but in the case of the solid fat crystals it seems plausible that they simply create discontinuities in the gluten network and provide a physical barrier to cross-linking of protein molecules. The specialised role that fat plays in the structure formation of laminated products is discussed below.

Mechanisms of structure formation and expansion in baked products

Bread and fermented goods

The importance of the development of a gluten network to the creation of the final cellular structure of bread and fermented products has been described above. After the initial foam of air bubbles has been created in the dough a number of significant changes take place. The first starts during mixing and, in some cases, may be completed before mixing has finished. Initially the gas bubbles being incorporated into the dough comprise a mixture of mainly nitrogen and oxygen, but the activity of the baker's yeast present in the dough quickly reduces the oxygen concentration in the gas bubbles leaving the nitrogen behind (Chamberlain and Collins, 1979). The nitrogen gas bubbles which remain in the dough play a critical role in breadmaking.

Baker and Mize (1941) studied the origins of the gas cell in bread dough and showed that the carbon dioxide gas that is generated as a result of fermentation in the dough by baker's yeast was not able to form a gas cell on its own and so was not the creator of the cell structure that is seen in the final baked product. The nitrogen gas bubbles that remain trapped in the gluten act as nucleating sites and the carbon dioxide gas that is produced during fermentation gradually diffuses into them. As the nitrogen gas bubbles receive the carbon dioxide they begin to expand and the bulk of the dough grows larger.

The degree to which the dough can expand is directly controlled by the rheological properties of the dough, not least by the degree to which the gluten proteins are hydrated and the gluten network developed. It is because of the need to expand that gluten structures need to be extensible. If the dough is too viscous (i.e. lacks water) or is too elastic, dough expansion is restricted. In practice the balance between the various rheological properties is crucial.

The initial expansion of dough bulk is slow and highly dependent on the dough temperature and level of yeast present, in addition to the contribution of the dough rheology. Once it has been initiated it is very difficult to slow down or stop the fermentation process. It is possible to retard the dough by chilling, while deep freezing is required to stop it altogether (Cauvain, 1998a).

During the gas production and expansion phase the gluten network is gradually stretched thinner and thinner. After some time the expansion of individual gas bubbles brings them into close proximity with others and coalescence of bubbles may occur. This coalescence is encouraged by foam drainage in the lamellae between the gas cells (Wilde, 2003). As a consequence of coalescence, the size of many of the gas bubbles increases, but this is not necessarily the case for many of the smaller ones. The internal pressure of some of the smaller gas bubbles is such that the carbon dioxide cannot diffuse into them and they do not increase in size. In the case of very small gas bubbles the internal pressure may be so great that they cease to exist, and the air/ nitrogen gas contained within them diffuses into the aqueous phase of the dough.

It is clear from the above remarks that fermentation in bread dough brings about significant change in its gas-bubble population. The initial gas-bubble population is mainly controlled by mixing conditions and the interactions with some ingredients. As the result of fermentation, the average size of the gas bubbles increases dramatically, typically from around $100\,\mu$m before baking to $2\,$mm in the baked product.

In addition to this expansion of size there is also a broadening of the distribution. In part the latter is considered to be a consequence of disproportionation, a process in which the internal pressure of individual cells plays a major role. In principle, the larger the gas bubble the lower its relative internal pressure and the easier it will be for the carbon dioxide to diffuse into it. The practical result may be summarised as being an expansion of the larger bubbles at the expense of the smaller ones. Coalescence increases the sizes of gas bubbles and lowers their relative internal pressures and so drives disproportionation for as long as the yeast remains active.

The activity of baker's yeast reaches its maximum at around 40°C, but is not finally inactivated until around 55°C (Williams and Pullen, 1998). This means that following the transition of a dough piece from the prover to the oven, gas production is still possible. It is at this time that there is still the potential for significant dough expansion, but the expansion-restricting effects of the foam-to-sponge conversion will be encountered. Before that point is reached, coalescence of gas bubbles and the influence of disproportionation remain key features of the dough system.

Cakes and sponges

The creation of a foam structure in cakes and sponges owes much to movement of the mixing tool through the ingredients. As the mixing tool sweeps through the ingredients, air is dragged into the mixture on the trailing edge. As the air is enveloped by the batter a number of mechanisms contribute to the air-bubble stability and, to a lesser extent, their size. Continued agitation can lead to the breaking up of larger air pockets to create smaller bubbles. As already discussed, fats and emulsifiers play key roles in the stabilisation of the gas bubbles so incorporated. Such stabilisation mechanisms are important in keeping the bubbles trapped in the batter (Fig. 5.7), otherwise the relatively low viscosity of the system and the natural buoyancy of the air bubbles would allow them to rise to the surface of the batter and be lost to the surrounding atmosphere.

The buoyancy of the air bubbles is increased if the temperature of the batter rises and through receiving carbon dioxide from the reaction of the baking-powder ingredients. In a well-stabilised batter, buoyancy

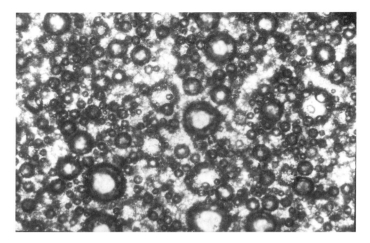

Figure 5.7   Air bubbles (dark rings) trapped in a sponge-cake batter containing GMS and oil.

of the gas bubbles is not a problem, provided that the batter is not agitated. Continued mixing and pumping of batters creates a shearing action which reduces the stability of the emulsion and can allow the escape of gas bubbles. The two mechanisms of coalescence and disproportionation occur in cake batters in a similar manner to that described for bread doughs. Coalescence and growth of bubble size increase the buoyancy properties and risk de-aeration of the batter.

The gas-bubble populations created during the mixing of cake batters appear to have narrower distributions than commonly seen in bread dough, and this seems to limit the effects of disproportionation. The overall impact is that, while expansion of gas bubbles occurs during baking, the final product structure is commonly composed of cells of similar size, even in the regions near to the crusts. In summary, cake batters can be seen as an air–fat dispersion in an aqueous phase, the latter comprising dissolved sugar and dispersed flour particles.

Biscuits and cookies

The potential to form foams in biscuits and cookies is restricted by the limited formation of a gluten structure. In addition, the low water levels used in the dough preparation limit the potential for air dispersion into the fat and its subsequent dispersion into an aqueous phase, as would be seen with cake batters. It is probable that there are small contributions to biscuit structure from gluten-forming and fat-stabilising mechanisms but, since significant expansion is not expected from biscuits and cookies, the lack of foam formation is not a problem. However, the incorporation of air does occur in the preparation of biscuit and cookie doughs because without it the product would lack the ability to increase in size during baking. Accompanying this lack of rise would be a loss in the crumby, short-eating character of the product.

So how does this air get incorporated into biscuit dough? Some is carried into the dough along with ingredients such as flour, sugar and fat, and a proportion is incorporated into the dough during mixing. Since there is no significant gluten development to trap air bubbles the fat plays a significant part in the dough aeration process, though the degree of overall aeration that is achieved is relatively low. In the manufacture of semi-sweet biscuits the limited gluten development which is achieved plays a greater role in dough aeration than in the manufacture of short-dough biscuits, while in the case of the latter type fat probably plays a greater role than in the case of semi-sweet biscuits.

Short and sweetened pastry

A similar situation exists in the manufacture of short and sweet pastes to that discussed for biscuits and cookies, not least because of the similarly high levels of fat and sugar in typical recipes and limited water levels added during paste mixing. Once again, gluten development is limited and offers little to paste aeration, and the contribution of the fat is small.

In some traditional mixing processes the limitation of gluten development is encouraged by blending the flour and fat together in a creaming process before other ingredients are added. This is an attempt to waterproof the flour by smearing the fat onto the flour proteins. In practice, the effect is minimal since, once the water has been added to the flour-fat mixture, continued mixing can lead to toughening of the paste, presumably through a degree of gluten development. In a second variation for sweetened short pastries, the fat and sugar are creamed together. This variation is somewhat harder to understand in that the fat–sugar mixture reduces in density with extended mixing times.

The rationale behind multi-stage mixing methods for the manufacture of pastry is hard to establish, not least because studies have shown that mixing processes based on all-in (mixing all of the ingredients together at one time) techniques yield satisfactory quality (Taylor, 1984). It is likely that multi-stage mixing methods were established when the quality of ingredients was less reliable than today, and that the methods have persisted through to modern times.

Savoury pastry

Gluten development is also limited in the manufacture of savoury pastes, only by the presence of high levels of fat, there being no sugar used in the formulation. Little air is entrained in the manufacture of the paste and, indeed, since boiling water and sometimes hot fat are used for the mixing stage there would be a tendency for trapped air to be lost, at least in the early stages of the mixing cycle. As the paste cools after the addition of the hot ingredients there is the potential for some air entrapment but, in general, savoury paste remains dense in nature.

Laminated products and crackers

The mechanisms by which, to a limited extent, the structure of laminated products and crackers is formed, differ considerably from those of other baked products. The formation of separate and discrete layers of dough and fat is critical and requires considerable care in the manufacturing process (see Chapter 6). Aeration of the base dough is not usually sought during mixing even though the development of a gluten structure is needed. This is probably another historical or traditional view which has not been challenged. The integrity of the dough layers is important because it is necessary to restrict the loss of gas when the product is in the oven. The generation of water vapour in puff-pastry products is largely responsible for the gas pressures that force the dough layers apart, with the movement of the steam to the surrounding atmosphere being impeded by the fat.

Yeast may be added to some of the individual products that fall into this group, such as croissants and Danish pastries. In these products the creation and expansion of product cell structures follow similar lines to that described above for bread – namely that oxygen is lost from the dough and the remaining nitrogen gas bubbles act as nuclei for the carbon dioxide produced by the yeast. There is also a contribution to the expansion of such laminated products in the oven from the same mechanism seen with puff pastry.

One difference between unyeasted laminated products and the yeasted varieties is that the yeast fermentation, especially during proof, physically disrupts the layering that has been created. The balance between expansion from baker's yeast and from the laminations has a significant effect on the final qualities, most noticeably the flakiness, of the product. The breakdown of layers tends to contribute to a less flaky, more bun-like eating character.

Flat breads

Many of the flat breads that originate from the eastern Mediterranean, the Middle and Far East are unleavened yet they have a characteristic form and structure. All such products are made from a bread-like dough. Some contain yeast and are fermented while others are not. Though a bread-like dough is formed there is relatively little in the way of a sponge-like structure in the baked product. (The naan breads of the Indian sub-continent probably come closest to this form.) Instead the key characteristic of flat breads is the formation of a pocket-like feature between the upper and lower surfaces of the product (Fig. 5.8). This comes from a baking technique that rapidly seals both upper and lower surfaces of the baked product, creating a barrier to the loss of water vapour and the generation of sufficient steam pressure to blow the upper and lower surfaces apart. Baking times are very short for such products, usually only a couple of minutes at very high temperatures. Flat breads tend to be hearth-baked on very hot surfaces.

Doughnuts

The mechanism for structure formation and expansion that applies to doughnuts depends on whether it is a yeasted or powder-raised form. In the yeasted form, the incorporation and stabilisation of gas bubbles is based on the formation of a gluten structure augmented by a higher level of fat than that seen in bread. If emulsifiers are present in the formulation, they too will aid bubble stability. The expansion of gas

Figure 5.8   Pocket-like feature of flat breads.

bubbles in yeasted doughnuts follows much the same principles as described for bread and fermented goods.

In the powder-raised, or cake, doughnut the fat and emulsifiers (if present) play a similar role to that described for cake batters. The impact, on both types of doughnut, of frying is discussed in Chapter 7.

Bagels and steam breads

These two groups of products have quite different product characteristics but share a common process mechanism in that boiling water is used to develop and set the final product structure (see Chapter 6). Bagels are made with a yeasted dough, but expansion of the structure is limited by comparison with bread. Traditionally, bagels are ring-shaped with a dense, firm and chewy eating character. The shiny crust comes from immersion in boiling water, which, in some cases, may also contain sugar.

Dough-based products that are steamed are common in China and throughout the Far East. A fermented dough is used, which, together with the relatively low heat transfer during steaming, gives a light and aerated structure. There is no colour formation on the final products which may come in a variety of shapes, some of which may contain savoury or sweet fillings.

Hot-plate products

A specialist group of products are baked on a hot-plate or griddle rather than in an oven. This group includes both yeast-raised and powder-raised products. The former group includes crumpets (Fig. 5.9), pikelets and muffins while the latter group includes various forms of pancake and scones. They may be made from fermented dough, e.g. muffins, fermented batters, e.g. crumpets and pikelets, powder-raised paste, e.g. scones and powder-raised batters, e.g. pancakes. In all cases, when the products are ready for baking individual units are deposited directly onto a hot-plate. Hoops or other containers may be used to limit product flow and retain final product shape. The final products are usually flat and thin or have a drum-like shape. A common characteristic of hot-plate goods is the very open cellular structure that results from the heating process employed (see Chapter 7).

Hot-plate products are usually reheated before serving and eating, commonly by the toasting or grilling of an unbaked or lightly-baked surface. The reheating often requires that the product be split into two portions. If this is not the case, then the upper surface (as with crumpets) is only lightly baked. In practice the individual units will be

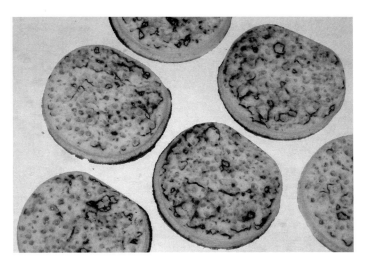

Figure 5.9   Crumpets.

deposited directly onto the hot-plate and turned part way through the baking process to achieve the required degree of colouration on both surfaces. These products tend to have short microbial shelf-lives and, because they tend to have high water content, are susceptible to bacterial contamination. Sugar levels in most hot-plate products are low.

Chapter 6
Interactions between Formulation and Process Methodologies

Introduction

The manufacture of all baked products is based on complex interactions between ingredients, formulation and processing methodologies and capabilities – change one aspect of the relationship and the nature of the interaction changes, resulting in one or more changes in product quality. The processing methodologies used in the manufacture of baked products today are the result of many years of, mainly, trial and error research. There have been specific scientific studies of many of the processing elements involved, but much of this work has concentrated on individual aspects of the process, such as mixing, forming, etc., and so most developments tend to be modifications of existing technologies rather than 'step' changes.

There is also a tendency for new process and equipment developments to be narrowly focussed on one specific baked product, after which attempts are made to extend the apparent benefits to a wider range of products. It has often been the case with such developments that the existing product technology has had to be adapted to enable the new technology to function. This approach commonly leads to changes in existing product characteristics which are unacceptable at a production or even consumer level.

Similar problems occur when new equipment is developed, particularly those pieces of equipment associated with handling the intermediate product (i.e. dough, batter, paste) before it is converted to baked product. One of the problems is that, while engineering requirements may be precisely specified, those of the product are harder to define. Most doughs, batters and pastes display non-Newtonian behaviour, which makes it hard to define their rheology with the degree of precision on which it is necessary to base equipment designs. Thus, the opportunities for step changes in processing technology for baked products are limited.

While the details of the processing technologies used for the sub-groups of baked products are diverse, there are some relatively common stages in the transition from ingredients to baked product. The common elements are:

- Mixing – the intimate blending of the ingredients
- Dividing/scaling/depositing – the sub-division of the bulk of the intermediate product into unit pieces
- Forming/moulding/shaping – the manipulation of the unit piece to conform to a particular product concept
- Expansion and relaxation – modification of the rheological properties of the intermediate to prepare it for baking
- Baking – the transformation to the final form of baked product

The main processing methodologies

Mixing

The importance of energy

The first significant process in the manufacture of any baked product is the blending together of the ingredients used in the recipe. A number of significant changes take place during this stage, and they begin with the solubilisation, hydration and dispersal of the various ingredients and their components. In all contexts, water in its various forms plays a key role, as has been discussed previously.

The dispersal and intimate blending of the ingredients depend on the mixing action employed. In the distant past mixing would have been done by hand, but now it is most commonly done using some form of mechanical mixing device. There are still exceptions, for example, bread dough may still be mixed by hand on the Indian sub-continent and in other parts of the world. The mixing mechanism employed in the manufacture of all baked products introduces specific changes that characterise many of the baking processes and bakery products.

Mechanical mixing is carried out in a confined container – the bowl – through which a mixing blade, or blades, pass in a defined motion. There are many variants of mixing bowl and blade design but all are configured to achieve the dispersal objective. Where they differ, however, is in achieving two other key aspects of mixing – passing energy to the blend of ingredients and the incorporation of gas (mainly air) into the mixture. While the transfer of energy is an integral part of developing a gluten network and, in this sense, is essential in the manufacture of bread and fermented products, the incorporation of air is fundamental to the manufacture of a wider range of baked products.

The importance of transferring energy to dough during breadmaking is such that it might almost be considered to be an ingredient in itself. In general terms, the greater the transfer of energy to the dough during mixing the greater the improvement in dough gas retention and therefore the greater the bread volume. Eventually, however, a point is reached when transferring more energy confers no extra gas retention and, in some cases, gas-retention properties may be lost. In the latter case, the dough may described as over-mixed, a condition that is analogous to the dough breakdown discussed in Chapter 5.

The most common way to increase energy transfer during mixing is to increase mixing time. However, this does not change the rate at which energy is transferred and only applies until the resistance of the dough decreases as its temperature rises above 35°C or so. It is clear that energy is being transferred to the dough during mixing because the temperature of the dough mass will rise, and the longer the dough is mixed the greater will be the final temperature. Indeed, it is possible to measure the increase in dough temperature of the ingredients from the start to the end of mixing, and bakers have used this relationship to calculate the water temperature required at the start of mixing, based on a knowledge of the required final dough temperature and the temperature of the other ingredients (Cauvain and Young, 2000) (see Chapter 8).

It may be necessary to make small adjustments to the dough temperature calculation formula in order to compensate for the effects of the mixing bowl and ambient conditions in the bakery, but usually such effects are small by comparison with the mechanical transfer of energy. It is possible to approximate the total quantity of energy transferred to the dough during mixing using knowledge of the ingredient specific heats, their masses and temperatures and the final dough temperature. An example of such a calculation for a spiral-type mixer is given in Table 6.1. The results are expressed in units of Watt hours per kilogram of dough (Wh/kg) since this has become a common expression over the last 40 years or so in the baking industry (to convert to J/kg multiply the value by 3.82).

Heat of hydration of flour (Wheelock and Lancaster, 1970) = 1.45
$\times 1000 = 1450$ cal

Heat input due to mechanical energy = total heat − heat of hydration
$= 11\,905 - 1450 = 10\,455$ cal

1 Wh is the equivalent of 859.8 calories

Table 6.1   Calculation of energy consumption when using a spiral-type mixer.

Ingredient	Initial temp. (°C)	Final temp. (°C)	Temp. rise (°C)	Weight (g)	Specific heat (cal/g/°C)	Heat added (cal)
Flour	20	28	8	1000	0.4	4 000
Water	15	28	13	600	1.0	7 800
Others	20	28	8	150	0.7	105
Total				1750		11 905

$$\text{Thus, } 10\,455\,\text{cal} = 10\,455/859.8 = 12.16\,\text{Wh}$$

$$\text{Energy input} = 12.16/1.75 = 6.95\,\text{Wh/kg dough}$$

The example given in Table 6.1 shows that, for a mixing time of 10 minutes (2 on slow speed and 8 on fast), the total energy transferred to the dough was about 7 Wh/kg. A shorter mix time would transfer less energy and a longer mixing time would transfer more energy. However, as discussed above, the transfer of more energy during dough mixing does not necessarily equate to improved bread volume. In part, the quality losses experienced with extended mixing times come from the high final dough temperatures that would be achieved. Even when the final dough temperature is controlled to an acceptable level, by using ice and water or a cooling jacket, for example, extended mixing times can yield poorer-quality products. This is because the optimum level of energy for any given dough depends to a large extent on the type of flour that is being used. Ultimately, the link is back to the wheat variety and, in broad terms, the optimum work input to the dough increases as the protein content of white flour increases and vice versa.

The design of a mixer also has a significant effect on the quantity of energy that can be transferred to the dough for a given mixing time. The key to energy transfer in many mixers is the degree of friction that arises because of the interactions between the dough, the mixing tool and the bowl. In this respect, mixing tools are often designed to squeeze and stretch the dough through narrow gaps created between the tool and the sides of the bowl. In other forms of design the dough may be screwed towards the base of the bowl or squeezed and stretched between pairs of mixing tools. Most mixer designs use all of the different elements to greater or lesser degrees.

Differences in mixer tool and bowl design account for only part of the variation in the energy transferred to the dough during mixing. A significant element in the rate of the energy transfer comes from variations in the mixing speed. Vertical- and continuous-type mixers commonly have the highest rate of energy transfer because they typically carry out mixing at higher speeds. In addition, such mixer types are equipped with internal baffles that impede the movement of the dough and contribute significantly to the squeezing–stretching interactions to which the dough is subjected. Because of the high rates of energy transfer, vertical- and continuous-type mixers tend to have much shorter mixing times than many other mixer designs.

The importance of energy in dough development was recognised may years ago by scientists and technologists working in the British Baking Industries Research Association (BBIRA) based at Chorleywood in the UK (Cauvain and Young, 2006). Their work was to lead to the introduction of the Chorleywood Bread Process (CBP). The CBP was characterised by the transfer of a defined level of energy to the dough within a defined time. They recognised the importance of both the total energy requirement and the rate at which that energy was delivered. The latter is more important than has previously been appreciated.

When introduced in 1961, the CBP was defined by the requirement to deliver 11 Wh/kg dough in the mixer within 2–5 minutes of mixing, and the BBIRA scientists showed that increasing the rate of energy transfer (while keeping to the same total energy and within the 2–5 minute period) gave improvements in dough gas retention. Later work reported by Cauvain (Cauvain, 1998b) confirmed that higher rates of energy transfer were beneficial even when the total energy was greater than the originally specified 11 Wh/kg. Chin and Campbell (2005a and 2005b) have also confirmed the importance of the rate of energy transfer to the dough. They found evidence that implied that dough development at higher speeds in a CBP-type mixer (energy input to the dough was $40 \, kJ \, kg^{-1}$) was more efficient (Chin and Campbell, 2005a) and that dough aeration and its rheological characteristics were dependent on both the total and the rate of work input (Chin and Campbell, 2005b).

In the CBP, dough mixing carries on until the predetermined level of energy has been transferred rather than for a predetermined time. This means that variations in the loading of ingredients into the mixing bowl will not result in variations in bread quality. Thus, if a full mixing load is 200 kg ingredients, then a total of 2200 Watt hours (200 × 11) will be required to complete mixing in say 3.5 minutes. If a half-mix is attempted, then only 1100 Watt hours will be required. This does not mean that a half-mix will be completed in half of the mixing time (1.75 minutes), because the transfer of energy depends on the interactions between dough and the mixing tool. A smaller dough batch will result in a different interaction, and usually the rate of energy transfer is reduced, so that reductions in mixing times are not as great as might be anticipated. Dough consistency will also affect the rate of energy transfer, with stiff dough taking less time to develop to its full Watt-hour allowance than soft dough.

There have been significant changes in wheat varieties (along with changes in improver formulations) since the initial introduction of the CBP. Many of these changes are associated with the strength of the gluten that is developed during mixing. Along with these stronger wheat varieties has come a realisation that their optimum energy lies beyond the 11 Wh/kg dough level. An example is given in Figure 6.1 for a past UK strong wheat variety, and the illustration shows that, even in UK lidded sandwich-type bread, improvements in volume were achieved when the work input level was raised from 11 to 17 Wh/kg (final dough temperature for both examples was 30°C). Similar illustrations have been reported elsewhere (Cauvain, 1998b).

It remains important to deliver the required energy within the 2–5 minute time bracket as originally defined for CBP. Therefore, in order to achieve work inputs as high as those illustrated it is necessary to raise mixing speeds. For the samples illustrated the mixing speed was 600 rpm which is somewhat higher than the typical 300 rpm of CBP-compatible mixers.

Low-speed mixing, even for a long period of time, imparts relatively little energy to the dough and so contributes relatively little to dough development. If used in breadmaking, it is common for the bulk dough which comes from the mixer to be set aside in a warm environment in order to ferment. During this fermentation period, the bulk of the dough increases as carbon dioxide is evolved and the rheological

Fresco

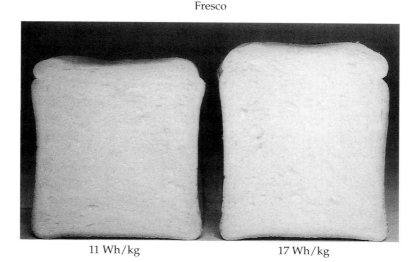

11 Wh/kg   17 Wh/kg

Figure 6.1   Effect on bread quality of increasing work input level.

properties of the dough are modified by natural enzymic actions. The fermentation conditions should be controlled in order to get optimum and consistent results. The precise length of fermentation time depends on a number of factors, including the level of yeast and salt in the recipe and the temperature at which the fermentation is carried out. There is a close relationship between flour strength and the length of fermentation time. High-protein flours that develop strong gluten networks require longer fermentation times than those with lower proteins.

Mixing-energy requirements for baked products other than bread dough are less well defined. In part this is because the requirement for a developed gluten network is considered to be less critical to final product quality. This assumption is largely true for cakes, biscuits, cookies and most pastes. The production of laminated products, however, does require a degree of gluten development. Traditionally, the base dough for such products is given less mixing than for bread dough, on the basis that the subsequent sheeting continues the development of the gluten structure. Indeed sheeting has been and is still used in the manufacture of bread dough. The contribution that the sheeting process makes to dough development is further discussed below.

The relationship between energy transfer and dough temperature has been exploited in the control of the mixing of semi-sweet dough and is claimed to deliver more consistent biscuit doughs to the sheeting stages (Chamberlain, 1979). In the case of such products, the end of mixing was defined as being that moment during mixing at which the dough mass reached 40–42°C, if sodium metabisulphite (SMS) was present as a reducing agent, and 44–46°C if SMS was not present. This approach to defining the end point of mixing has largely been confined to this one area of baking.

Gas incorporation

In the preparation of cake batters, the movement of the mixing tool pushes the material aside and a void is created behind the trailing edge. As the batter flows into the void that has been created, small pockets of gas (air) are entrained. These air pockets can remain trapped in the batter because they become stabilised by the surface-active materials which are present in the recipe. These typically include the egg albumens, emulsifiers and, as discussed above, fat.

The continued movement of the mixing tool sweeping through the batter continues to entrain air and the density of the batter falls. Eventually a point is reached when the batter is not capable of holding more air and the density reaches a minimum. The minimum density achievable depends on the quantity of surface-active materials which are present. In broad terms, the greater the quantity of surface-active material in the recipe the lower the minimum density that can be achieved, but a mixture of surface-active materials does not always ensure an additive effect. For example, Cauvain and Cyster (1996) illustrated the effect of adding GMS to an oil-enriched sponge-cake recipe and showed that without GMS the egg albumens largely stabilised the foam. When a low level of GMS was added the foam collapsed in the oven, but cake volume recovered as the level of GMS increased.

The length of mixing time has a profound effect on cake-batter density – the longer the mixing time the lower will be the batter density, at least until a minimum density is reached. With extended mixing, the movement of the mixing tool sweeping through the batter disentrains some of the air which has already been trapped. Eventually, during the mixing process, a point is reached when the level of air being entrained equals the level of air being disentrained. This equilibrium coincides with the minimum batter density and is unique for a given recipe and type of mixer.

If the batter is stable its density will not change once the minimum is reached. However, many batters are not stable, especially if they contain baking powder. Soon after mixing, the components of the baking powder begin to react and carbon dioxide gas is released to start the process of inflating the trapped air bubbles. The disentrainment that occurs with continued mixing allows some of the gas bubbles to escape, along with air and any of the carbon dioxide that may be present. The air may be replaced during entrainment but the carbon dioxide cannot be replaced once the baking powder has reacted. In consequence, the ratio of air to carbon dioxide in the batter changes with mixing time as the concentration of the latter falls. The impact of such changes can be seen in the data presented in Figure 6.2 which show that, while there is a continual loss of carbon dioxide with increased mixing time, it is not until after about ten minutes of mixing that the combination of loss of carbon dioxide and disentrainment of air result in an increase in batter density.

If the bubble-stabilising mechanism in the batter begins to break down with continued mixing, it will also contribute to the disentrainment of air and the batter density will rise. Cauvain and Cyster (1996) showed that the breakdown of this mechanism and the loss of carbon dioxide could occur in the case of sponge-cake batters containing GMS mixed with a planetary-style mixer. In these circumstances, extended mixing times lead to loss of cake volume and quality that is consistent with sponge-cake recipes containing little or no baking powder. Key characteristics of such products are large numbers of bubbles on the cake surface, a rounding of the angle between the cake side and its

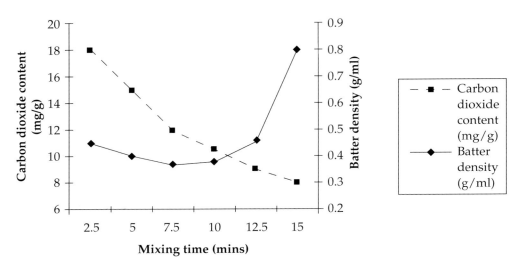

Figure 6.2 Loss of carbon dioxide from cake batter during mixing.

base (chamfering) and crust that is readily detached from the product crumb.

In most cases, the different types of mixer that can be used in the preparation of cake batters deliver similar product qualities, provided that batter densities are matched. Two different types of mixer stand apart from the others in the context of batter mixing, the **pressure whisk** and the **continuous mixer**. The former comprises a vertically-mounted mixing chamber in which a mixing tool (beater or whisk) moves in a planetary motion. The chamber is commonly subjected to positive pressure during the mixing cycle, which has the advantage of increasing air incorporation and reducing the cell size in the final product. This type of mixer is most commonly used in the manufacture of sponge-type cake products. Because of the increased air incorporation it is common to reduce the level of baking powder used in the recipe to maintain a constant batter density.

The impact of positive pressure on the final cake structure is the opposite of that observed when bread dough is mixed under positive pressure (Cauvain and Young, 2006). As discussed below, finer crumb cell structures in bread products are normally obtained when dough is mixed under negative pressure. The differences in the effects of mixer headspace pressures during mixing are closely related to the lower viscosity of cake batters and the lack of gluten formation by comparison with bread dough.

The continuous mixer comprises a much smaller mixing chamber than the planetary or horizontal bowl forms. In the continuous mixer a pre-blended batter is pumped into the mixing chamber, which comprises a central rotor set to revolve within two fixed stators. Both sides of the rotor and the inner faces of the stators are fitted with a series of concentric pins, which leave a narrow gap through which the batter may pass (Fig. 6.3). This mixing action imparts high shear to the batter and tends to create a smaller average bubble size than would be seen with other mixer types.

In addition to the high shear, rotor–stator interaction, gas may be introduced directly into the mixing chamber and the residence time of the batter in the mixing chamber can be regulated using a back-pressure device. In total, this mixing action is more efficient than the planetary and horizontal bowl forms and yields products with greater uniformity. Commonly, the level of chemical aeration in the preparation of cake batters with a continuous mixer can be reduced without loss of product volume.

With the continuous-type mixer, the introduction of pressure into the mixing chamber is through the back-pressure device. There are mixers suitable for the production of cake and other batters where the pressure in a planetary-style mixing chamber may be adjusted directly. Commonly, cake batters would be mixed under positive pressure, which causes the gas-bubble size to be reduced and the loss of carbon dioxide limited. The end result is that the products have a finer, more uniform cell structure and the level of baking powder used in the recipe may be reduced without loss of product volume.

The action of a mixing tool passing through bread dough performs a function similar to that discussed above for cake batters. Again, both entrainment and disentrainment processes occur and equilibrium between the two may be reached. As with the mixing of cake batters, there is a potential for the loss of carbon dioxide from the matrix with extended mixing. In the case of bread dough, this would come from any early activity of the yeast in the recipe. However, two factors make significant contributions to the restriction of loss of carbon dioxide

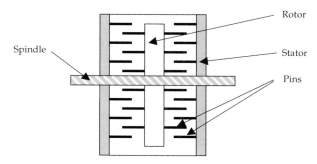

Figure 6.3   Diagrammatic representation of the cross-section of a mixing head of a continuous mixer/aerator.

during the mixing of bread dough. One is that the yeast takes some time to start producing carbon dioxide gas. This is referred to as a lag phase, and during this period the yeast will adjust to the surroundings before starting the fermentation process. The temperature of the dough plays a part in controlling the fermentation process.

The second significant contributing factor is the more viscous nature of bread dough by comparison with cake batter, because this reduces the risk of air bubbles attaining sufficient buoyancy to escape from the dough matrix. The high viscosity of dough comes about because of the reduced levels of added water and the development of the gluten network. Thus, while dough mixing times may be longer than those experienced with cake batters the visco-elastic properties of bread dough largely keep gas bubbles trapped in the dough.

The gas bubble populations that may be found in bread dough are more significantly affected by mixing conditions than might be seen with the mixing of cake batters. In breadmaking processes that have no fermentation of the dough in bulk (often referred to as 'no-time' dough-making processes) the gas-bubble population that is created in the mixer provides the basis of the cell structure in the crumb of the final product (Cauvain, 2001a).

The type of mixer influences the gas-bubble population in the dough. Vertical, high-speed and z-blade mixers tend to give a narrow range of bubble sizes and smaller average size than is seen with spiral-mixed dough (Cauvain *et al.,* 1999). The differences in the final product reflect the gas-bubble populations in the dough, so that the spiral mixer yields bread with a more open and random cell structure. This is an important aspect of bread-dough mixing, since it is not easy to reduce the size of the gas bubbles in the dough in post-mixing processing. In fact it is unlikely that the gas-bubble size is reduced at all in post-mixing processing. The nature of the gas-bubble population may change but usually this comprises the elimination of larger bubbles and a narrowing of the range of bubble sizes which remain in the dough.

Many of the CBP-compatible mixers are fitted with some form of atmospheric pressure control of the mixing chamber. When first introduced, a key feature of the CBP was that the dough was mixed at pressures lower than atmospheric, typically 0.5 bar* (Cauvain and

---

* Confusion over pressure units can exist because of the way in which they are expressed. In part this arises because gauges fitted to mixers often express atmospheric pressure as being 0. A partial vacuum may be given as 0.5 bar vacuum and positive pressure may be given as 0.5 bar pressure. In this discussion, atmospheric pressure is taken as being equal to 1 bar (or full vacuum = 0). Thus, a figure of 0.5 bar is 0.5 below atmospheric pressure, 0.3 bar is 0.7 bar below atmospheric, and 1.5 bar is 0.5 bar above atmospheric pressure.

Young, 2006). The aim of using reduced pressure during dough mixing was to reduce the gas-bubble size and the average cell size in the crumb of the final product. As the list of permitted oxidants in the UK was restricted to ascorbic acid, the commercial trend was to delay the introduction of the partial vacuum until part-way through the mixing cycle. The intention was to provide greater opportunity for the ascorbic acid to work before the level of air being mixed into the dough was restricted by the application of the partial vacuum (Marsh, 1998).

Detailed investigation of the role of air in the development of bread dough at the Flour Milling and Baking Research Association (FMBRA), Chorleywood, revealed that it was possible to use a combination of positive and negative pressures to achieve a wide range of bread cell structures (Cauvain, 1995). Where a fine cell structure was required in the product, the first stage of the mixing would be run under positive pressure to optimise ascorbic-acid-assisted oxidation and the second part of the cycle run under negative pressure to yield a fine and uniform cell structure in the final product. Products which required a more open cell structure could be made using higher pressures in the mixer headspace (Cauvain, 2003).

While much discussion on the aeration of cake batters and bread dough has centred on the incorporation of air, it is worth noting the potential for gaseous mixtures other than air. Work on bread dough at FMBRA, Chorleywood, had shown the potential for oxygen enrichment of the mixer headspace (Chamberlain and Collins, 1979). The optimum combination appeared to be a mixture of 60% oxygen and 40% nitrogen (Cauvain, 2004b), with the nitrogen bubbles filling the crucial role of nucleating sites for the carbon dioxide and the increased oxygen concentration aiding the ascorbic-acid-assisted oxidation. With this mixture of gases there was no need for the application of partial vacuum to achieve a fine cell structure in the final product.

The incorporation of gases during the mixing of biscuit and cookie dough and paste appears to be of relatively limited value, probably because the creation of a foam is not an integral part of the structure-forming mechanisms.

Single- and multi-stage methods

Over the many years that cakes have been made a number of different mixing methods have evolved. The simplest method comprises blending all of the ingredients together in a single-stage process. The exception to that rule would be if fruit or other particulate materials were present in the recipe, and they would be held back to be added once the batter had been completely formed. This single-stage, or all-in, mixing method has become increasingly common, and, in a significant number of cases, superseded multi-stage methods of batter preparation. This has become possible because of the improved functionality and reliability of modern ingredients, which has lead to better mixing control. Multi-stage methods are based on separating particular ingredients, either to prevent the formation of gluten or enhance the foam-formation potential of, say, the egg. A number of multi-stage mixing methods might be applied to the mixing of cake batters (Figs 6.4 and 6.5). A common theme in several of the multi-stage mixing processes discussed so far is the delay of the evolution of carbon dioxide gas. Examples are present in the manufacture of cakes and biscuits.

Multi-stage mixing processes are common in the manufacture of biscuits, cookies and pastes. In these cases a common theme appears to be the desire to limit the uptake of water by the wheat flour and the limitation of gluten formation. The creaming of the fat and flour as one of the mixing steps appears to be a direct attempt to waterproof the flour and limit its water uptake.

In another form of multi-stage mixing, savoury short pastes may be prepared using 'cold' or 'hot' mixing methods. In the former case, all of the ingredients are held at bakery temperature for mixing, while in the latter case the water and/or the fat (oil) are heated before being added to the other ingredients. The advantage of the hot-ingredient methods over the cold mixing methods is that they tend to give a crisper paste in the final product and one which is less susceptible to moisture migration. There is a view that the crisper paste comes from a partial gelatinisation of the starch when hot water is used.

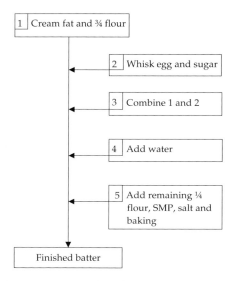

Figure 6.4   Flour-batter mixing method for cake batters.

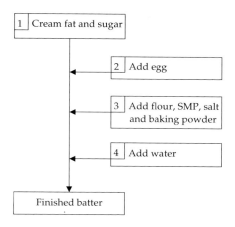

Figure 6.5 Sugar-batter mixing method for cake batters.

The manufacture of chou paste is another example of a hot, multi-stage mixing method. In this case there is a deliberate intent to gelatinise the starch in the wheat flour by mixing it with boiling water. Gelatinisation of the starch–water mixture, or roux, considerably increases its liquid-holding capacity. Liquid egg is blended into the roux to form the chou paste ready for depositing and the combination of the high water content and egg albumen forms the hollow centre which characterises chou products, such as éclairs.

There are few examples of multi-stage mixing methods applied to bread production. The main example of multi-stage mixing in the context of breadmaking is the preparation of part of the dough ingredients in advance of the main mixing process. To some extent this is based on ancient technologies utilising portions of old, fermented dough in order to leaven a mix of new ingredients.

Even though modern strains of baker's yeast are very reliable, the concept of a 'mother dough', 'sponge' or 'sour' remains in place. The concept allows the natural fermentation processes to develop particular flavour notes in the fermenting dough which are carried through to the final product (Calvel, 2001). The flavour, usually acid, comes from fermentation by the micro-organisms present naturally in the flour and the air in the bakery. Lactic acid bacteria make a significant contribution to the flavour notes as well as other micro-organisms. After the pre-fermentation stage, typically lasting 4–24 hours, the fermenting material is re-mixed along with the rest of the ingredients. A common term for this type of technology is **sponge-and-dough** and its use is widespread (Cauvain, 1998b). In addition to the change in flavour, the sponge concept contributes to the modification of dough rheology.

A further example of multi-stage mixing applied to bread production is the delaying of the addition of salt until towards the end of the mixing cycle, which is sometimes used to help the breadmaking potential of some flours.

Dividing/scaling/depositing

On the commercial scale no baked products are mixed to deliver a single unit size. This means that in practice the large bulk of the mix must be divided into smaller units for further processing. The main aim of all dividing/scaling/depositing processes is to deliver the unit size product for further processing without significant change in the intrinsic properties of the matrix concerned. The dividing process is commonly achieved by filling a chamber of known dimensions with a dough, batter or paste of known and fixed density. This relationship between chamber volume and matrix density is important, because most bakery products need to be manufactured to a given weight. In some cases this is for legal weight-control reasons while in others it is so that variations between individual products will be limited.

It is inevitable that some changes will occur as the result of the shear and pressure experienced by the dough/batter/paste during the dividing process. In those matrices which are foam based (e.g. bread dough and cake batters) the effect will be to de-stabilise the bubble structure and to allow the escape of carbon dioxide gas. Naturally, the design of the dividing equipment needs to be such that it minimises the damage concerned.

The dividing chamber will be fed from some form of hopper arrangement which holds the bulk of the material to be divided. This means that some time will pass between the first unit passing through the divider and the last. During this time, changes in the rheological properties of the matrix can occur. Once again the main changes will be associated with the release of carbon dioxide gas. In the case of breadmaking, the dough density will fall and the expanded gluten network will become more susceptible to 'de-gassing'. Usually dividing times are kept as short as possible.

Forming/moulding/shaping

After the bulk of material from the mixer has been divided into unit-sized pieces, it is common for the individual pieces to undergo some change in form or shape to fit the particular product concept. At this stage there are a wide variety of procedures, largely unique to particular sub-groups of baked products and each with its own particular history of evolution. The simplest of forming techniques is applied to cake batters since, in order to bake them, the individual deposits are placed directly into a pan or container. There are a few batter-style products which may be baked free-standing (e.g. sponge drops, Swiss roll) but they are the exception.

The shaping of a dough piece in bread manufacture is typically a two-stage process, often separated by a short rest (Marsh, 1998). It is not unusual for the dough piece to be moulded first into a round ball shape (Fig. 6.6) and later into some form of cylinder. There may be a short rest period, known as first or intermediate proof, between the two moulding stages (Fig. 6.7).

In both moulding stages the rheological properties of the dough are very important in deciding the final product quality. It is especially important that the relatively delicate bubble structure in the dough piece is not damaged during moulding otherwise loss of quality may occur. Damage to the gluten membrane that separates the gas bubbles allows them to coalesce more readily before baking and can lead to the formation of large holes (Cauvain and Young, 2001) and discoloured, firm-eating patches in the crumb (Cauvain and Young, 2000).

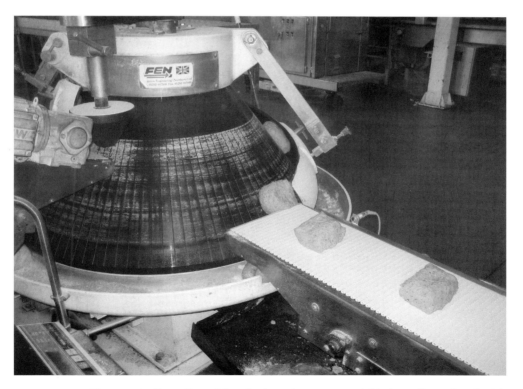

Figure 6.6 Rounding of dough pieces in a commercial bakery. Reproduced with permission of Frank Roberts and Sons Ltd.

Figure 6.7   Resting of dough pieces in a commercial first prover. Reproduced with permission of Frank Roberts and Sons Ltd.

The interaction of the dough with the moulding equipment in the manufacture of bread and fermented goods relies on a combination of appropriate engineering design and dough rheology, particularly as controlled by the level of water used in the recipe. Unlike hand moulding, machines cannot yet respond to differences in dough rheological properties and accordingly adjust their pressures in the moulder. The gas bubbles in the dough have been likened to a basket of eggs (Collins, 1993), with the objective of moulding being to convey those eggs to the pan without breaking any.

Some damage to the cell structure is inevitable, though it can be limited by the design of the moulding equipment. Many of the final moulder designs seen in use are based on the presumption that degassing of the dough at this stage is desirable. This assumption is based on the processing of doughs that have undergone a period of fermentation in bulk before dividing. The gas levels in such doughs may be as high as 70% by volume at the dividing stage and as low as 20% by volume after leaving the final moulder. In contrast, no-time doughs, such as the CBP, have relatively little gas in them at dividing, typically less than 20% by volume (Cauvain and Young, 2006). This being the case, the de-gassing impact of moulding is relatively limited and the moulding step is essentially one of shaping the final product.

A common practice in the final moulder is to sheet individual dough pieces between one or more pairs of rolls (commonly three or four). If the dough piece is round entering the rolls then typically it becomes an elongated pancake on leaving them. At this point the usual procedure is to roll the pancake of dough into a rough cylinder, which is then shaped by squeezing the piece between a board and moving belt (Fig. 6.8). The sheeting rolls are contained behind the screen at the top right of the picture and the pressure board with the moving belt is in the left-middle. A curling chain sits in the gap between the sheeting rolls and the pressure board. There are a number of detailed variations on this theme but the principles of operation for the different equipment designs remain very similar (Marsh, 1998).

Sheeting the dough piece through pairs of rolls imparts further energy to the dough and slightly modifies the gas-bubble population of the piece. If carried out correctly the sheeting procedure will eliminate any large unwanted gas bubbles leaving behind a narrower range of sizes and yielding a finer cell structure in the baked product. If an open cell structure is required in the final product, the conditions of the moulding stage need to be adjusted to retain the larger gas bubbles. Treating the dough gently then becomes crucial in determining final product quality.

The use of sheeting rolls is widespread in the manufacture of baked products. It is important to recognise the potential that they have to transfer energy to the product being sheeted. Breadmaking procedures in some parts of the world use the passage of the dough backwards and forwards, along with folding and turning, to develop the dough structure (Kilborn and Tipples, 1974). Sheeting procedures are, however, more common in the manufacture of laminated products and biscuits.

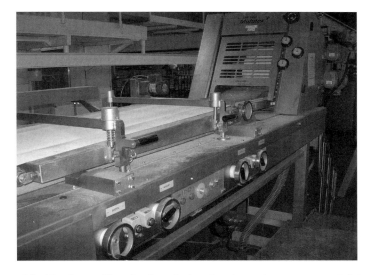

Figure 6.8 Final moulder for bread dough pieces in a commercial bakery. Reproduced with permission of Frank Roberts and Sons Ltd.

The characteristic structure and eating quality of laminated products arises from the development of alternate and discrete layers of fat and dough. There are several variations on the manufacturing process but the end result of the lamination process is very similar (Cauvain, 2001b). The rheological properties of the base dough are important in forming intact sheets of dough with suitable extensibility. Equally, the rheological properties of the fat play a critical role. The laminating fat must also remain intact but must be plastic enough to deform under the sheeting pressures. The integrity of the dough layers is critical in the expansion of the product in the oven. The key properties of the laminating fat have been discussed earlier.

After the initial sheeting of the dough and fat layers they are folded to increase the number of layers – for example, a paste comprising two fat layers and three dough layers can be folded to create four, six or more fat layers depending on the technique employed. Two of the most common laminating techniques used in smaller bakeries are the French and the English (Fig. 6.9). In large-scale manufacture the laminating fat is extruded onto a layer of dough and another one placed on top or the laminating fat extruded onto the centre of a dough sheet and the sides of the dough sheet folded over to cover the laminating fat. In both

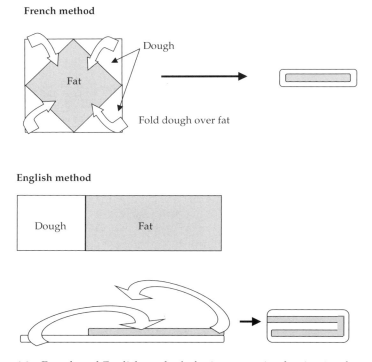

Figure 6.9   French and English methods for incorporating laminating fat.

cases the initial paste comprises one fat layer and two dough layers. Whatever the initial laminating procedure, the dough layers do not increase in the same ratio, because folding brings two layers together. It is common, therefore, to refer to the number of fat layers in the paste as defining the degree of lamination.

The process of sheeting may be carried out to reduce the paste thickness prior to more folding to increase the number of fat layers. Initially, pastry lift will increase with increasing number of fat layers but, after reaching a maximum, will fall with further lamination. The loss of lift seen with increasing lamination arises because of the breakdown of the integrity of the dough and fat layers, which permits the ready escape of steam in the oven. In addition to the effect of layering on lift there are contributions from the strength of the flour (stronger flours give increased lift) and the qualities of the laminating fat (higher melting points give increased lift).

During the sheeting process, the gluten structures in the dough tend to become aligned in the direction of sheeting. If this is not corrected, shrinkage of the dough sheet may occur at 90° to the sheeting direction. To combat this effect, the manufacturer of such products uses a combination of **relaxation** (see below) and **re-alignment** of the paste through 90° to even out the stresses in the sheet.

Many types of biscuit are made by sheeting the paste from the mixer through pairs of rolls and then cutting out the individual pieces from that sheet ready for further processing or baking (Manley, 2000). Such products are usually only sheeted in one direction because of the limited gluten formation which occurred during mixing and the relatively plastic nature of the paste. Any undue elasticity in the sheet manifests itself through eccentricity of the biscuit shape. For example, round shapes may become oval. In some cases the cutting die employed will be deliberately cut to allow for shrinkage of the piece to the required final shape. The main processing techniques used in biscuit manufacture are summarised in Figure 6.10.

Savoury and sweet paste products may also be subjected to sheeting. Commonly, the method is applied to the formation of the lids for pies. The development of a gluten structure in such pastes is very limited and so the creation of a sheet of paste becomes easier and there are fewer problems with eccentricity of the pieces after cutting.

Most paste products are formed using some type of pressing process. Commonly referred to as **blocking**, it is done using a die and a mould of required shape. A piece of the paste is placed in the mould and the blocking device lowered to squeeze the paste to the required shape. Any excess paste is squeezed out of the mould and trimmed to give a clean shape. In most cases the mould acts as the baking pan, in part to prevent the product shape collapsing and in part because, once formed,

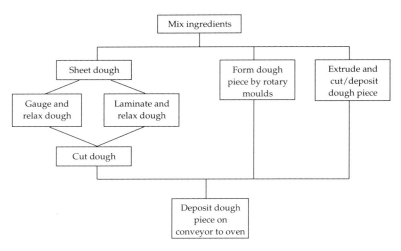

Figure 6.10   The main processing techniques used in biscuit manufacture.

the paste unit cannot be removed from the pan without destroying the required product shapes.

The manufacture of short, sweet biscuits also relies on the use of a mould to create the required shape. The presence of relatively high levels of sugar and fat in the recipe restricts gluten formation and yields a soft, plastic paste. The pieces are formed in a rotary moulder (Manley, 2000), which uses a large drum into which are cut impressions of the biscuit surface features and shape. The biscuit paste is fed into a gap between a roll and the drum and portions of it fill the impressions. As the drum rotates, suction from a rubber-coated lower roll draws the unit pieces out onto a belt which carries them away for baking. A wide variety of shapes and surface patterns can be created using this technique. Rotary moulding may be used in the manufacture of short paste pie lids with motifs on the surface.

Expansion and relaxation

In many cases, usually bread dough and pastes, the passage of baked products from mixer to oven is interrupted by a stage of limited activity. A common aim of this interruption is to modify the rheological properties of the material to prepare it for baking and to obtain improved product quality.

In the manufacture of bread, the moulded dough pieces are transferred to a warm and moist environment in which the yeast continues to produce carbon dioxide gas and inflate the nitrogen gas-bubble nuclei. Provided the gas is retained in the dough, it will expand and may more than double its original size in a defined time period. The process employed is commonly referred to as proof. In addition to the expansion of the dough the gluten structure relaxes – that is it becomes less elastic and more extensible. This change means that the transition to the oven is less injurious, particularly where the product shape is concerned. The enzymic activity from the flour and yeast in the dough contribute to the relaxation of the gluten structure.

In the manufacture of any baked product in which gluten structures are formed, relaxation is of benefit to final product quality. The impact of dough relaxation is most often seen in the manufacture of laminated products, and in such cases is closely linked with the strength of the flour. High-protein, strong flours tend to yield elastic glutens which contribute to dough shrinkage after sheeting. One way to reduce this problem is to allow for a resting period between thickness reduction processes. In general, the stronger the flour the greater the need for resting periods and the longer they should be. Even short pastes and some biscuit types benefit from short resting periods before blocking and cutting. As with proof in bread doughs, the relaxation period leads to better control of final product shape.

Baking

The transition from dough, batter or paste to the baked form requires the input of considerable energy. The changes which take place in products when they bake are many, varied and complex. They will be discussed in more detail in Chapter 7, but may be summarised as follows:

- Evolution of gases
- Inactivation of enzymic and yeast activity
- Expansion of the unit piece
- Setting of the structure
- Reduction of moisture
- Formation of crust colour

Frying

A few bakery products, e.g. doughnuts, are fried rather than baked. The process involves the partial (float frying) or total submersion of dough, batter or pastry in hot oil. As described previously (see Chapters 3 and 5) there are two main types of doughnut, depending on whether they are yeast or powder aerated. The yeasted doughnut will have undergone a period of proof, which contributes to the expansion of the gas bubbles which were incorporated into the dough at the mixing stage. On reaching the fryer, the changes which take place are essentially similar to those described above for baking and will be discussed in more detail in Chapter 7.

Boiling and steaming

There are a few instances where heat transfer using water is the main mechanism by which the product structure is formed and set. The main products which are made this way are bagels and steam breads. Bagels are a ring-shaped dough product that is immersed in boiling water (sometimes with a little sugar syrup present), rather than being baked in an oven, to form and set the structure. The subsequent baking merely contributes to colouration of the product. The immersion in boiling water/sugar syrup helps the formation of a shine on the outer crust, an essential feature of bagels. The boiling process for bagels has some similarities with frying in doughnut production.

The use of boiling water, or more correctly steam, is an integral part of the production of Chinese steam breads. In this case the product is not placed directly in the boiling water but is suspended over the boiling water and is exposed to the diffusing steam. The product temperature does not rise above 100°C and so there is no colour formation, but a thin, delicate and slightly chewy crust forms on the product.

Using re-work

In a number of process stages materials may be generated which are a consequence of particular manufacturing processes and not offered for sale. Most commonly, such materials are generated in sheeting, cutting and blocking processes. For example, individual round-shaped biscuits may be cut from a dough sheet leaving behind a network of unused dough. It is common practice to re-use such materials, provided there are no product safety or quality concerns. In such cases their storage and re-use, in terms of time, temperature, quality and quantity, should be carefully controlled in order to avoid introducing quality defects. In many cases, re-work (as it is often called) should be considered to be an ingredient with specified characteristics. It is usually considered best to incorporate re-work into the virgin material at the mixer in order to ensure uniform dispersion and optimum control, though some operations may feed the re-work back into production at the sheeting stage. The factor that most often decides where the re-work should be added is the degree of gluten development that may have occurred in the material or is likely to occur with re-sheeting.

The use of re-work should be limited as much as possible in the manufacture of fermented products. Yeast activity leads to the continued evolution of carbon dioxide and the eventual depletion of sugars in the dough and loss of the crust-colour-forming components in the dough. There will also be changes in the rheological properties of the gluten network of the dough which commonly contribute to loss of its gas retention. If fermented re-work must be used, then its level of addition should be severely limited and it is important to ensure thorough mixing with the fresh ingredients. Failure to ensure thorough incorporation of fermented re-work will result in variable product quality (Fig. 6.11). The inefficient incorporation of the fermented re-work shows up as lighter-coloured patches of product or even within the same individual product.

The contribution of ingredients and formulation to the evolution of current processing methodologies

Currently, processing technologies used for the manufacture of subgroups of bakery products often have quite specific conditions and require closely-specified ingredients. The close relationship between ingredients, recipe and processing contributes to the wide diversity of baked products. However, the dependence of one aspect of this triumvirate to another is not always fully appreciated and often restricts the view of what is the right combination for a particular product. It is possible that a change of one aspect of the ingredient-recipe-process triumvirate may well be balanced by changes in one or both of the other aspects. There are numerous examples in baking of how this relationship works.

In breadmaking, a significant part of the concept of dough development (which equates to dough gas retention) is built on the relationship

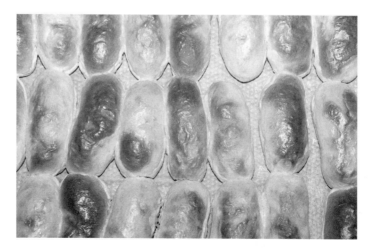

Figure 6.11   Inefficient incorporation of fermented re-work.

between flour strength and mixing energy. The development of the CBP showed that an increase in bread volume was achieved compared with the same protein content flour used in an optimised bulk fermentation process (Cauvain and Young, 2006). This was to offer the opportunity for millers and bakers to reduce flour protein content by about 1% while maintaining bread volume. Alternatively it offered the opportunity to increase the size of the loaf that was made. In practice, both opportunities have been taken advantage of in the UK industry to manufacture a range of bread and fermented goods. In the USA, the sponge-and-dough process has evolved to use flour with high protein content, the sponge component making contributions to both flavour and, perhaps more importantly, helping to modify the rheological character of the dough after final mixing. The introduction of flour with a lower protein content would not be able to deliver the high specific volume products that are required.

The ability to differentiate aspects of processing and ingredients is perhaps best seen in the manufacture of puff pastry. Processing methods that use high protein flours have been evolved, but, because of their tendency to yield elastic glutens, it is necessary to introduce resting periods to modify the gluten rheology. Originally developed with hand pinning and later pastry brakes (mechanised rolling equipment) the same concept has been encapsulated in modern plants dedicated to the manufacture of puff pastry. However, if a lower-protein flour is used then the need for an extended resting period is reduced and overall processing time can be significantly reduced. This effect is illustrated in Figure 6.12, which shows relaxation curves for two flours. The 'optimum' processing window in rheological terms is delineated.

The data show that a longer relaxation time is required for the stronger of the two flours to reach the optimum area, but once there it changes relatively slowly with increasing resting time. On the other hand the weaker of the two flours yields a paste which requires very little time before it is ready for processing but almost as quickly passes through the optimum processing period. In practical terms, these data reveal that shorter processing times can be utilised by choosing an appropriate flour, in this case weaker, but overall the process would be less tolerant to delays or stoppages. In this example, for puff-pastry production, the balance to be achieved is then between through-put rates, tolerance and product quality. The last should not be neglected since weaker flours tend to give less lift in the final product. To some extent loss of lift could be compensated for by increasing the numbers of fat layers in the paste. Key to deciding the balance between the different contributing factors will be the characteristics required in the final product.

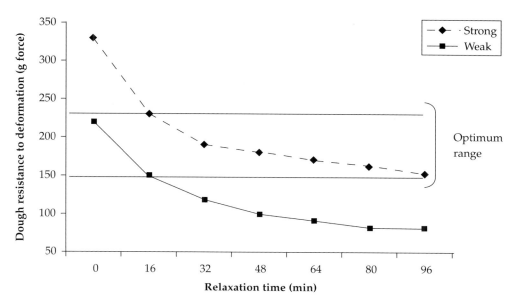

Figure 6.12 Changes in paste rheological properties for laminated product manufacture.

In many cases the development of processing technologies merely reflects the mechanisation of hand processing of traditional materials and recipes. The design of bread-dough moulding equipment for pan breads is perhaps one of the best examples of such an evolutionary process, which has only recently been challenged. As described above, it is common after dividing to mould the unit pieces to a roughly round shape, rest the dough for a few minutes and then remould it to a roughly cylindrical shape. These actions mimic closely the hand processing of dough. The ball shape is probably historical since it tends to be the natural shape when moulding two dough pieces at the same time, one with each hand, to speed up dough processing. Traditionally, the first moulding stage would also have contributed to the de-gassing of the dough pieces, which helped develop a finer crumb cell structure in the final product. The stress to which the dough pieces had been subjected adversely changed the dough rheology and made it less suitable for moulding to a cylindrical shape, so the pieces were given a short rest between the two moulding stages.

In challenging conventional thought on the processing of bread dough it is best to start at the end of the final moulder. Mainly for historical reasons, we have pan bread of particular dimensions. In UK sandwich-bread production four-piecing of bread dough is commonly employed (Cauvain and Young, 2001). As the dough pieces are placed in the pan, the length of each of the four pieces cannot exceed the width

Figure 6.13 Four-piece bread dough assembled for panning. Reproduced with permission of Frank Roberts and Sons Ltd.

of the pan (otherwise they cannot be fitted in). An example of four dough pieces assembled ready for placing in the pan is shown in Figure 6.13.

In order to get four pieces of the appropriate size for the pan, the total length of the cylinder of dough reaching the blades that cut a single piece to create four needs to be four times the length of each of any of the four individual pieces. This simple calculation gives the length of the cylinder which must be delivered to the separating blades during final moulding. At the front of the final moulder, the ball passes through the sheeting rolls and is curled to form a rough cylinder. Squeezing this rough cylinder out to the size required at the end of moulding requires pressure, but excessive pressure can damage gas-bubble structures and adversely affect product quality. In these circumstances, the rheological properties of the dough and the design of the pressure board are crucial in determining the outcome.

The main deficiency of current final-moulding techniques is the creation of a round dough piece and the first mould often given to the dough. Without the first mould the resting period can be reduced or eliminated and the rheological properties of the dough are more suited to final moulding. However, critical to getting the best-quality product is ensuring that the dough pieces enter the rolls on the final moulder as uniformly as possible. Creating a round shape is one of the ways of ensuring that uniform delivery, and so the argument becomes circular and self-justifying. There are alternative ways of dealing with dough processing as has been shown (Cauvain and Young, 2006).

Similar arguments to those discussed above could be made for quite a number of baking technologies. The comments are made, not to denigrate the achievements that others have made in the development of current technologies, but rather to show that only through a thorough understanding of the ingredient-recipe-process interactions can we provide the springboard for new products and process technologies. On occasions it may require the crossing of the artificial boundaries we have created to separate the sub-groups of baked products and adapting a particular technology to serve an alternative purpose.

Chapter 7
Heat Transfer and Product Interactions

Introduction

Modern baked products, in their many shapes, have a long history with deep-rooted symbolism, and because they are so familiar to all of us it is sometimes easy to forget the intimate relationship between form and the essential character of the product. In many cases there will be a strong regional character to products, and there will be more recent developments associated with them. The laminated product that we call 'croissant' provides us with a suitable example: it can be found as a complete circle with ends touching, horn-shaped with ends open (Fig. 7.1) or straight and cigar-like in shape (Fig. 3.15, p. 68). Even the profile of the shape will vary according to whether it is considered right to have well-defined shoulders or not. The traditional croissant form has now been extended to include mini-croissant and filled croissant. The eating qualities will run from the brittle and flaky to the soft and bun-like depending on preference. Butter flavours will dominate in some parts while in others margarine-based products will be acceptable. The same basic laminated product technology would have been used to make the variety of shapes, with slight adaptations to ensure that the required shape and form are achieved.

One of the critical factors in achieving the wide variety of bakery-product forms is the input and extraction of heat. All baked products are subjected to at least one heating stage – baking – and one heat-extraction stage – cooling. Key factors which control the transfer of heat in baked products include the thermal conductivity of the material and the dimensions of the product. In baking and cooling, heat has to pass to and from the centre of the product in order that the required changes take place. Thus, the normal mechanism is for the surface of the product to heat or cool and then heat is conducted to or from the centre of the product. In a few cases, convection may play a role, for example in the baking of cake batters, but within the product conduction is the main heat-transfer mechanism.

Figure 7.1   Croissant shapes.

In baked products the transition from foam-to-sponge and the loss of moisture are critical to final quality. In some cases, the former is more important than the latter, while in others the reverse is true. In baking, all products will lose moisture. Some moisture losses will occur during cooling though bakers usually take steps to reduce such losses as much as possible. In all heat-transfer stages product size, shape and form have significant impact on the ultimate product quality.

Both the intermediates and the final baked products may be subjected to the transfer of heat and not just for the purposes of baking. There are occasions when the normal manufacturing process is interrupted and the unbaked form may be chilled or even deep-frozen for storage before completion of the baking at a later date. In all heat-transfer situations the relatively poor conductivity of the intermediate and the baked products has a profound impact on final product quality. Rask (1989) provided data on dough and bread for thermal conductivity and specific heat. The thermal conductivity of dough and bread is much lower than that of metals in part because of their water content and in part because of their low density.

Heat transfer processes

The transfer of heat in the manufacture of baked products occurs at a number of stages. These include:

- Refrigeration and retarding
- Proving
- Baking
- Cooling
- Deep freezing

Refrigeration and retarding

Refrigeration of bakery-product intermediates may be used to aid processing or slow down or delay particular reactions. In the manufacture of laminated products and some pastry products it is common practice to cool the dough or paste. For example, chilling laminated pastes during manufacture reduces the risk of the laminating fat turning to oil and creating problems with processing. Refrigeration is most commonly used in the manufacture of all-butter laminated doughs and pastes and may involve the transfer of a mass of dough or paste or, perhaps more conveniently (at least for the products), the reduction of the temperature in the processing environment.

Retarding is a specialised form of refrigeration that is often applied to doughs containing yeast (Cauvain, 1998a). There are a number of advantages in being able to 'time-shift' production and retarding technology has become widely employed for overnight storage of fermented dough. A key difference between retarding and refrigeration is that, in the case of the former, the humidity levels in the retarding unit are maintained to be similar to that of the dough, i.e. around 90%. If this were not the case, the loss of moisture from the dough would cause the formation of hard skin on the surface of the dough. This skin would restrict expansion later in processing and cause significant quality losses.

Many different sizes of dough product may be retarded, but the technology is most successful in those which have a small diameter relative to their surface area. The chilling of the centre of a dough piece from, say, 25°C to typical retarding temperatures of between −5 and +3°C can take some time. For bread-roll size pieces 60 minutes or more may be required, while for pan-sized loaves the time is more likely to be 4–6 hours. Yeast activity in the dough piece will continue even at temperatures as low as 3°C. Thus, when the dough piece enters the retarder, yeast activity near the surface of the dough quickly ceases. In the centre of the piece, however, carbon dioxide gas is still being produced and the dough piece seeks to expand. It is not until the whole of the dough piece is cooled to below 3°C that expansion ceases.

Chemically-aerated bakery products may also be refrigerated or retarded in order to slow down gas evolution from the baking powder.

Products which may be manufactured using this approach include scones and cake batters. While the same considerations with respect to heat transfer apply to chemically-aerated products as to yeasted dough, there will be little release of carbon dioxide from the chemical components of the baking powder.

Proving

The processing of dough through a prover is a technique used only in the manufacture of bread, fermented products and some yeast-raised pastries (e.g. croissants and Danish pastry). The dough is held in a warm and moist environment in order to encourage the production of carbon dioxide by the yeast. Baker's-yeast activity reaches it peak at 40–43°C, and it is with temperatures in this range that provers commonly operate. Dough entering the prover usually has a lower temperature than that of the equipment. Typically, dough temperatures will vary within the range of 25–32°C, depending on the breadmaking method employed and the temperature of the bakery. In some hot climates dough temperatures may rise to as high as 35–36°C.

Whatever the actual temperature of the dough pieces, they are usually lower than that of the prover at the point of entry. In the prover the dough temperature rises quickly at the surface and more slowly at the centre. The shape and form of the dough piece has a direct impact on the rate at which the dough temperature will rise, with units with narrow cross-sections warming faster than those with thick cross-sections. Because dough pieces with narrow cross-sections tend to prove more rapidly, the yeast level may be lowered in order to extend proof time. The reason for doing this is that relaxation of the dough piece is an integral part of the proving operation. As has been described earlier, the changes in dough rheology that occur with time are helpful in controlling expansion in the oven.

By the end of proof, the temperatures at different points in dough pieces with narrow cross-sections (e.g. baguettes) tend to have equilibrated to that of the prover. However, there will still be a difference in the time for which the yeast has been working at its optimum rate. In effect, the ends of a long thin cylinder like a baguette, as well as its surface, may be over-proved by comparison with the centre of the dough. This difference accounts for the practical tip given to bakers about how to judge when a baguette is proved: the dough is gently pressed with the fingers and the recovery of the surface after taking the fingers away is observed. An under-proved dough springs back quickly while an over-proved dough does not recover its shape, and an optimally-proved dough slowly recovers its shape. In practice, the baguette is never touched at the end of the piece because it has had more proof than the rest of the dough. The proving state of a baguette is always judged by pressing towards the centre of its length.

Dough pieces with large cross-sections, such as pan breads, almost always leave the prover with a temperature differential between the surface and the centre. The size of the differential can have a significant impact on the behaviour of the pieces in the oven. The lower the dough temperature entering the prover the greater the temperature differential is likely to be when it leaves. The temperature differential can be minimised by raising the initial dough temperature, but there are practical limits. These are mostly dictated by the ability of dough-moulding equipment to handle the softer dough that would come with the increased temperature.

Baking cake batters

The manufacture of cakes represents one of the simplest production operations in the bakery, with only three major stages: mixing, depositing and baking. Cake products come in many sizes and shapes, with the majority being held in some form of pan or container for baking. A few cake types may be baked as free-standing products, but the low viscosity of the batters and its tendency to flow readily mean that such products can only take the form of thin sheets (e.g. Swiss roll) or small shapes (e.g. sponge drops and sponge fingers).

The free-standing forms must be transferred to the oven quickly in order to bake the necessary shapes. Because such products are thin by comparison with their surface area, heat transfer is rapid and the products are quickly set. The rapid transfer of heat is aided by high baking temperatures (that is high for cake baking). Baking times are kept short, in part to avoid charring of the product surface and, more critically, to keep the final product moisture content as high as possible to retain soft eating characteristics.

Cake batters held in pans for baking have relatively large surface areas through which heat can be transferred. The thermal conductivity of the pans is much greater than that of the batters and so they represent no significant barrier to passing heat on to bake the batter. Conduction plays a large part in cake baking as heat is transferred from the surface towards the centre of the product. However, as the temperature of the batter begins to rise its viscosity falls and the fluidity of the batter allows for the development of convection currents within the pan up to the point at which the batter sets. Cake batters, like all baked products, set from the outer surfaces inwards and so any convection currents that form will do so towards the centre of the product. The centre portion of a cake batter will always set, which is why one practical means of assessing when a cake is baked is to lightly press it in the centre and observe its behaviour. Some bakers consider that the sound that the cake makes if touched during baking indicates when it is fully baked: a slightly wet or 'squelching' sound indicates that the product is not baked.

Studies using coloured cake batters (Cauvain, unpublished) have shown that there is an initial movement of the fluid batter towards the base and then it begins to rise up the sides of the pan (Fig. 7.2a). In some cases, if the batter was able to remain fluid for a long time into the baking cycle (that is, if it has a high gelatinisation temperature and low viscosity), it was possible to see continuation of the convection current towards the top crust and then downwards again to the centre of the cake as shown in (Fig. 7.2b). The differences in flow illustrated in Figure 7.2 were typical of high-ratio cakes made with chlorinated cake flour (a) and untreated cake flour (b). The restriction of batter flow in the case of the cakes made with chlorinated flour could be ascribed to the release of amylose from the starch granules at an earlier stage of the baking process than for the untreated cake-flour batter. In examples of high-ratio cake batters made with untreated cake flour that showed the complete circulation pattern, the products would collapse after they left the oven. This phenomenon is discussed in more detail in the section at the end of this chapter.

The important mechanisms that operate during cake baking may be summarised as follows:

- As the temperature of the batter increases the starch granules begin to swell. As the temperature of gelatinisation is approached, amylose begins to leach out into the sucrose solution and the viscosity of the batter increases. The temperature at which starch gelatinisation

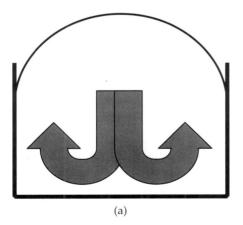
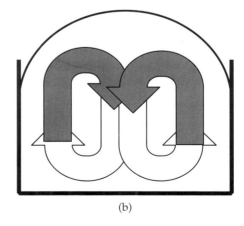

(a)   (b)

Figure 7.2 Convection currents in cake batters: (a) chlorinated, partial; (b) untreated.

occurs depends on the concentration of the sucrose solution and it is higher with increasing sucrose concentration. Usually gelatinisation occurs at around 80°C.

- The proteins in the batter coagulate. Typically this will occur at 70–80°C, though the presence of sucrose may raise the setting point by one or two degrees. Thus, the protein coagulation temperatures are quite similar to one another in cake batters.
- Carbon dioxide gas is released from solution in the batter and from the continuing reaction of the baking-powder components. The rate of release depends on the acidulant chosen, and the quantity of gas on the level of baking powder.
- Gases trapped in the batter expand with heat
- Moisture is lost
- Maillard reactions contribute to crust-colour formation

To understand the impact of size, shape and form on baking it is necessary to understand that the changes that take place in the oven are dynamic and occur at different times at different points in the product cross-section as the heat penetrates. Collectively, the changes in the batter structure equate to the foam-to-sponge conversion which has been discussed previously. All of the surfaces of the batter make this transition within a few minutes of entering the oven, including the formation of a thin crust on the upper surface. The progression of the heat front into the batter is fastest from the surfaces in contact with the pan. The upper crust remains relatively thin for a long period of time and this means that while the centre of the batter remains fluid there is an upwards pressure which may break through the crust. When all of the batter is finally set, expansion of the batter ceases and there is a slight contraction of the product as the internal gas pressure is equalised with that of the surrounding atmosphere.

The flexible nature of the top crust and the internal pressure of the expanding batter account for the peaked shapes and cracks that are often seen on different cake types (Fig. 7.3). This effect is relatively acceptable on small products, like cake muffins, but becomes less acceptable as the size of the product increases. Thus, in the case of large slab cakes a smooth unbroken surface is expected and so the baking conditions have to be adjusted accordingly to provide a lower temperature and longer bake time. Thin products, like Swiss rolls and sponge cakes, heat relatively quickly and uniformly so there is less opportunity for convection currents to be set up in the bulk of the batter. In these products the inclination towards forming a domed or peaked shape is lessened, though it may occur if the recipe is unbalanced or the baking conditions are inappropriate (that is, if the temperature is too high or there is excessive air flow across the top of the product, or both).

Figure 7.3 Cracks on cake surface.

At the end of baking, the cakes have a low-moisture crust and a much higher moisture crumb. Cakes are not expected to have a hard crust, so equilibration of the moisture gradient is encouraged. As a cake crust is thin, little water needs to be lost to achieve this equilibrium and the moisture content of the crumb is not significantly lowered. Loss of moisture from the cake to the atmosphere tends to occur at a low rate because moisture migration to the atmosphere is limited by the low water activity of cake products.

Baking bread doughs

The transition from foam-to-sponge in bread dough follows similar lines to those described for cake batter, with the exception that the high viscosity of the gluten network prevents the formation of convection currents within the dough piece. The important mechanisms that operate during bread baking may be summarised as follows:

- Carbon dioxide gas is released from solution in the dough, and from the final burst of activity of the yeast, until the temperature reaches 55°C
- As the temperature of the batter increases the starch granules begin to swell and gelatinisation occurs around 60°C

- *Alpha*-amylase activity increases and may attack the gelatinising starch. This activity will continue until the amylase is inactivated at 60–90°C, depending on the form used (see Chapter 4).
- Other enzymes which may be present are inactivated
- The gluten proteins in the dough coagulate at 70–80°C
- Gases (including water vapour/steam) trapped in the dough expand with heat
- Moisture is lost
- Maillard reactions contribute to crust-colour formation

During bread baking, the heat front advances from the surface towards the centre of the dough piece in a fashion similar to that described for cakes. Expansion from the last burst of yeast activity at the centre of the dough piece can be considerable, and far greater than that seen in cakes. The upper crust is more rigid and fixed than in cakes and so any splitting of the crust tends to be along the sides of the dough piece. This 'oven spring' or 'oven break' is seen as desirable in many forms of bread and usually shows as a white or paler line or area on one or both of the long sides of bread products. Large-diameter dough pieces are more likely to show oven spring or break because of the longer time needed for the heat to penetrate to the centre of the dough and inactivate the yeast. Oven spring in bread doughs during baking may be difficult to control. A significant contributor to the uniformity of the break is the rheological properties of the dough. If the dough has been optimally proved then oven spring tends to be uniform. Over-proved dough lacks oven spring while under-proved dough tends to exhibit uncontrolled spring and oven break.

There are techniques to improve the control of oven spring. One is through the use of surface cutting or marking of the dough just before baking, which creates points of weakness for the expanding dough (Fig. 7.4). The dough used to make the loaf on the left was not cut at the end of proof and, as a result, the oven spring is uncontrolled and one-sided, while the loaf on the right was cut along the length of the dough piece and has a controlled expansion and uniform shape.

It is most common to cut the surface of free-standing or oven-bottom breads such as bloomers and baguettes and some pan breads. The characteristic patterns so created have now become part of the traditional product appearance (Fig. 7.5). Other benefits of cutting dough before baking include more rapid heat penetration and an increase in the ratio of crust to crumb in the product – since the crust is a significant contributor to bread flavour a more flavourful product is the result.

Another technique used to control oven spring is the introduction of steam or water vapour at the start of the baking process. The

Figure 7.4   Control of bread oven spring by cutting.

Figure 7.5   Variations in cutting patterns on oven bottom bread.

condensing water increases the flexibility of the product surface and allows a more uniform expansion. The resulting crust has a shiny appearance and, if done correctly, the product has a thinner and crisper crust. Steam is most commonly introduced in the baking of free-standing breads, rolls and baguettes.

The penetration of heat all around the pans that hold the baking dough is important in yielding a uniform bake colour and shape. In many larger bakeries the pans may be strapped together for convenience of handling. The gap between adjacent pans and the positioning of the strapping must be such as to allow sufficient hot-air movement around each pan, otherwise quality losses from poorly-baked and -formed breads may occur. Similar consideration should be given to the strapping of cake pans, but the problems tend to be less acute because of the lower bake temperatures used.

There is a significant moisture gradient between the crust and crumb of bread products by the end of baking. Equilibration takes place quite readily and provided that no moisture is lost to the atmosphere the crust readily softens. In many bread products, especially those of smaller size and diameter, the loss of moisture from the crumb to achieve that equilibrium is significant and contributes to the firming of the bread crumb during storage. The water activity of bread is high enough to permit the ready evaporation of moisture and, unless wrapped, bread will go hard quickly and become inedible.

One product that has become increasingly popular is part-baked bread, in which the structure of the product is formed but the crust is only lightly coloured. In order to achieve the required effect it is necessary to reduce the final proof time and the baking temperature. The lower baking temperature is required in order to avoid excess colouring during the first bake but effectively extends the period of yeast activity at the beginning of the bake and so a compensatory reduction in proof time is required. A second bake, usually at the point of sale or in a food-service environment, warms the product and completes the colouring process. The products involved usually have a small cross-section in order to ensure heating of the product core without excessive colouring of the surface.

Baking biscuit and cookie doughs

The different forms of biscuits and cookies are baked directly on the oven band and, being small thin units, they are rapidly baked at relatively high temperatures. Some expansion of biscuits does occur during baking, as gases are liberated from any aerating agents and by thermal expansion. The softening of the dough, especially the sugar solution and the fats, makes the biscuit pliable enough to grow in size for a short while. Since the products are free-standing, expansion can be in any of the three dimensions of the product. Spreading occurs particularly in biscuit formulae with high levels of sugar present, for example in ginger snaps, and needs to be controlled if the products are not to become too thin. The setting of some biscuit structures may be governed by the foam-to-sponge conversion, but in many cases the high sugar and low water levels probably inhibit full gelatinisation of the starch.

The major changes during the baking of biscuits are the darkening of the surface colour through the Maillard reaction and the considerable loss of water. The final moisture content of the product is commonly 1–4%. Even in a product as thin as a biscuit it is still possible to have a moisture gradient in the product after it leaves the oven. As moisture migrates from the moist centre to the drier surfaces, the contraction and expansion which follows causes cracks to occur following lines of microscopic weakness in the products. This problem is referred to as 'checking' and in some cases the biscuit may break completely in two (Cauvain and Young, 2001). All shapes of biscuit can suffer from this problem.

Baking pastry products

There are a wide variety of sizes and shapes of pastry products and most are baked as a composite with a filling of some kind. For the pastry, the transition from unbaked to baked form involves the movement, usually loss, of water and, to a lesser extent, fat. There appears to be relatively little evidence for gelatinisation of starch because of the low water content. The portions of paste in the composite product are similar in thickness to many biscuit products and so it is likely that they bake relatively quickly; however, the overall baking time for the composite products is much longer because the bulk of the product will be the filling. Thus, large pies will take longer to bake than small ones, though the pastry coating in both cases may be baked in the same length of time.

The relationship between the outer paste and filling is a complex one and involves the migration of moisture between the two. It is almost always the case that the filling moisture content is higher than that of the paste at the start of baking but the direction of moisture movement is controlled by the loss of water from the paste to the atmosphere and the water activity of the filling. Heat is conducted through the paste to the filling in which convection currents will certainly occur. The evaporation of moisture from the filling can lead to absorption of water by the paste, but the paste can usually lose that water to the atmosphere, mainly through the lid since it is not protected by the container that holds the paste.

There is evidence from work on apple pies that some moisture may move from the paste to the filling during baking (Cauvain and Young, 2000) (Fig. 7.6). The data reveal an increase in the apple-filling moisture content immediately after baking, which reverses during subsequent storage as the moisture migrates to the paste and then the atmosphere. It is possible that the low water activity of the apple filling (with its high sugar concentration) was responsible for the absorption of water by the filling.

Baking laminated products

The mechanism behind lift in laminated products is based on the evaporation of moisture (mainly from the dough layers) and its impedance by the laminating fat. The volume of steam generated at standard pressure in a 10 g puff pastry can exceed 2 l but some of it quickly makes its way to the outside atmosphere, and not all of it will provide useful lift. Most laminated products achieve their maximum lift by halfway through the baking cycle. The remainder of the time in the oven is concerned with the loss of water to reduce the moisture content to a few percent. This contributes to the dry and flaky eating quality which characterises laminated products.

The impact of the shape of laminated products and the interactions during processing often only become apparent in the oven. Shrinkage

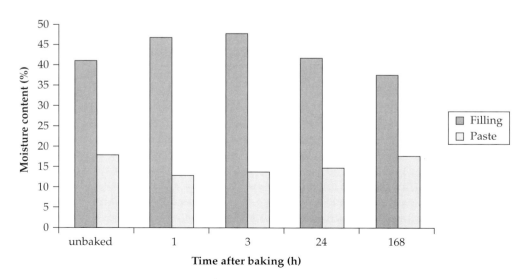

Figure 7.6   Moisture movement in apple pies.

can be a particular problem. As the fat begins to turn to oil and the dough layers lose moisture they contract. The degree and direction of contraction reflects the stresses and strains to which the paste was subjected during sheeting and lamination, and the shape of the product. In the case of vol-au-vent rings, shrinkage often makes the product assume an eccentric shape, while squares may become rectangular and croissants, which are expected to be circular or horn-shaped, typically tend to straighten out. In addition to losing the desired shape, shrinkage of laminated products may lead to uneven lift.

To overcome these problems, particular attention needs to be paid to the lamination and sheeting processes (Cauvain, 2001b). Such problems are exacerbated if the sheeting procedures are to run the paste in the same direction without turning. Shrinkage may be readily reduced by extending the relaxation periods, but the plant design and operation would need to be such that increased resting periods could be accommodated. The evenness of lift, and, to a lesser extent, shape, is sometimes controlled by puncturing the paste. This technique is sometimes called **docking** and is designed to create release points for the escape of steam. Docking helps control lift in a way similar to that of cutting bread dough to control oven spring in tight doughs.

Microwave baking

One way in which to transfer energy to baked products without the inconvenience of the effect of the poor conductivity of bakery materials is to employ microwave radiation. All electromagnetic radiation comprises an electric and a magnetic component and can be defined in terms of the strengths of these two fields. Microwaves are generally considered to be that part of the electromagnetic spectrum of 300×10^6–300×10^9 Hz. The ability of a material to be heated by microwave energy is significantly affected by its relative dielectric constant. Schiffmann (1993) listed the most important factors affecting the heating of materials by microwave energy:

- Moisture content – materials of higher moisture content usually have higher dielectric constant
- Density – air is effectively transparent to microwaves
- Temperature – the dielectric constant may increase or decrease with temperature depending on the nature of the material
- Frequency – the lower the frequency the greater the depth of penetration, but there are only two allowed industrial frequencies, 2450 MHz and 915 MHz, with the latter being the one most commonly chosen for food

- Conductivity – strongly influenced by the presence of ions in the material
- Thermal conductivity – still plays a part in overall heat transfer because microwaves may not penetrate to the centre of the food, depending on its dimensions
- The specific heat of the material

Since unbaked cake batters and bread doughs have high water contents they may appear to be ideally suited to heating using microwave energy. Unfortunately this is not always the case, because the dimensions of the product and its air content tend to counterbalance the benefits of the high water content. Thus, while Chamberlain (1973) found that large UK-style loaves (1 kg of dough in pan) could be baked in as little as two minutes with microwave energy, it was necessary to combine the microwave energy with conventional heating in order to deliver bread with acceptable characteristics of crumb softness and crust colour. The bread was baked in non-metallic pans in around eight minutes and an additional advantage of the process was that the rapid inactivation of the flour *alpha*-amylase activity would allow the use of low-Falling-Number UK wheats. The process never went into commercial operation because of lack of investment in the development of suitable non-metallic pans.

Outside of the home, microwave energy has been used to bake bread, to prepare part-baked products and for the baking of cakes. More recent developments have permitted the use of metallic pans, which has reduced a significant obstacle for commercial exploitation. The heating of fermented dough with microwave energy has also been used to accelerate the proving of dough pieces and in the thawing of some bakery products. Similar applications have also used radio-frequency. This latter technique is often used in biscuit and pastry baking to reduce the moisture at the product centre and give a more uniform moisture gradient. Using radio-frequency in this way can reduce or eliminate potential problems with checking of the products on cooling and storage.

Applications of microwave heating have been limited in commercial bakeries. In part this was because of the problems associated with the pan materials that could be used in the ovens. There were also problems associated with product dimensions and even shape. Despite popular belief, microwaves do not necessarily penetrate right to the centre of large products. Much depends on the wavelength being used and, as commented on above, there are restrictions on the wavelengths that are permitted, creating some problems with larger products. This may lead to non-uniform heating, particularly as the moisture content in different regions of the product changes. Ring and round-shaped products tend to fare better than rectangular products in microwave baking.

Frying doughnuts and other products

The transfer of heat to bakery products during frying depends on a number of factors, including the temperature of the oil, the type of frying and the shape and nature of the product. On entering the fryer, heat is transferred to the doughnut (yeast- or powder-raised) by conduction from the hot oil into the body of the product. For the yeast-raised doughnut the pattern of bubble expansion and coalescence follows in much the same way as would be seen for bread dough, though, because of the intimate contact between heating source and product, the time taken for the foam-to-sponge conversion is much shorter. Nevertheless, the conversion usually does take place, subject to some of the considerations discussed below. While powder-raised doughnuts are created in a similar manner to cake batters it is unlikely that convection currents are set up in the frying batter, and so most of the heat transfer will occur because of conduction.

There are two main frying methods employed in doughnut production: **float frying** and **submerged frying**. With float frying, the product is deposited (cake doughnut) or placed into the hot oil (yeast-raised). Depending on the density of the product it will float to the surface of the oil so that only part of it will be in direct contact with the heating medium. This leads to some variation in the changes in cross-section of the frying product. The lower product surface will heat more quickly than the upper surface and will therefore expand at a greater rate. As gases are released, the density of the product falls and it remains afloat. The upper surface, exposed to the bakery atmosphere, will begin to dehydrate and a dry skin may form. In order to get uniform expansion, the floating products are flipped part way through and the former upper surface becomes the lower surface for the remainder of the frying process.

Uniform expansion and colour are required features in doughnuts and many see the formation of a white ring around the circumference of the doughnut as a desirable feature. Since this ring has not coloured it has clearly not been exposed to the same degree of heating as the rest of the product surface. In fact it has probably spent relatively little time in contact with the hot oil. Clearly the density of the product is a critical factor in achieving this effect and in this context both gas production, and gas retention in the yeast-raised form, play a major role. The more gas that is produced and retained the lower will be the product density and the more prominent will be the white-ring formation. If the product is totally submerged for frying then heating will be more uniform. Since gas production will occur, the density of the product will fall and the natural buoyancy of the product will cause it to rise to the top of the hot oil. It is necessary therefore to provide a means of preventing the product from reaching the surface, and commonly the products are held in a cage of some form.

Most fried products have a relatively small diameter and large surface area. Commonly they assume a ball- or spherical-shape during frying. Large-diameter products, filled pies, for example, are difficult to fry because of the poor conductivity of the materials used in their manufacture. The rate of heat transfer can be speeded up for frying, especially in powder-raised doughnuts, by depositing a ring shape, which increases the surface area relative to the product diameter. This approach shortens frying times and speeds up the foam-to-sponge transition, but does not fundamentally change the nature of the conversion.

A common problem associated with doughnuts is the absorption of relatively large quantities of oil as the result of frying. This leads to greasiness when handling the doughnut and a greasy/fatty mouth-feel when it is eaten. As discussed above, when doughnuts first enter the fryer there is considerable expansion of the dough as the heat begins to penetrate the dough or batter. While the gas bubbles are intact and expanding the pressure inside the piece is greater than that of the oil or atmosphere and this will prevent the oil from penetrating into the product structure. It is only after the foam-to-sponge conversion has been made and the pressure inside the piece is equal to that surrounding it that oil can begin to penetrate the structure. Even then the escaping water vapour impedes the ingress of fat. Thus, the absorption of fat should only occur in the later stages of frying.

Baking on a hot-plate

In the baking of hot-plate products the initial heat is supplied by conduction from the very hot surface of the plate or griddle. This quickly sets the lower surface of the product. There is a rapid transfer of heat into the remainder of the product, and there is usually too little time for convection currents to be established in those products that are made from batters, such as crumpets. The rapid input of heat causes an immediate release of carbon dioxide and expansion of the gases in the batter or dough, but, as the structure is already beginning to set, the movement of the gases is upwards in the baking matrix. This upward movement is exaggerated by baking the products in a ring or hoop shape. The overall result is to create a series of vent-like tunnels, running from the base of the product right through to its upper surface. As the structure finally sets, the upper surface assumes a characteristic pocked-like appearance (Fig. 3.16, p. 70 and Fig. 5.9, p. 119).

The processes that contribute to structure development for this group of products depend heavily on the batter and the dough having large quantities of carbon dioxide readily available when the deposit first contacts the hot-plate. In the case of yeast-raised products this is achieved by using high levels of yeast and a period of fermentation prior to depositing. In the case of powder-raised products the type of baking powder may be adjusted to provide a rapid release of carbon dioxide by using the faster-acting acids. In all cases, the viscosity of the system is important in controlling the movement of the large gas bubbles upwards. Too low a viscosity and the gas may escape before the structure has set, yielding poor product volume. In the case of crumpets and pikelets, the product may have a 'blind' appearance, that is, it may not have pock marks on the surface. If the viscosity of the system is too high, the batter or dough does not readily flow and product shape suffers.

It is common practice to turn the individual products over part way through the baking process. The time at which the products are turned depends on the surface appearance desired. Crumpets and pikelets are not usually turned over until the upper surface has set and is just beginning to dry out. The baking time after the turn over is relatively short and relatively little surface colour is formed. This ensures that the products will brown when they are later toasted or grilled, yet remain relatively moist-eating. Muffins and pancakes are turned much sooner in the baking process and get a more even bake on both sides. These products traditionally have a smooth surface, but when cut (or more correctly, in the case of muffins, torn apart) the inner crumb will comprise many large holes and the cut surfaces resemble crumpets. The cut surface of the muffin is usually toasted to a light brown colour before serving.

Cooling

After leaving the oven, most baked products require a period of cooling (Fig. 7.7) before further processing and wrapping. As with all heat-transfer processes, the rate at which products cool depends on their dimensions and the temperature differential between the atmosphere and the product. Heat transfer to the surrounding atmosphere involves mainly convection and radiation. Heat is also lost through moisture evaporation but usually such losses are minimised. Most of the cooling in bakeries is carried out without refrigeration and relies on a flow of cool air across the product. The air movement will increase evaporative losses if the relative humidity of the air is lower than that of the product. Large-scale commercial cooling may use refrigerated and humidified air to speed up the process and minimise moisture losses (Wiggins, 1998).

Figure 7.7   Bread in a commercial spiral cooler. Reproduced with permission of Frank Roberts & Sons Ltd.

The temperature to which a product is cooled depends very much on what further processing may be required. In the case of bread that will be sliced it is necessary to ensure that the crumb is firm enough to withstand the mechanical effect of the slicing blades. This usually means that the core temperature of loaves should be in the region of 27–30°C before slicing. In this respect the relatively rapid re-association of the amylose in the starch as bread cools helps to firm the bread crumb (Schoch and French, 1947). The firming of bread crumb later in storage is mainly related to the retrogradation of the amylopectin portion of the starch.

One of the main reasons for cooling baked products is to prevent condensation after they have been wrapped. Any condensation within the wrapper may encourage microbial spoilage, particularly mould growth on the surface. The length of time taken for baked products to cool will vary according to size and shape but commonly takes from 30 minutes for small-cross-section products to several hours for large-cross-section and dense products. The latter category includes large fruited cakes.

Deep freezing

Bakery intermediate products may be deep frozen in order to extend their practical shelf-lives. Examples include frozen doughs and cake batters (Kulp *et al.*, 1995). Size, shape and form have a profound effect on the length of time that it will take a product to be frozen, larger products requiring longer times to achieve the frozen state than smaller ones. Cauvain (1998a) provided examples for bread dough units frozen in a blast freezer with an air temperature of $-35°C$ which showed that roll-sized pieces achieved a core temperature of $-10°C$ in 15 minutes, while large pan breads took 100 minutes to achieve the same core temperature. In large units of bread dough the relatively long time required to achieve the frozen state may even allow significant yeast activity to occur before it becomes dormant.

Unbaked biscuit doughs and cake batters may be frozen for long-term storage and bake-off at a later date. In such cases the high sugar levels in the recipe mean that the freezing point is very low. In some cases it can be as low as $-20°C$, so that products are barely frozen under typical deep-freeze storage conditions. There can be losses of carbon dioxide gas during the frozen-storage period, which will result in progressive loss of product volume with prolonged storage. In the case of cake batters, there is also a tendency for final product shape to become more peaked. This is similar to the effect that might be seen with scratch-baked cakes which are low in baking powder.

The deep freezing of part-baked and fully-baked products may be used for the longer-term storage of bread, cakes and pastries. A storage temperature of $-20°C$ is most commonly used and it is important that the products are cooled as quickly as possible before transfer to frozen storage.

Foam-to-sponge conversion and the collapse of bakery products

In the manufacture of bread and cake products, foam-to-sponge conversion is an integral part of the structure-formation process. One of the significant factors involved in the timing of that process is the gelatinisation of the starch in the wheat flour. This usually occurs at around $60°C$ but the presence of sugar will increase the gelatinisation temperature – the higher the level of added sugar the higher the gelatinisation temperature of the starch. If the sugar level is high enough then gelatinisation of the starch can occur after the setting of the protein structures.

On setting, protein structures lose their ability to hold onto gas bubbles and they will escape to the surrounding atmosphere. As the gas pressures in the batter or dough equalise with those of the surrounding atmosphere the product stops rising and may even shrink back a little before baking is completed. Cauvain and Chamberlain (1988) measured the height of dough baking in an oven with and without the addition of fungal *alpha*-amylase and showed that the maximum height for both dough pieces was achieved a short while before the end of the prescribed baking time (Fig. 7.8). The same measurements showed that not only was a greater maximum height achieved with the addition of fungal *alpha*-amylase but that it occurred a short while later than when using the recipe without added amylase. The delay in achieving the maximum height can be attributed to the presence of extra sugars generated by the action of the amylase on the damaged and swelling starch in the dough.

Higher levels of amylase addition commonly lead to collapse or caving-in of bread crusts. This is partly due to the presence of extra sugar but is more closely related to increased gas retention. This causes greater expansion of the inner crumb of the baking loaf and compression of crumb material against the developing crust. The collapse of

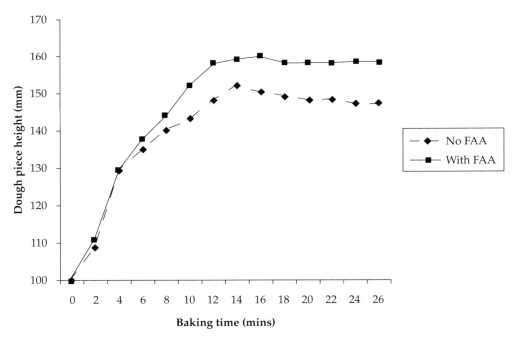

Figure 7.8   The effect of fungal *alpha*-amylase (FAA) on the height of dough pieces during baking (based on Cauvain and Chamberlain, 1988).

the loaf is not manifest until it begins to cool. This problem is almost always associated with breads baked in a pan. Free-standing breads and rolls may continue to expand and, if the force is great enough, may crack the crust which has formed.

Rolls, buns and doughnuts can collapse on cooling, leaving them with a wrinkled appearance. This type of collapse is associated with incomplete foam-to-sponge conversion and the presence of sugar in the recipe. Even though the protein structures have set, the late gelatinisation of the starch can leave some gas bubbles intact in the matrix. On cooling, the internal pressure of these intact bubbles quickly falls below that of the surrounding atmosphere, the structure can no longer support itself and it shrinks. The outer crust is less flexible (but not totally inflexible) and folds in on itself, assuming a wrinkled appearance.

Collapse of cakes on cooling may also occur because of incomplete foam-to-sponge conversion. This problem most commonly occurs when high-ratio cakes (see Chapter 3) are made with untreated flour and with larger-sized cakes baked in pans. Treatment of the wheat flour with dry heat or chlorine gas modifies the surface properties of the starch to encourage the earlier release of amylose from the starch granule. This restricts the fluidity of the batter in the oven and lowers its setting point.

If the foam-to-sponge conversion is not complete when the products leave the oven, it can be completed by subjecting them to a mechanical shock while still in the pans. The impact of this action is to burst any remaining intact gas bubbles instantly, with the subsequent equalisation of pressures. The effect of mechanical shock only works on products that have shrunk or collapsed on cooling, it cannot correct collapse that has occurred prior to cooling. Using a mechanical shock to cure collapse in baked products appears counterintuitive, not least because much advice is given to avoid mechanical shock during transfer from prover to oven or during baking. Collapse at these times is associated with instability of the bubble structure in the matrix and gas lost at such times cannot be recovered.

The use of mechanical shock to cure post-baking collapse does in fact have a sound basis in craft bakery practices. Often the problem is not seen when the same product recipe is baked in different forms. One well-known example used by the authors in practical training sessions is to bake a fruited-bun recipe as round buns on trays and the same recipe as bun loaves in pans. The round buns collapse and wrinkle on cooling while the bun loaves do not. This might be interpreted as a size-related phenomenon, but it has more to do with the fact that within a few seconds of leaving the oven the bun loaves are removed from the pan to prevent them sweating and the side and bottom crusts going soft. The most common method of de-panning bun loaves is to knock the pan on a suitable block to release them from the pans. The mechanical shock so delivered ensures complete foam-to-sponge conversion. In practical training sessions the authors then demonstrate the validity of this observation using a repeat bake of the fruited buns, dropping the tray on the floor immediately after removal from the oven. A perfect instance of science being able to explain bakery practice!

Ingredient, recipe and product interactions

A number of the ingredient and recipe choices made at the start of the manufacturing process have significant impacts later during processing. In some cases there are interactions which also involve product size, shape and form and these may lead to the adjustment of an ingredient level in order to optimise product quality. In many cases the interactions which precipitate a change involve the transfer of heat to or from the product concerned.

There is a strong interaction between gas production in cake batters and bread dough, and the product size. This is because of the variations in heat transfer that occur with products of different sizes. In the manufacture of cakes it is common to adjust the level of baking powder according to size, with smaller-sized units having proportionally higher baking powder levels than large-sized units. An example of variations in aeration with cake size is given in Table 7.1. To provide a direct comparison, only the variation in sodium bicarbonate level is quoted, to allow for the use of different acidulants (see Chapter 4). The adjustment of baking-powder level is based on the fact that it will take longer for the heat of baking to penetrate to the centre of products with a large cross-section relative to their area, e.g. a slab cake, than those with a small cross-section relative to their area, e.g. a cup cake or cake muffin.

Table 7.1 Sodium bicarbonate levels in different cake types.

Product	Dimensions (cm)	Level of sodium bicarbonate (% flour weight)
Unit cake	$15 \times 8.5 \times 8$	1.5
Slab cake	$30 \times 15 \times 6.5$	0.7
Layer cake	$45 \times 33 \times 6.5$	1.5
Cup cake	6×3	1.8
Fruited unit cake	$15 \times 8.5 \times 8$	1.0

The effect on cake quality of adding reducing sugars like dextrose and polyhydric alcohols like glycerol has been commented on earlier (see Chapter 4). The brown discolouration of the cake crumb that comes with increasing levels of addition is less noticeable in smaller and thinner products. Thus, levels of use can be higher in small and thin layer cakes. Along with the higher levels of use come benefits for product spoilage-free shelf-life, because of the lower water activity.

The addition of fruit to cake batters and bread dough increases the density of the products: the higher the fruit content the greater the density. If it is important to maintain a particular size (volume) or shape of a plain product, then deposit weight of the fruited form will need to be greater to maintain the required weighed size. The increase in deposit weight required will depend on the quantity and type of fruit used. There are size differences in the fruit pieces to consider, with raisins being larger than sultanas, which, in their turn, are larger than currants. If candied fruit, nuts, chocolate chips or other particulate ingredients are present in the recipe these too will have an impact on the deposit weight of batter required. Some examples of deposit weights and their respective densities are given for plain and fruited cake batters in Table 7.2.

Another example of the complex interactions that characterise baked products is the relationship between product, yeast level and temperature in the manufacture of retarded fermented products (see above). Optimising final baked-product quality depends on choosing the retarding and subsequent warming (proof) temperatures, and is strongly influenced by the nature of the product. The only practical recipe adjustment that can be used is yeast level; adjusting other ingredients inevitably leads to a reduction in quality. The larger the dimensions of the dough product (especially the diameter) the longer it takes to cool or warm uniformly, whatever the temperatures chosen. The impact of the delay in heat transfer to the centre of the piece allows

Table 7.2   Cake batter deposit weights.

	Dimensions (cm)	Plain		Fruited	
		Deposit weight (g)	Batter density (g/ml)	Deposit weight (g)	Batter density (g/ml)
Unit	$15 \times 8.5 \times 8$	300	2.35	340	2.67
Slab	$30 \times 15 \times 8$	1250	2.78	1400	3.11
Layer	$45 \times 33 \times 2.5$	1500	1.01	1700	1.14
Cup	6×3	22	0.78	25	0.88
Sponge sandwich	18×4	200	0.79	230	0.90

for considerable yeast activity in the case of the retarding phase and inactivity in the warming phase.

One way in which to reduce this particular problem is to adjust the yeast level. Ideally, less yeast would be used in the retarding phase and more in the warming phase. This is not practically possible, so the choice of yeast level is most commonly based on limiting gas production in the retarding phase and minimising the problems in the warming phase by adjusting time, temperature or both. Longer processing times in the post-storage phase for retarded dough (and to some extent frozen dough) can be readily accommodated in pre-programmable specialised refrigeration equipment known as retarder–provers. Using these, the sequence of cold and warm conditions can be pre-set, but the baker must still make the decision as to the amount of yeast to use. As a general rule, the larger products (e.g. pan breads) benefit from a greater reduction in yeast level by comparison with the scratch equivalent than do products of smaller dimension (e.g. rolls). If a batch of products entering the retarder–prover comprises both large and small, the conditions must be set to optimise the larger products.

In the manufacture of laminated products the degree of lift required is most commonly dictated by the nature of the product. There are a number of ways of controlling lift and they include the following:

- The type of laminating fat – the higher the melting point the greater the lift
- The type of flour – generally higher protein flours give greater lift because the dough layers are more likely to remain intact
- The processing temperature – lift with low-melting-point fats can be improved using lower processing temperatures
- The ratio of fat to dough – usually lift increases as the ratio of laminating fat to base dough increases until a maximum is reached and then there may be some loss of lift. This occurs because fat layers are so thick that they readily permit the escape of the water vapour which is the key mechanism behind laminated pastry lift.
- The number of fat layers – initially, as the number of fat layers increases so does lift, until a maximum is reached, and thereafter lift decreases. The loss of lift occurs because of the breakdown of the integrity of dough and fat layers.
- Relaxation of the dough – in the case of stronger flours better lift may be obtained by allowing the dough to have a period of rest during processing

There are many more examples of the complex interplay between ingredients, recipe and type of bakery product. The few examples chosen above serve to show the wide variety of choices that face the baker in the manufacture of baked products. Many of these interactions are particularly difficult to deal with because the rules which govern product quality are often not clear or indeed known. This makes problem-solving, quality optimisation and new-product development particularly challenging, as will be discussed in the final two chapters.

Chapter 8
Understanding and Manipulating the End-Product Requirements

The importance of records

Being faced with a product that does not come up to scratch causes bakers many headaches. Often considerable time, effort and money are required to identify the causes of the problem and find solutions in order to obtain the desired end-product quality. Unexpected quality variations are not the exclusive province of any particular size of manufacturing unit – they can occur anytime and anyplace. Nor are they exclusive to the production bakery – even in the best-controlled test bakery or laboratory unexpected fluctuations in quality can occur.

There is no magic to problem solving. It is normally achieved through critical observation, structured thought processes and access to suitable sources of information. It must be recognised, however, that baking is a complex mixture of ingredient and process interactions with a good sprinkling of human intervention! It is at this time that the experience of the baker can be put to effective use. Knowledge and understanding of how particular characteristics can be achieved in an end product help the baker to eliminate suspects one by one until the real culprit or culprits (since often a fault can have more than one contributor) can be isolated. It is possible to stumble quickly on the required solution by chance, but more often than not it is the haphazard approach to problem solving that is wasteful of time, resources and money. Successful and efficient problem solving or quality enhancement usually requires a methodical approach.

Bakers and product developers can go some way to helping themselves optimise product quality. Keeping good records of the effects of any changes made to ingredients, their quantities and processing (even if the effect is directional and not quantitative) can help to provide the information needed for problem solving. Whether problem solving in a traditional way or using the knowledge-based systems described later in this chapter, a consistent and methodical approach to what has been seen is essential. This is where a log or other record of the faults that occur and the appropriate solutions implemented becomes invaluable. Records should routinely be kept of recipes and any work instructions or product sheets associated with the manufacture of the product. In almost all modern bakeries, a formal production record will be set up for each of the product types and used by the manufacturing operatives to prepare the various items.

The importance of a formal record of what was actually carried out on a particular occasion cannot be over-stressed. While many operatives will keep to the prescribed formulation and processing recipe, small variations about a given value can occur, and lack of information of what the actual values were for a given mix makes problem solving more difficult. It is normal for standard production specifications to allow a degree of tolerance for weights and operating conditions. For example, a temperature specification for a cake batter may be stated as 20 +/− 2°C. However, such a specification allows for replicate batters to be 18°C or 22°C, and a 4°C variation, coupled with other small changes, may have a larger effect on final product quality than expected, not least in the rate of production of carbon dioxide through the baking-powder reaction.

A formal record of production can encompass many aspects including:

- Any variations in the source of the raw materials
  ○ Changes in flour or whole egg batches, or a new supplier of a particular ingredient
- Changes in analytical data
  ○ Even where these are still within acceptable limits, because the cumulative effect of small changes in a number of individual parameters can have a large effect on final quality
- The actual quantities of ingredients used compared with the standard values
  ○ In breadmaking it is common to adjust the amount of water added in order to maintain a standard dough rheology for subsequent processing. In other cases, deliberate changes from the standard formulation may have been introduced in order to compensate for some process change – for example, in bread dough the yeast level may be adjusted to compensate for a change in prover temperature so that final proof times do not vary.
- The processing conditions
  ○ Mixing times, energies, ingredient and batter or dough temperatures. Once again, the values may fall within acceptable ranges but still have a cumulative effect.

- Process equipment settings that may vary according to operator preference or because of other variations in other factors
  - For example, an unavoidably higher laminated-paste temperature may result in greater damage to the laminated structure, which may require a compensatory adjustment to roll gap settings during sheeting
  - Process timings; baking or cooling times
- Changes in packaging materials

The record may be simplified by using the standard recipe as a *pro forma* against which to record variations. Such techniques have been commonly used to record dough divider weights and can be readily adapted for any aspect of bakery production. The record may be on paper or using suitable computer-based programs.

In addition to the recipe and process records it is very important to have a formal record of finished-product quality. Once again it will be common to have some form of product specification with appropriate tolerances against which to make an assessment. Such techniques are commonly the province of the Quality Control Department. The degree of detail recorded will vary. For use in problem solving the formal product specification or quality control record may require some adaptation and enlargement as small, but commonly accepted, variations may hold the vital clue to the cause of a particular problem. The techniques which may be used to measure baked product characteristics have been described earlier (see Chapter 2).

Optimising baked-product quality through test baking

One of the most common methods used to identify the causes of quality defects, to optimise product quality and develop new products is the use of test baking. The premise for such a method is that it is possible to simulate the conditions that would be observed in commercial practice. Once a standard method has been established, the practice is to apply deliberate perturbations to ingredients, recipe and processing conditions and examine the results against a given hypothesis. This approach has provided the answers to many difficult problems and enabled the development and refinement of many of the bakery rules that are in use today. However, the practice of test baking is not without its problems and must be carried out in a disciplined manner in order to gain benefit from the exercise. Poorly-conceived, controlled or executed test baking can be misleading and result in considerable wastage of time, effort and raw materials.

In order for test baking to be truly effective it is necessary to recognise that in many cases its fundamental basis is unsound. The principal difficulty lies with the fact that it is almost impossible to reproduce on a smaller scale processes and interactions that are likely to occur on the larger scale. Scale-up factors with the same equipment will lead to different interactions with a standard set of ingredients and a given recipe. Once it is accepted that the best use of test baking is that it acts as a guide to what will eventually be seen in commercial practice, its value increases. Usually directions of change for a given effect will remain the same whether carried out in the test bakery or on the manufacturing plant. For example, increasing the level of ascorbic acid to make bread by the CBP with a small-scale mixer will show the same effect as that of a larger mixer, namely a progressive increase in bread volume until a maximum is reached. The absolute level of ascorbic acid at which maximum bread volume will be reached is determined by the relationship with available oxygen and, in turn, by the ratio of mixer headspace volume to dough volume. If this complex relationship is not exactly the same for both small and large mixer then the optimum level of ascorbic acid will be different for both machines.

Good experimental design, control, systematic working and record keeping are the key to the success of test baking. Statistical design and analysis have important roles to play in providing reliable interpretation of complex interactions, and many different approaches have been used (e.g. Street, 1991). However, there can be a temptation to assume that only information derived from a statistically designed and analysed study has any significant value. Such an assumption ignores the value of trends in data, which can be readily seen by the simple plotting of graphs or the use of histograms. It is also perfectly possible to use statistics to derive correlations between parameters which have no real meaning in practice.

A significant problem in test baking often comes from apparently poor reproducibility between samples and batches. This arises in part from the inherent variability that may come from the composition and quality of the raw materials. While raw-material suppliers will try their best to ensure uniformity of properties it should be remembered that in most cases baking deals with natural raw materials and they are subject to natural variations. The most obvious example is wheat flour, where it is perfectly possible to have two flours with the same protein content but yielding very different gluten qualities.

In any test-baking procedure it is important to understand the typical variability which will occur. This will be the sum of all of the potential ingredients' quality, recipe quantities and process variables. Most critically it will also include the variability in the ingredient-recipe-process interactions. To gain an appreciation of the variability associated with a given test-baking procedure it is necessary to appreciate:

- The within-batch variability – It is always advisable to make more than one product from a given test batch. The precise numbers of replicate products required depends on many factors, but in practice is most likely to be associated with the quantity of raw material available or the operating capacity of test-baking equipment.

- The batch-to-batch variability – Making replicate batches is always advisable, but once again practical limitations may become more important than statistical considerations.

- Time-related or day-to-day variability – Many test-baking pro-grammes are so large that they will take several hours, days or even weeks to complete. Time-related variations may occur because of changes in ingredient properties, for example yeast activity reduces with age and conditions of storage (Williams and Pullen, 1998), and both flour and fat performance are known to change with time. Variations in the test bakery may also occur during a given day: practical bakers know, for example, that the first couple of bread doughs in the day need slightly warmer water than will be used during the rest of the day in order to achieve a given final dough temperature. Such effects can be reduced using temperature control of the testing area. In extended test-baking programmes there is variability associated with having to change from one batch of an ingredient to another, but even when the same ingredient is avail-able, day-to-day variation can occur.

When setting up a test-baking method it is useful to put in place a series of trials, with standard ingredients and a given recipe, that encompass the three sources of variability referred to above. For example, a bread test bake may produce four loaves from each batch. This could be replicated five times covering a typical production period (e.g. six hours) and on several days of the week. This may seem like a lot of work, but establishing the variability that a given test bake is likely to yield provides a strong base on which to judge future tests. All the relevant objective and subjective assessment methods should be included as part of the initial study.

One problem that does bedevil test baking is the assessment of final-product characteristics. Few bakery products, if any, are homogeneous throughout their bulk. Many product characteristics are assessed by first cutting the product to provide a surface or a slice. Even the slice may be further sampled, for example to take a core for texture profile analysis (see Chapter 2). With baked products no two products' surfaces, slices or cores are identical, and so measurements on replicate samples are bound to be variable. In the case of texture profile analysis, the characteristics of the sample may be profoundly influenced by features hidden beneath the surface, e.g. holes or hard cores. Once again, evaluating a number of samples taken from a given product will provide useful data on typical variability.

In the bread test bake referred to above it may be necessary to make measurements on samples taken from several points in the loaf in order to obtain an average value. Choosing the sample location and the number of samples to take is not easy. While a statistical-based approach is helpful, it should be recognised that many features associated with baked products are not random in nature but are associated with particular processing techniques.

The four-piece loaf that is used to make sandwich bread in the UK provides an example of the problems associated with choosing sampling points. The main features of the four-piece loaf are shown in Figure 8.1. The manipulation through the final moulder to create the four pieces that characterise the four-piece loaf was discussed in Chapter 6. There are two major contributors to the characteristic structure which is formed during proving and baking. The first is the combination of sheeting and curling and the second is turning the dough pieces through 90°. The position of the curls within each dough piece is shown by the dotted lines in the cross-section through the assembled loaf in Figure 8.1. The combination of the effects of sheeting and the pressure of the upward expansion at the joins of the individual pieces creates a different structure to that at the centre of the individual pieces. When the loaf is sliced, the individual cells at the joins tend to be more elongated and shallower while those in the centre of a piece tend to be more rounded and deeper.

In these circumstances, the surface or slice chosen to measure can have a profound effect on the interpretation of the measured data. A pragmatic approach to this situation could be to assume that the right

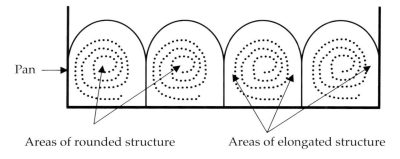

Figure 8.1   Main features of a four-piece loaf.

half of the loaf will be mirrored by the left half, so a possible sampling strategy could be to take four individual measurements: two at the joins and two at the centre of each of two pieces (Fig. 8.2). A fundamental problem with sampling, though, is that no two slices through or surfaces of baked products with a cellular structure are identical. Some data obtained from C-Cell that illustrate the problem (see Chapter 5) are given in Table 8.1.

It is clear from the above discussion and examples that establishing a sound test-baking procedure, with a clear understanding of the degree of variability which might be expected for a given procedure, is an important tool in product optimisation and new-product development. Given the inherently variable nature of test baking over extended periods of time (e.g. due to having to change batches of raw materials), it is prudent to include a standard bake on a given day. If there is a risk of drift within a given baking day, the inclusion of two standard bakes, one at the start and one at the end of the day, will be helpful. Starting the test-baking day with a mix that is not part of the assessment can be helpful in making sure that equipment, baking conditions and even personnel are ready for the trials, so that the first proper test bake is not compromised.

The long-term variability that may be seen in the standard or control test bake can be a problem. The variability arises mainly from the combination of small natural variations of the ingredients used, which are compounded by the different sources of variability in the test method. One way of coping with such variability in some of the data is to make comparisons with standard product properties. For example, the standard or control product volume may be taken as 100% and other test volumes compared with that volume and expressed as either above or below 100 accordingly. This method should only be applied

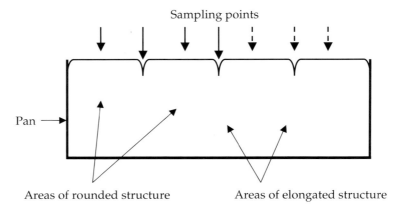

Figure 8.2   Sampling points on a four-piece loaf.

Table 8.1 C-Cell data for four-piece bread.

Slice number	Slice area (mm²)	Slice brightness	Number of cells	Cell diameter (mm)
1	12 794	146	9290	1.65
2	12 739	150	9247	1.69
3	12 537	154	9090	1.75
4	12 441	154	8661	2.00
5	12 472	154	8792	1.90
6	12 345	153	8648	1.88
7	12 332	152	8447	1.95
8	12 312	154	8309	1.88
9	12 478	156	9196	1.74
10	12 507	156	9517	1.74
11	12 445	153	9241	1.73
12	12 260	151	9124	1.66
13	12 226	151	9367	1.65
14	12 303	154	8917	1.83
15	12 227	155	9670	1.70
16	12 424	154	9235	1.72
Mean of all slices	**12 428**	**153**	**9046**	**1.78**
Standard deviation for all slices	*164.91*	*2.40*	*383.68*	*0.11*
Mean of slices 1–8	**12 496**	**152**	**8810**	**1.84**
Standard deviation for slices 1–8	*184.04*	*2.75*	*364.75*	*0.13*
Mean of slices 8–16	**12 359**	**154**	**9283**	**1.72**
Standard deviation for slices 8–16	*116.71*	*1.83*	*233.74*	*0.06*
Mean of slices 2, 5, 7 & 9	**12 505**	**153**	**8920**	**1.82**
Standard deviation for slices 2, 5, 7 & 9	*169.73*	*2.50*	*375.60*	*0.12*

when the absolute volume of the standard test bake product falls within the expected range of variation.

Once standard test-baking methods have been established and evaluated for their reliability, they may be used in a number of different ways:

- **Troubleshooting** to find the causes of quality defects by the deliberate and systematic variation of ingredients, product recipe and processing conditions
- The **optimisation** of product quality through perturbation of an existing product
- The **evaluation** of new ingredients, equipment and processing methods compared with current conditions
- **Identification** of ingredient, recipe and process factors that control product character through planned test-baking evaluations
- The **development** of new products

Control of baked-product characteristics by manipulation of ingredients, formulation and processing methods

There are some opportunities to adjust baked-product characteristics through the manipulation of the rules that govern the ingredient–recipe–process interactions. The rules are complex and imperfectly elucidated, however. To find the underpinning rules it is necessary to find suitable sources of information. Of the limited number of publications providing information in a suitable form, the rules of recipe balance in cake-making are perhaps the most well known (Street, 1991). There are numerous examples of published studies that contain the basis of other rulesets, but they are often not as clearly stated as those which have been defined for cake recipes. This means that most of the relevant information remains in the hands of the expert, who has learned through experience and trial and error the rules that apply to particular products and their manufacture.

As discussed above, structured test baking is a useful tool by which to establish the basic rules that govern product quality, but such activities are time- and resource-consuming. Much relevant information is available in the many publications that are available concerning baked products. Frequently the problem is that the information is hidden and often narrowly focussed so that its potential for wider application is lost. Quality optimisation and new-product development both rely on access to relevant information and a critical interpretation of the information that is presented.

The functionality of many of the ingredients used in baking has been introduced in Chapter 3 and discussed in more detail in Chapter 4. The headings used for Tables 3.1–3.7 illustrate the functionalities for the main ingredients listed, and provide a limited basis for understanding interchangeability between ingredients. The tables do not, however, address the recipe or process interactions. The reason they do not do so is that the level of detail required for even a small portion of baked-product manufacture is immense. In many cases few of the interactive rules are known. In the final analysis, it is the ability of the scientist and technologist to identify and link critical factors into a knowledge-base which identifies the routes for quality optimisation and product innovation. Despite the apparent negativity of the foregoing comments an example will serve to show that much can be achieved by assembling existing information.

The manufacture of the laminated product known as puff pastry relies on the formation of separate and discrete layers of dough and fat. In the base dough, the development of gluten structure with good extensibility and limited resistance to deformation is a critical factor in determining pastry lift. As has been discussed, the lift depends on the integrity of the dough layer, since holes in the dough structure readily permit the escape of the steam that is the main contributor to pastry lift. The proteins of the wheat flour allow the development of the necessary gluten network and are directly related to wheat type (recognising that agronomic and environmental factors do have an impact on the potential for gluten formation). In general terms, higher protein wheat flours will yield better lift (provided the gluten quality is satisfactory).

The availability of suitable wheat flour for the manufacture of puff pastry may be limited in some parts of the world. For example, the protein content may be too low. In such circumstances what would be the options for the baker? Some of the options and the thinking behind them may be described as follows.

The flour protein content could be adjusted, through the addition of **dried gluten** as a recipe ingredient. The required protein deficiency in the flour could readily be identified from analytical data and the level of dried gluten to be added calculated from the protein content of the raw material.

The quality of the dried gluten must be such that it can re-hydrate and provide functionality similar to that of the indigenous wheat proteins. The extraction and drying processes employed to separate wheat protein from the starch mean that the extracted product does not have the same composition as the indigenous proteins. In particular, some of the water-soluble proteins are lost, and drying may impair the gluten-forming properties. Nevertheless it is possible to provide a product which contributes much of the functionality of indigenous wheat protein. The product is commonly referred to as 'vital' wheat gluten to show that it has the necessary functionality.

The next step is to decide whether the dried gluten should replace part of the existing flour or be included as an additional ingredient. In the manufacture of puff pastry the ratio of base dough to laminating fat is one of the factors that controls lift, and a change in that ratio will have an impact on the degree of lift that will be achieved.

After meeting the required protein contribution, the next step is to determine the new level of water which needs to be added to the base dough. The water absorption capabilities of dried, vital wheat gluten are greater weight for weight than wheat flour and so a small increase in dough water level will be anticipated, whether the dried gluten replaces part of the flour or is an additional ingredient. Once the level of dried gluten addition and extra water have been determined it may be necessary to adjust the quantity of laminating fat to maintain a constant base-dough-to-laminating-fat ratio.

The manufacture of puff pastry with gluten-fortified flours is perfectly feasible. The degree of improvement in pastry lift for a given level of added dry gluten depends on the quantity and qualities of the protein in the starting flour. Small changes in the rheology of the base dough may occur, which may require adjustment of the processing conditions. The dough layers in puff pastes are particularly susceptible to damage during sheeting. If the base dough has higher resistance to deformation, as might occur in gluten-fortified flours, then there may be a tendency for the gluten network to be more readily broken down. If additional water has not been added to reduce the dough resistance then there may be a tendency for the paste to become more elastic with greater shrink-back after leaving the sheeting rolls. This will affect the subsequent laminating process and may require the narrowing of subsequent roll gaps to maintain optimum production capabilities. Narrower roll gaps lead to greater pressure which, in turn, leads to more damage to the base dough layer and the potential negation of the benefits of the addition of dried gluten.

If the addition of dried gluten was not an option, other means of increasing pastry lift may be sought. These include increasing the ratio of laminating fat to base dough or changing to a laminating fat with a higher melting point. While these changes may restore pastry lift they will also bring other potentially unwanted changes in product quality: specifically, they will make the products more fatty to eat, and the higher-melting-point fat confers a waxy mouth-feel.

In breadmaking, the addition of ascorbic acid is used to increase dough gas retention and product volume. Such improvements may be seen as analogous to increased lift in puff-pastry manufacture and, indeed, the addition of ascorbic acid to a base-dough recipe will increase lift. However, although the increased lift tends to be accompanied by increased shrinkage and shape distortion in puff-paste products, the same effects are not seen in breadmaking. The differences in the effect of ascorbic acid performance may be attributable to the ascorbic acid interactions with air during mixing. In breadmaking the ascorbic acid effect is largely confined to the mixer, since there is only limited exposure to fresh oxygen during bread-dough processing. In contrast, the sheeting and laminating processes employed in puff-paste manufacture expose significant areas of the paste to air and so increase the potential for further oxidation of the dough by the ascorbic acid.

Conventional wisdom in the manufacture of puff paste is that the base dough should not be fully developed in the mixing stage. Increased dough development to levels similar to that seen in bread dough leads to undesirable rheological properties in the base dough: the dough becomes too elastic and then requires significant rest periods during processing. In breadmaking, over-mixing of the dough leads to breakdown of the gluten structure and the loss of gas-retention properties. As has been discussed, sheeting imparts energy to the dough (Kilborn and Tipples, 1974) and sheeting plays a much greater role in dough processing in the manufacture of puff paste than in breadmaking. If an over-mixed dough is subjected to appropriate sheeting, then it begins to develop a more cohesive gluten structure but with different rheological properties. The complex interplay between energy transfer at different rates has been studied before (Kilborn and Tipples, 1975), though usually in the context of the potential for 'unmixing' dough by disorientating a developed dough structure through slow-speed mixing.

This example for puff-pastry manufacture shows that there are often opportunities to adjust product quality by manipulating the ingredient-recipe-process interaction. The contrast between the requirements for gluten development in bread dough and the puff-paste base dough also shows that the rules that govern a particular characteristic are complex, so that an understanding of one product does not necessarily give an understanding of another. Some modification of the rule has to be applied. However, with an understanding of the principles that underpin the manufacture of baked products, quality optimisation can be more systematic and not just achieved through trial and error.

Optimising baked-product quality through the application of knowledge-based systems

In recent years there has been a lack of experienced bakers and baking technologists. Bakers have not had the luxury of time to acquire knowledge about different product types. More immediate sources of information and tools have been required. One technology that has come to the aid of the baker is computing science. Collecting knowledge about baked products and the contributions made by ingredients and processing to final product quality, and creating a software program that can augment the baker's own knowledge, has enabled bakers to take a more efficient and methodical approach to optimising end-product quality. The field of computing science used was that of knowledge-based systems (KBS). A knowledge-based system incorporates heuristic knowledge (rules-of-thumb, best guess, intuitive modelling, directional changes, etc.) gained from intelligent sources of knowledge. These sources can be human experts, recognised literature, company databases, etc. Such systems are sometimes known as Expert Systems.

A KBS can only be developed if knowledge about the technology of the product is known and made available. Such knowledge can be represented, structured and encoded into a software program or system. Such systems can be used by bakers to reach their goals more rapidly. They can be used for more informed decision support so that products either under development or in production can better meet the expectations of the baker. Several systems have been developed since the inception of this aspect of computing technology in the 1980s. Some have remained as in-company systems whilst other commercially-available systems have saved the baking industry considerable sums of money.

Knowledge-based systems for bread products

In 1990 the Bread Faults Expert System was one of the first commercially available systems developed using this computing technology (Young, 1998). The domain chosen was the 800 g white pan bread made by the Chorleywood Bread Process (CBP). By answering a series of questions about the product, the user could get suggestions for curing the deficiency or enhancing the product. In the following ten years, computing technology advanced considerably, and in 2001 a more powerful knowledge-based system was developed by baking technologists and computer scientists at CCFRA.

In this system, aptly named *Bread Advisor*, information that linked recipe, processing conditions and product quality for a range of fermented products manufactured by any of five major processing methods was collected and made available. The knowledge was encoded and the system could be used to investigate the causes of problems in the product, either at the dough stage or at the finished-product stage. It could be used to investigate directional changes in processing parameters, and advice could be sought. Visual images were used to illustrate defects so that rapid diagnosis of faulty products could be achieved.

Using the Bread Advisor

The scene is set by choosing the product type and processing method by which it was manufactured. During the consultation, these two parameters define a product profile that is built and carried forward to other parts of the system. The product profile holds the information needed by each of the elements of the system as they are reached. For example, if the problem in question was in a free-standing bloomer-style product exhibiting collapse, made using a spiral mixer and a no-time dough process, then these selections are made from the list of products and processes. The processes list includes:

- Chorleywood Bread Process
- No-time dough

- Bulk fermentation
- Sponge and dough
- Flour brew

Generic product types include:

- Pan breads
- Lidded or unlidded
- Free-standing (e.g. oven-bottom/hearth breads)
- Sticks (e.g. baguettes)
- Soft rolls
- Crust rolls
- Twisted rolls
- Hamburger buns

The generic types are representative of the major product types produced throughout the world and, in effect, represent products of different dimension types. Images can be viewed of the high-lighted product type (Fig. 8.3).

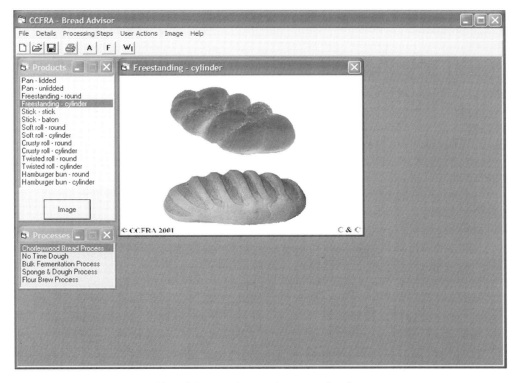

Figure 8.3 Identifying product and process details.

Fault diagnosis or quality enhancement

The *Bread Advisor* mimics the way a human being might diagnose a fault or set out to improve the quality of a product. We identify the problem, try to ascertain the causes, gather information to eliminate them and from there consider the options for corrective action or improvement for the most likely causes of the fault. On many occasions the manifestation of a particular problem does not necessarily have a unique and identifiable cause, and so there may be other intermediate steps to take into account in determining the real cause of the problem. This situation can be described schematically as follows:

PROBLEM $\Rightarrow$ PRIMARY CAUSE $\Rightarrow$ CONTRIBUTING FACTORS
$\Rightarrow$ CORRECTIVE ACTION

Or in more simple terms as:

What is seen $\Rightarrow$ why $\Rightarrow$ because of . . . $\Rightarrow$ corrective action

Using the *Bread Advisor*, the first step is to choose the fault or the attribute chosen for improvement. The faults are divided into categories to assist in finding the fault quickly. These categories are diverse and include:

- Aroma
- Crumb – faults that occur inside the product, e.g. holes, texture, structure, colour
- Dough – faults that occur during the processing of the dough, e.g. sticky or soft
- Eating qualities (for both crumb and crust)
- Flavour
- Shape – concavity, low shoulders, lack of oven spring
- Surface – crust colour, spots, blisters and wrinkles

Faults such as low volume or collapsed product are included in a catch-all category called General (Fig. 8.4). If the product exhibits several faults, they can each be selected and viewed in a selected category. The software is intended for use internationally and, as the naming or terminology of faults is often unique to the country and product, an image of a fault can be seen by clicking the image button for the fault in question.

Faults or product-quality deficiencies rarely have a single cause. However, faults can be split into those which are considered primary, or principal, causes (the 'why') and those which have 'contributed' (the 'because of . . .') to the faults in question. A user can easily and quickly

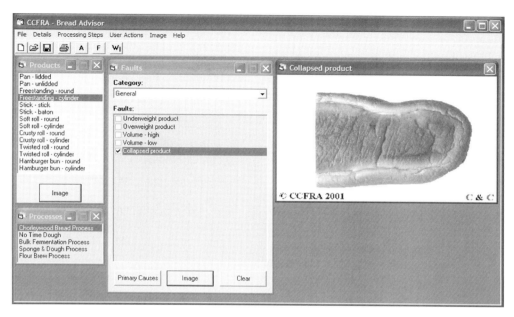

Figure 8.4 Identifying the fault.

obtain them by clicking the Primary Causes button. This action reveals a further pop-up window with such causes ranked in order of likelihood, the most likely being listed at the top (Fig. 8.5). The list of primary causes can be considered and checked out with the processing conditions that were used.

Factors that might have contributed to any of these causes can be displayed when the cause itself is checked and the Contributing Factors button selected (Fig. 8.5). At the end of a consultation, the baker has a list of suspects (in the case of the collapsed bloomer – lack of gas retention and eleven factors that might have contributed to it) which can be investigated, along with the local circumstances that the product underwent to reveal the cause or causes of the fault. As a result, the necessary corrective action can be taken to improve the product quality.

For an experienced baker, the fault-diagnosis function of the *Bread Advisor* considers all the necessary information and offers a quick and thorough investigation of the possible causes known to produce the faults in breadmaking. Unlike a human, the software never forgets or overlooks a possible cause. For novice bakers, the same aspect offers knowledge about the causes of faults from which they can build their own knowledge base about bread faults. Suspects can be eliminated quicker when processing conditions are checked and the 'once in a lifetime' fault flagged for investigation.

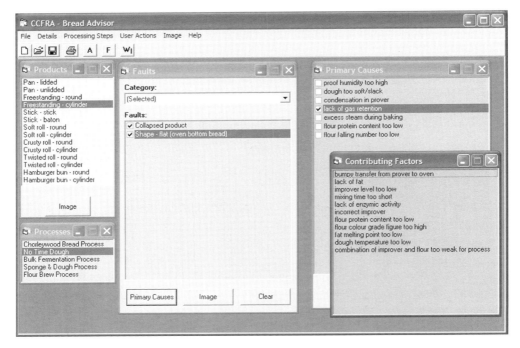

Figure 8.5   Primary causes and contributing factors.

Processing details

Investigating the suspects can also be done using the software. In the Contributing Factors list of the collapsed-product example, 'Mixing time too short' is flagged as a suspect. By inputting the known processing details about the mixing stage these can be checked for acceptability for the product in question. The generic settings given by the software are only those relevant to the process chosen. Where the input values for the mixing stage of the bloomer are at variance with the requirements for the process and product, information is displayed giving the range of values in which the parameter (in this case mixing time) should lie to achieve acceptable product quality, along with a message giving details of consequences to the product quality (Fig. 8.6). Such information is useful in isolating the cause of the fault and to the novice who may be unsure of the settings required for the product.

Other useful software tools for fermented products

It is important to know the correct conditions for mixing fermented products to ensure that the ingredients are dispersed well and the

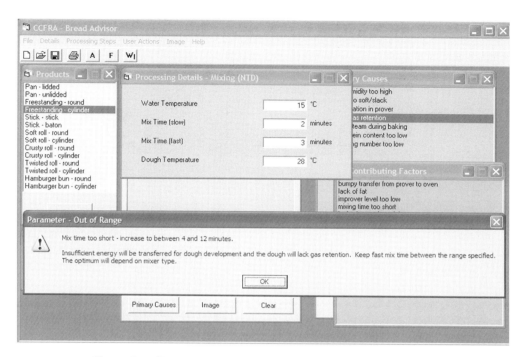

Figure 8.6   Examining process variables.

gluten network is formed (see Chapter 6). Getting the appropriate water temperature, heat rise and energy input are essential to consistent product quality. Such calculations have been included in the *Baking Technology Toolkit* (CCFRA, 2004), a software tool with which to calculate these parameters.

For the energy calculator the quantity, temperature and specific heat of each of the ingredients is taken into account when the energy calculation is made (Fig. 8.7). Similarly, the initial water temperature required to achieve a particular end of mix temperature and the dough heat rise during mixing can be ascertained. Such calculations can be tedious and prone to error and often the raw data are not held at the baker's fingertips. Using software of this nature, then, can help the technologist to deliver more precise and controllable mixing to benefit consistent production.

Knowledge-based systems (KBS) have been less widely adopted in the food industry to control production. Very few KBS have been developed for on-line process control for baked products. At-line control has been attempted to a greater degree. The *Retarding Advisor* was such a KBS (Young and Cauvain, 1994).

The retarding process (see Chapters 6 and 7) for fermented goods allows bakers to time-shift production to meet peak sales demands,

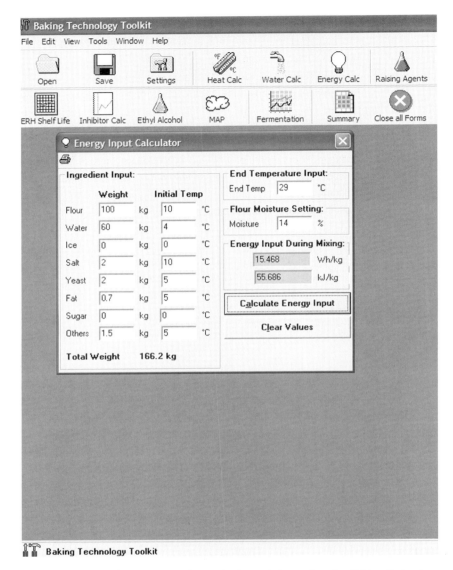

Figure 8.7 Calculating energy input during mixing using the *Baking Technology Toolkit.*

eliminate night working and to give staff more sociable working patterns. Retarding delays the fermentation process by storing the product dough units at a low temperature, between −5°C and +4°C, in a specialised refrigerated cabinet. The same cabinet is later used to raise the dough temperature (20–45°C) so that the product undergoes the proof period required. The complex relationships between ingredients, formulations and between temperature, time, yeast level and bulk of dough in the cabinet are all taken into account using the *Retarding Advisor* to give the baker the optimum settings for the products to be retarded. These settings can then be downloaded to the cabinet. An intermediate step allowing a 'what-if' scenario of different, equally viable, settings to be examined by the baker before they are downloaded is also given (Fig. 8.8). The consequences of choosing one set of retarding conditions over another are displayed, enabling the baker to make a more informed decision. In addition to the at-line control, the *Retarding Advisor* could be used off-line to explore the causes of poor quality, using a detailed fault diagnosis with corrective actions indicated.

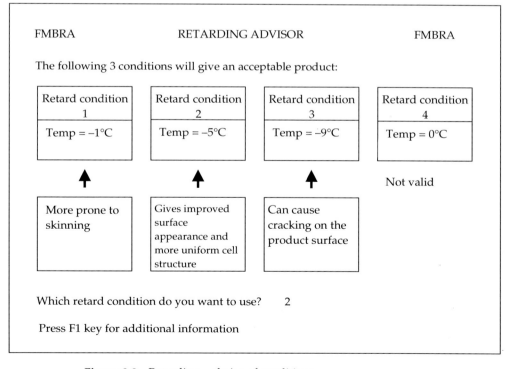

Figure 8.8   Retarding – choice of conditions.

Knowledge-based systems for cake products

A knowledge-based system has also been developed for the diagnosis of quality defects in cakes. Using *FAULT DoC* (Petryszak *et al.*, 1995), faults in cakes and sponges can be diagnosed in a similar way to that using the *Bread Advisor* though, since this software was developed in the early 1990s, the use of images showing fault characteristics is limited. *FAULT DoC* is one of three modules within the *Cake Expert System*, the other two modules deal with cake recipe balance (*BALANCE*) and water activity (*ERH CALC*™).

Before using any diagnostic tool of this nature a thorough assessment of the product should be undertaken. The more accurate the description entered the better the diagnosis might be. Diagnosis can be requested at the batter or at the finished-product stage of production. The cake (cake: high or low ratio; sponge: high or low fat), its type (plain, chocolate, white or fruited) and size format (small/cup, layer, unit or slab) are selected. Using graphical representations the current shape in comparison with the desired shape is given.

There follows a series of three fault category screens for crust, crumb and other faults. In each of these screens the user has the option to select the most appropriate descriptors for the product, e.g. external characteristics such as chamfered bottom corners, wrinkled top crust, internal characteristics such as crumb colour, tunnel holes and other characteristics such as taste (e.g. too sweet) and textural properties (e.g. dry eating). The information describing the product is then used to identify the possible causes for the divergence of quality and a weighting of their likelihoods is given. These causes are displayed either in a complete list or, more usefully, as those causes that are production related, ingredient quantity related or ingredient quality related, that being the order in which the baker might choose to attempt to rectify the product quality (immediacy).

Determining raising or leavening agents in cake and biscuit/cookie products

Finding the right combination of raising or leavening agents to achieve the lift required has often been considered a 'black art'. Developers often defer to the expertise of their suppliers to provide raising agents with the right characteristics and are resigned to the extra cost that this entails. However, the chemicals used in baking powders react in a very predictable way, both in the quantity and rate of evolution of CO_2 at specific temperatures (see Chapter 4). The data required for all of the common bicarbonates and acids used in leavening agents, so that gassing rates of their combinations can easily be determined, have been encoded in a *Raising Agent Tool* as part of a suite of useful calcula-

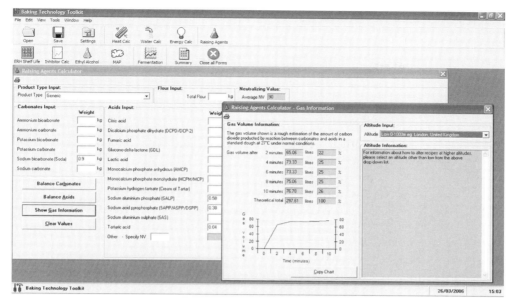

Figure 8.9   Gassing curves in the Raising Agents Calculator.

tor tools in the *Baking Technology Toolkit* (CCFRA, 2004). Using this software tool, a product developer can design a leavening agent to give a particular boost to the carbon dioxide levels at the appropriate time in the setting of the product's structure. For example, if a raising agent made up of sodium bicarbonate, sodium acid pyrophosphate (SAPP) and sodium aluminium phosphate (SALP) (a combination of a medium- and slow-acting baking powder) is chosen, using the software the levels of acids can be balanced to ensure that neutrality will exist in the product when the gassing reaction is complete. The gassing curves for the proportions of the different reactants SAPP and SALP can be displayed (Fig. 8.9). The tool allows experimentation with different combinations of chemicals, and provides information to help product developers balance the raising agents in a formulation. The tool can give advice on the acceptable amounts and types of chemicals to add to different types of product recipes. The tool also acts as an information bank about the properties of the most commonly used raising agents.

Advice and help in using knowledge-based software

General advice and help is also included in the software described in this chapter. At any stage, users can learn how to navigate around the software in order to reach the relevant topics quickly. In many cases the advice and help is context-sensitive and can be displayed when needed. The information displayed can augment the user's own knowledge.

Chapter 9
Opportunities for New Product Development

Processes involved in the development of baked products

The start

There may be a number of drivers for the development of a new baked product. They include:

- Market- (consumer)-driven requests for new products or enhancement of existing products
- Marketing Department-driven requests for new products or enhancement of existing products
- Problem-driven enhancement of existing products
- Ingredient- or process-driven opportunities for new product development or enhancement of existing products
- Eureka!-type identification for new product development or enhancement of existing products

The product-development brief

The initiation of a brief for new product development may come from a number of sources, including those discussed above. The brief will tend to be an amalgamation of different requirements and will typically include:

- A list of required and permitted raw materials – the ingredients
- Identification of any limiting factors which would apply to the recipe/formulation – e.g. a chocolate cake must contain cocoa solids
- Identification of any process limitations – e.g. the type of equipment available or likely to be required
- Key aspects of presentation to the consumer – e.g. size, shape, colour, finishing, shelf-life (both sensory and microbial), hazard analysis, packaging and transport

- Legislation requirements
- Identifications of any cost limitations
- The timescale for development of concepts, prototypes and launch
- Any development costs and their implications

The product-development process (Fig. 9.1)

The first key steps in the product-development process, whether it is the development of a new product or the enhancement of an existing one, are identification of the differences between desired and existing product features and choosing the appropriate knowledge bases to work with. In the case of product enhancement, the appropriate knowledge-base is largely defined by the baked-product group, e.g. bread,

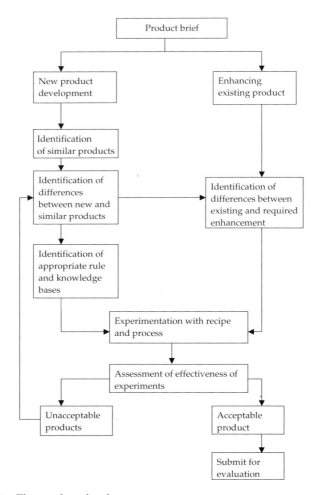

Figure 9.1   The product development process.

cakes, biscuits. Product enhancement does not normally require the developer to stray far from the rules which define product character. Thus, making cakes with a longer shelf-life only requires an understanding of which ingredients will have the greatest impact on shelf-life and then adding them or manipulating ingredient levels to achieve the required shelf-life without unduly compromising other product characters.

In genuine new product development, the boundaries between baked products often need to be broken or at least extended beyond those which normally apply to specific product groups. The problem for the development bakery technologist is how to identify which rules used to define one product group might have value when applied to another product area and to what extent the boundaries of rules can be extended.

Ultimately, all of this has to be done within the constraints of a typical product-development programme, which includes budgetary constraints. The latter has a profound impact on the process applied to new product development. It predicates against the extended experimental phases that would be necessary in order to develop a comprehensive and robust set of rules that could be applied to all bakery products. In view of the difficulties faced by development technologists, there is a tendency to stay within relatively tight boundaries and thus restrict new product development – or the technologist makes a few wild guesses and carries out a limited number of experiments. If lucky, then a new strand of product development may be initiated, but all too often the results of the experiments are equivocal and the approach is soon abandoned.

Characterising the product

Before developing a new product it is necessary to be able to define the characteristics that are sought in the final product. This is often the most difficult task, but is a necessary first step in the innovation process since it will provide the skeleton on which the flesh of the new product can be laid. It will help in identifying the ingredients, processes and equipment that will be of most use and where to seek a recipe on which to base development trials.

Typical product characteristics might encompass:

- Size, shape and density
- Cellular structure
- Eating qualities
- Flavour
- Shelf-life

The characteristics of existing product types can be defined so that their domains, or boundaries, can be specified and then used when moving from one product type towards the new one. The ways in which these characteristics are created (from the elements contributing to the characteristic) form the known routes that point the way to the desired characteristics in the new product and provide the base on which to create it.

Examples of known product characteristics might be:

- Bread
  - Eating qualities – soft, moist, chewy
  - Flavour – bland, acidic
  - Shelf-life – <7 days (short)
- Cake
  - Eating qualities – soft, fragile, crumbly
  - Flavour – sweet
  - Shelf-life – 7–70 days (intermediate)
- Biscuit
  - Eating qualities – hard, crunchy, chewy
  - Flavour – slightly sweet, sweet
  - Shelf-life – >170 days (long)
- Laminated
  - Eating qualities – flaky
  - Flavour – slightly sweet, savoury
  - Shelf-life – 7–70 days (intermediate)
- Pastry
  - Eating qualities – short, crumbly
  - Flavour – sweet, bland
  - Shelf-life – 7–70 days (intermediate)

A 'tree' can be created for each of the characteristics (Fig. 9.2). The tree covers bread, cake and pastry products and embraces many aspects of ingredient, recipe and process. At the lowest level of the tree there is knowledge about each of the ingredients and how they affect the defined characteristic for the known product at the top of the tree. Ingredient knowledge at this level can be compared with that contained at the lowest level for another product-characteristic tree. Each box of the tree needs to be populated with relevant information, which may include hard and soft information. An example of hard information might be that when the cake moisture content falls below 18% the product is considered to be too dry-eating. Soft information is often knowledge on direction rules, for example, lengthening the mixing time will reduce batter density, but it is not possible directly to correlate

For any product – (key: T = type; L = level)

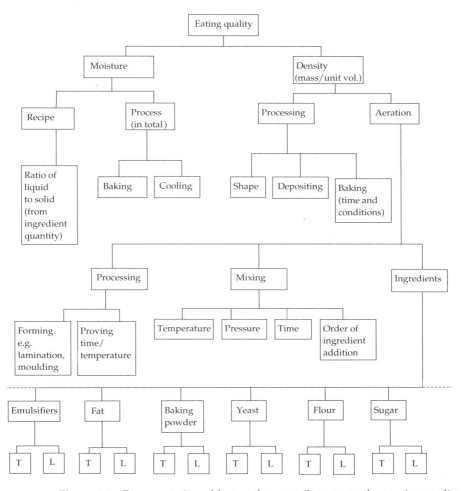

Figure 9.2 Representation of factors that contribute to product eating quality.

the effect of a one-minute increase in mixing time on batter density without carrying out appropriate trials.

One way of using the tree approach is to start from the bottom with the ingredients and work upwards. For example, a knowledge of the type of sugar used in the recipe (e.g. granulated or powdered) leads directly to information relevant to its contribution to aeration, which, in turn, links with information on product density and then from there to a specified aspect of eating quality. For a cake, this might define whether it contributes to a soft, fragile or crumbly eating quality. Similarly, the time taken to mix will affect the aeration, which will in turn affect the density and eating quality. The cooling regime will affect the moisture retained in/lost from the product, which in turn will affect how soft the eating quality is. Where there is an element that affects two different aspects of the product characteristics, e.g. baking affects both moisture and density, then each of these will need to be examined and balanced for the new product.

The tree concept may equally be used from the top down. In some ways this is the more useful mode because it starts with a definition of the end-product quality. Once the requirements for the end product have been defined, the elements that make contributions to the required qualities can be identified. These elements will be a mixture of process and ingredients. Identification of the required processes helps identify the equipment that needs to be used. Ingredient specifications and quantities are chosen based on knowledge of their contributions to particular end-product characteristics. This 'top down' approach may be summarised as:

'What do I want to make?'
'How am I going to make it?'
'What am I going to use to make it?'

When a new product moves from concept to reality it is inevitable that some determination of the quantities of the chosen ingredients must be made. In some cases, an original recipe might be modified slightly to move the product character in a particular direction. The majority of new products of this nature are variations of a tried and tested formulation and the task of reaching the new product is relatively straightforward, though still requires some effort. For a totally new product the task is much harder and the functions of the ingredients and the determination of quantities required are more difficult to envisage and achieve. Technologists must rely on access to suitable information sources, their experience and imagination to develop new products. During the development of a new product, whatever it is, there is a balance that must be reached which combines the ingredients and the processing conditions to deliver the desired product characteristics.

Potential for new product development using IT methodologies

There are many reference materials technologists can use to find recipes to use as a starting point, including those given in Chapter 3. For each of the many different product types the appropriate rules concerning the ratios of ingredients will need to be identified and applied. In the past, calculations were done on scraps of paper, perhaps with the aid of a calculator, and many iterations of modification, test baking and assessment may have been necessary before the product reached the marketplace.

The advent of IT and computing technologies has made the technologist's product-development task easier and faster. Formulations can be stored in database or spreadsheet format and calculations can be made very easily. In addition, the recipe information can be converted into a suitable form for the product label (composition and nutritional information). The specification of each of the ingredients, including costs, can be linked to the recipe so that all the product information is held centrally.

In the entire new product development cycle, the central iterative process, which requires a balance to be achieved between the ingredients, recipe and processing methods, is crucial to successful innovation. The rules that govern the traditional products need to be clearly understood and applied. Many of the rules involve mathematical calculations, some simple and others more complex, so that great care is needed when undertaking the balancing process. The computing areas of knowledge-based systems and other IT programs have been put to good effect for many bakery products and their development. A few of these systems will be described in order to give the reader a flavour of what is possible and what is available.

Cake product development using IT systems

The complex rules of cake (flour confectionery) recipe balance have been discussed earlier. A *Cake Expert System* was developed at FMBRA and later at CCFRA (Young *et al.*, 1998; CCFRA, 2002). This three-module system deals with recipe balance (*BALANCE*), shelf-life (*ERH CALC*™) and fault diagnosis (*FAULT DoC*). In the technical development of a new cake product each of these modules can be used to enhance the development process and to move more rapidly to the final product specification. The software can be used without making up the product and so reduces the number of test bakes required, ensures the safety of the product and leads the developer to the desired product in a shorter time scale. Consequently, such a system can help in the realisation of true bottom-line savings.

When embarking on a new development, the *BALANCE* module can be used to check that the product ingredients are in the correct proportions (ranges) for the type, shape and size of previously-specified finished products. The module contains all the rules connected with the ingredient functions for a type of cake product. Images of the product are displayed throughout the balancing process, to show the result of keeping the ingredients in or out of balance. Such visualisation can assist the developer in understanding how certain features are arrived at.

A recipe can be selected from a library of traditional cake products as a starting point, and the recipe can then be manipulated to develop the desired characteristics (Fig. 9.3). Alternatively the technologist's first concept recipe can be entered and the ingredient quantities manipulated. The program considers the quantities of each ingredient according to its function in cake making and checks whether their ratios are within the ranges defined for the type, size and shape of the cake being developed. To help the product developer, the ingredients are categorised according to their function in cake making. For example, the flour category contains all those ingredients which will take up water, e.g. flours, fibres, oatmeal, starches. The fruit category contains all the commonly used fruits, e.g. currants, raisins, etc., and also other ingredients that are of a particulate nature, such as nuts and glace cherries. At any point the recipe can be saved and recalled, making calculations very efficient.

The rules of cake making are applied in a pre-set order of ratios : sugar : flour, fat : flour, egg : fat, raising agents : flour, fruit : flour, other

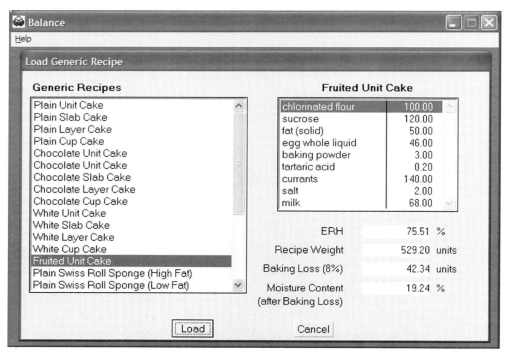

Figure 9.3 Recipe selection.

minor ingredients and finally the liquid(moisture):flour. At each check the relevant ratio is calculated and a check made to ascertain whether the ingredient falls within the range for the product under development.

As each ingredient changes, the total recipe balance changes: for example adding an ingredient containing a high proportion of moisture will require the total amount of moisture to be reconsidered. If the ingredient under examination is outside the acceptable range for the product, a message, with the relevant range for the ingredient (relative to the quantity of flour) is displayed. The user can then enter a new value for the ingredient so that the recipe becomes balanced for that ingredient (Fig. 9.4). If an ingredient is outside the upper range value then the program will display the maximum permissible quantity, which the user can accept or alter. Likewise, if the ingredient is below the lower range value then the minimum permissible quantity is displayed.

In addition to the range values, other characteristics that might be present when the ingredient is out of balance are listed: for example, if the raising agents are too low then characteristics of the resulting cake (lack of volume, peaked shape, tunnel holes in crumb, etc.) are listed. By using this feature, product developers can expand their own

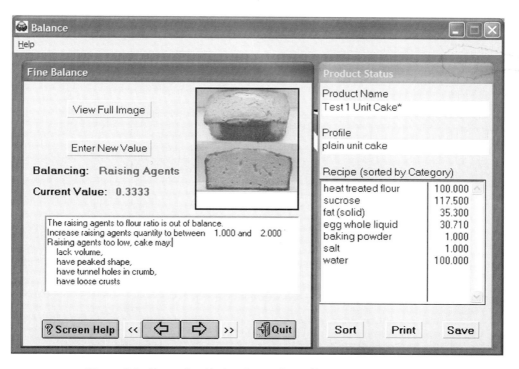

Figure 9.4   Example of balancing an ingredient.

knowledge about the use of that ingredient in the product under development. As the quantities are altered so the proportions of other ingredients change. The program takes these changes into account and makes it easy for the user to balance each of the ingredient categories 'on the fly'. If an ingredient category is balanced when it is first encountered then a simple message to that effect is displayed and no action need be taken unless the user specifically wants to alter it.

At the test-baking stage, those product qualities which are lacking can be described in the *FAULT DoC* module and the product characteristics fine-tuned using information displayed. Once all the categories of ingredient are balanced, a comparison between the initial and final recipes is shown and also the parameters of the formulation: for example, the ERH (equilibrium relative humidity), recipe weight, baking loss and moisture content after baking, along with the mould-free shelf-life, given for 21°C and 27°C. Such parameters can be used to make comparisons between recipes and will eventually become part of the product specification when it goes into production.

When developing new products, the directional changes that can be made to an ingredient level can be difficult to determine. A useful visual feature of the software is the Ingredient Range chart (Fig. 9.5). This shows, in a bar format, where each of the major ingredients lies in the broader scenario of the total recipe. In the example shown, the moisture/liquid level is at a minimum whilst the egg solids are at the maximum. If the product is proving too costly, the chart shows the option that some of the egg could be replaced with water or other liquid (by moving each ingredient within its range) and the product

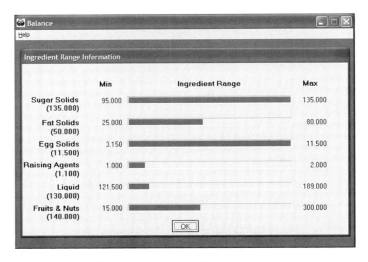

Figure 9.5   Example of ingredient range effects.

would still give an acceptable bake, provided both the egg solids and the liquids remain in the ranges shown.

At any point the recipe can be saved to be recalled at a later stage. There are other useful features, including a Sort button, so that the recipe can be displayed in any of the formats – ingredient category, ingredient level, alphabetical, Baker's % or total weight %. The ingredient-level format is useful for labelling information, when the ingredients need to be listed in descending quantity order. It is a small step to link the recipe data in spreadsheet format to costing information, processing values, etc.

Software for determining process settings

Very little software is known to the authors that would be of specific use in the technical development of the processing aspects of baked products. For plant engineers there are numerous software systems for designing plants to meet the proving and baking conditions required for the product once they are known. However, the determination of these criteria still falls to the product developer with their implementation on the plant being the domain of the engineer. In the *Baking Technology Toolkit* (CCFRA, 2004) (see Chapter 8) there is a series of tools to enable calculation of heat rise, water temperature and energy input during mixing of dough.

The *Bread Advisor* system (CCFRA, 2001) (see Chapter 8) has a module in which the developer can ask 'What if . . . ?' questions connected with directional changes at any of the processing steps: for example, 'What if I reduce the first proof humidity?' (Fig. 9.6). Using this facility, the developer can get an idea of the effects of such changes at any of the processing steps. However, there is no attempt in this software to give absolute values for the parameters under investigation, with ranges giving the developer only an indication of the boundaries of acceptability for the product.

Ensuring product safety using software

The deterioration of product quality by spoilage from moulds, rancidity, contamination, etc., is inevitable once the product has left the oven. In the field of mould contamination and growth much work has been done to determine the mould-free shelf-life (MFSL) of a product (Cauvain and Young, 2000). Controlling the water activity, a_w, or equilibrium relative humidity (ERH) is key to knowing how long a product will last before it starts to exhibit mould growth. Knowing this value helps in the determination of a use-by date (after production) that can be printed on the packaging.

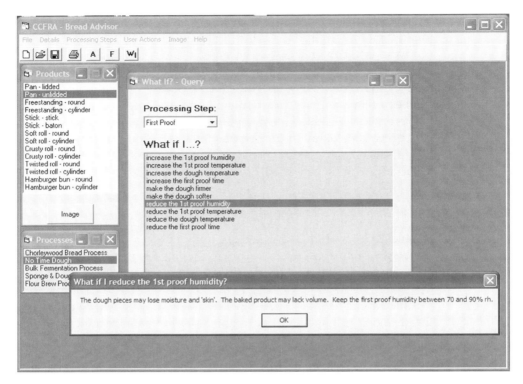

Figure 9.6 . Example of 'What if . . . ?' question in the *Bread Advisor*. ·

Often the commercial side of product development requires the developer to create a product that lasts for a sufficiently long time to allow economic distribution to the retail stores and for display on their shelves and storage in the consumer's home. The ingredients and baking conditions have an influence on the a_w/ERH of the product. As described in Chapter 2, a_w/ERH is a measure of how well the water in the product is held by the mass of ingredients. The lower the value the more tightly the product holds on to the moisture within it. If the moisture is tightly held then that same moisture cannot be used by moulds for growth. The lower the a_w/ERH the stronger is the force holding on to the moisture and consequently the longer the mould-free shelf-life.

Because of their properties (e.g. sucrose equivalence, molecular weight, water content), ingredients hold on to water in different ways (Cauvain and Young, 2000). It is possible to sum their individual effects so that an a_w/ERH can be calculated and the shelf-life determined. The product developer can then manipulate the recipe towards the desired a_w/ERH by altering the quantities and by controlling the moisture loss during baking, cooling and storage. The calculations can be done with a calculator, provided each of the data values and quantities are known for an ingredient. In the 1990s, the opportunity was provided at FMBRA (Cauvain and Young, 2000) to develop a program to calculate the ERH or a_w from a product recipe and baking conditions, and the software *ERH CALC*^{TM} (CCFRA, 2002) was developed. The resulting software has been enhanced since first launched and other features pertaining to a product's shelf-life, such as the addition of mould inhibitors and packaging considerations, have been included.

In essence, *ERH CALC*^{TM} can be used to determine the a_w/ERH and MFSL of virtually any food product. The developer can choose and enter ingredients to make up the product recipe from a comprehensive list of common ingredients (Fig. 9.7). Ingredients unique to a company can be added to a separate database within the program to customise product information. The baking, cooling and storage moisture loss can be given along with the proposed storage temperature so that the calculated a_w/ERH can be determined and the link made to the MFSL (Fig. 9.8).

Information such as product baked weight and moisture content is given, and the developer can consider these in the wider requirements

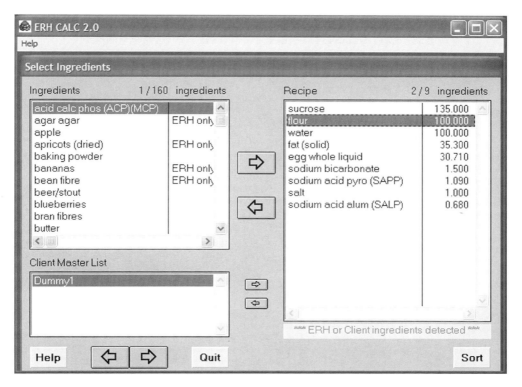

Figure 9.7   Choosing ingredients from a list in *ERH CALC*^{TM}.

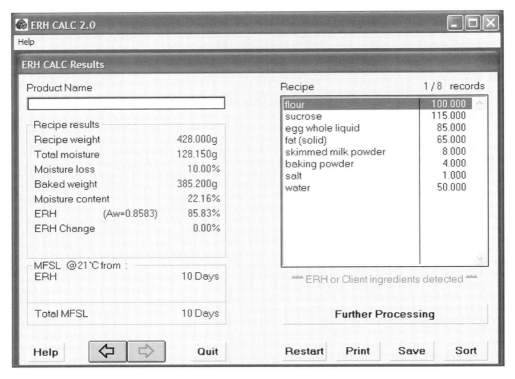

Figure 9.8   Example of result screen from *ERH CALC*™.

of the final product. Component parts of a multi-component product (e.g. an iced cream cake) can each be assessed, so that spoilage from moisture migration can be avoided. In the past, the a_w/ERH might have been measured physically, using a water-activity meter. However, to do this the product needs to be made up, whereas with the software the a_w/ERH can be calculated many times using different ingredient quantities. The accuracy of the software is equivalent to the accuracy of a water-activity meter (+/− 2%).

As the developer nears the desired product character by manipulating the ingredients but is unable to achieve the required MFSL, then the software can be used to determine the amount of inhibitor (potassium sorbate or sorbic acid) needed to ensure the extra shelf-life (Fig. 9.9). Where a solution is sought for the problem of moisture losses during long-term storage of the packaged product, in order to reduce the margins of error in the MFSL, the developer can investigate moisture losses through packaging films of different transpiration rates using *ERH CALC*™.

In the *Baking Technology Toolkit* (CCFRA, 2004) there are small calculator tools. These can be used to determine additions of ethyl alcohol

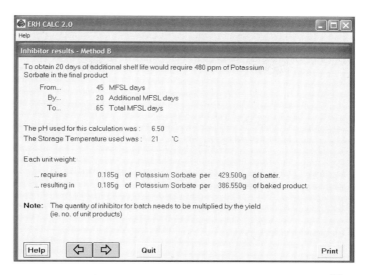

Figure 9.9   Example of mould inhibitor calculation from *ERH CALC™*.

for preserving products, the amount of gas flushing with CO_2 necessary to extend shelf-life by a required amount and an estimation of the fermentation-free shelf-life for certain products.

HACCP software

When developing products it is prudent to consider what hazards there might be in terms of contamination, production methods and well-being for the product. A hazard analysis and critical control point (HACCP) analysis should be undertaken. At the least, this can be a paper exercise with the results detailed in the company quality-control documentation. However, there are several commercially-available software programs which make the task easier and ensure that the outcome is automatically saved.

Company-specific knowledge

Every company has specialised knowledge of its own products, and this can be captured and encompassed in software so that it is not lost and can be used by others. For example, information about the functionality of ingredients such as enzymes, fats, leavening agents, etc. could be captured and developed into software tools. The *Leavening Agents Toolkit* (see Chapter 8) is an example of the type of small generic program that might be produced within an individual company by capturing the appropriate ingredient rules.

The first step in putting together such a software system is to assemble and systemise the appropriate information. Thereafter it is a matter of deciding the appropriate form for the output. The development of knowledge-based systems requires an iterative approach. These systems are seldom, if ever, achieved by the technologist providing a full specification for coding by the IT specialist. This is because there are usually many gaps in the knowledge which are not always apparent at the specification stage. Also many of the rules used by individuals tend to have a high degree of uncertainty associated with them. Knowledge-based-system development, through prototyping, tends to be more effective.

Software tools of the type described above enable faster product development. Experimentation can be done at the PC without risk of failure, and the feasibility of ideas for the potential product can be tried out at little cost. Context-relevant text can be available at the click of the mouse button and the supporting information displayed can augment the user's own knowledge. However, software to develop a product with certain attributes such as 'it looks like . . .', 'tastes like . . .' or 'eats like . . .' is not yet available. The building blocks for product shelf-life exist (through determination of water activity), and certain known characteristics for cake products are achievable through *BALANCE* and for fermented products using *Bread Advisor*. However, software with links back to recipe and process from textural and consumer demands is some way from being reality.

Using structure assessment in innovation

All baked products rely on the development of key features that underpin the structure of the final product and thus many of the key characteristics, not least eating quality. The structures of baked products are diverse, ranging from the sponge-like structures of bread and cakes through to the layered structures of laminated products to the dense and compact structures of biscuits and cookies. The ability to assess product structure and to combine that assessment with the appropriate ingredient, recipe and process rules can provide a sound basis not only for quality optimization but also for new-product development. As with all baked products, having the ability to create such links provides the technologist with powerful tools. The length of time we take to identify the cause and the corrective actions needed in product development varies considerably from occasion to occasion and from individual to individual, and is more likely to be related to our accumulated knowledge and experiences rather than cold, logical reasoning. Our ability to recognise and match subtle patterns is probably so intuitive that we are seldom aware that we are doing it.

Much of the value of structure assessment is built on our ability to recognize patterns in the products we make and the data we capture as human beings. With the development of the C-Cell instrument for capturing images of the internal structure of baked products, the analysis of such data can now be put to effective use for both quality optimization and innovation. The C-Cell instrument holds data describing a product slice in electronic format (see Chapter 5). These data can be put together as smaller sets relevant to a particular purpose, e.g. data pertaining to the patterning of the cells seen in the slice or to the external features (height, concavity, etc.). Such data might be examined and manipulated in a diagnostic knowledge-based system to facilitate quality enhancement.

Likewise, using C-Cell, the internal slice data, such as cell-wall thickness, cell diameter, etc., could be linked with textural features and consumer acceptability. Where such data are known to be associated with particular eating qualities, and where the processing and ingredient characteristics which lead to these textures are embodied in a knowledge-based system, the product developer would have a very powerful tool with which to innovate. With full use of C-Cell's data, the road between new-product development and routine quality enhancement becomes a 'multi-way' thoroughfare with information from any direction feeding the others. For example, representative slices data for a product might be assessed using C-Cell. The product may also be assessed against certain other criteria in the normal quality-control environment. The textural information (gained using an instrument) and consumer acceptability (assessed by consumer panels) of the product, along with the relevant processing data (under what conditions the structure was formed) could all be linked using a knowledge-based system. Even in its simplest form, as a directional rule-based system which identifies that, for a given change in input, the direction of a given product character will change (go up or down, become positive or negative, etc.), such an approach would be a valuable tool for moving new product development into uncharted domains and could bring the ability to design a product which 'eats like . . ., 'tastes like . . .' etc. closer to reality.

The first lesson we learned in developing computer-based systems was that baking is an interactive science – if you alter just one aspect of your product, whether that be ingredient or processing step, the alteration can have consequences in more than one place. The second lesson was that if you take a subject in bite-sized pieces you can produce computer programs which will be useful in the working environment. The third lesson was that when you give bakers computing tools of this nature they open up their imaginations and you learn their wish list very quickly. The need for baking technology software is definitely there.

Matching patterns in baking for innovation

The acquisition of data and its analysis are an integral part of the manufacture of baked products. The data are necessary for ensuring consistency of raw materials and processing to deliver the required final product. Analytical data is also commonly collected on the final product. With the potential for capture of so much data it might be assumed that models can be built for the whole of the baking process from start to finish, from raw material to baked products. This is not the case.

In most instances, the links between raw-material properties, processing parameters and final-product quality appear tenuous, except for some narrowly-constrained products. The problem is that many of the relationships between these remain hidden from immediate view. This is often true for analytical data gathered on bakery raw materials. The problems are exacerbated by the nature of some of the testing methods used. This is especially true for wheat flour where many of the evaluation methods still used have little relevance to current bread-manufacturing procedures. Yet despite these limitations the data still have value.

The analytical, process and product data gathered in baking is of great value to the expert technologist, who is able to interpret the information in the context of quality optimisation. Here it is very much a case of pattern matching, a human skill that still exceeds the abilities of any machine or software. In the context of new-product development it is prediction or interpretation of results that is required, and in these circumstances pattern matching can play a major role.

The process of pattern matching might be visualised using the concept of spider diagrams (see Chapter 1). An example of how the process might work for bread manufacture is illustrated in Figures 9.10a,b,c. The process starts (or ends, depending on which way you approach the diagram) with the characteristics of a given wheat or mixture of wheat varieties and proceeds through the flour-milling process, which supplies one of the key raw materials for the baker. Based on the flour properties, a pattern of recipe and process conditions, which aims to deliver a particular group of defined properties in the final product, is established.

The illustrated example combines hard and soft data in individual diagrams. The key to the successful application of this approach is based on achieving a particular pattern at each stage of the overall process. Variations from the normal pattern are quickly recognised. In the development of new products, reverse engineering from a group of specified final-product characteristics can help in determining many of the necessary ingredient, recipe and process requirements and

Wheat characteristics

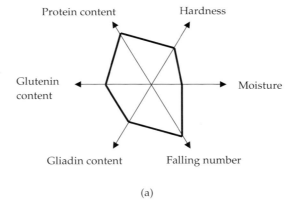

(a)

Flour characteristics

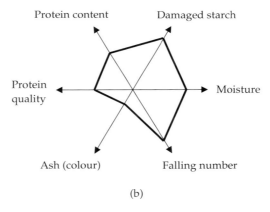

(b)

Dough and bread characteristics

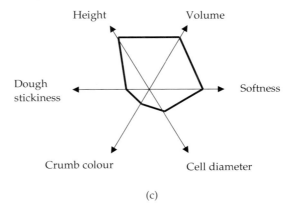

(c)

Figure 9.10 Examples of pattern matching for bread production: (a) wheat, (b) flour and (c) dough and bread.

is the specific nature of sub-groups of baked products, characterised by their specific ingredients and recipes, which are combined with specialised processing methods. It is the special nature of the ingredient-recipe-processing interactions which delivers the special characteristics that distinguish breads from biscuits and pastries from cakes. This is the classical world of bakery products, commonly defined and mostly discussed in terms of the classical boundaries that have been developed over many years. It is possible to say that as bakery products have evolved over the generations the various sub-groups have diverged and some may say become fossilised.

There is no doubt that the range of bakery products we see today have a common origin in the crushing of wheat, mixing it with water and heating it. From those simple beginnings have sprung a myriad of products and complex technologies. Given their common origins, there is clearly a case for re-considering similarities between baked-product sub-groups. As has been discussed several times, the genuinely new bakery products are those that cross the boundaries between existing product groups. It is intriguing to consider that the classical bakery products that we know today must have at one time been revolutionary and boundary crossing. Who first thought of adding sugar to the flour–water mix to turn bread into a proto-cake? How was the technique for laminating fat into dough discovered? Perhaps by accident, but it does not really matter how they came about – they did and food production changed.

The consumer attitude to bakery products remains positive, despite health scares. In the more developed parts of the world, traditional bakery products are well established, so consumer focus is on innovation. For the manufacturers of baked products, market share is about developing new products without compromising traditional product quality. The demands of legislation and food safety have added new pressures, but it is still the pleasures associated with eating bakery products that drive development in the marketplace.

In less developed parts of the world the emphasis remains very much on providing nutrition for large parts of the population, and the more basic wheat-based products play a major role in meeting those nutritional needs. As the basic nutritional needs of such people are met, the introduction of new products soon follows. Traditional products are quickly supplemented by new and exciting ones. This has always been the way with bakery products and there is no reason that it should not continue to be so. Innovation based on a sound understanding of the principles involved will continue to satisfy humankind's appetite for a diverse range of bakery products for many years to come.

References and Further Reading

References

AACC (1995) *Approved methods, Vol. II*, AACC, Minneapolis, MN.

Anderson, J. (1995) Crust colour assessment of bakery products. *AIB Technical Bulletin* XVIII, Issue 3, March, AIB, Manhattan, KS.

Baker, J.C. and Mize, M.D. (1941) The origin of the gas cell in bread dough. *Cereal Chemistry*, **18**, 19–34.

Baker, J.C. and Mize, M.D. (1942) The relation of fats to texture, crumb and volume in bread. *Cereal Chemistry*, **19**, 84–94.

Bent, A.J. (1998) Speciality fermented goods. In: *Technology of Breadmaking* (eds S.P. Cauvain and L.S. Young), pp. 214–39. Blackie Academic & Professional, London.

Bernardin, J.E. and Kasarda, D.D. (1973) Hydrated protein fibrils from wheat endosperm. *Cereal Chemistry*, **50**, 529–36.

de Boer, L., Heermans, C. and Meima, R. (2005) Reduction of acrylamide formation in bakery products using *Aspergillus niger* aspargine. In: *Using Cereal Science and Technology for the Benefit of Consumers* (eds S.P. Cauvain, S.E. Salmon and L.S. Young), pp. 401–05. Woodhead Publishing, Cambridge.

Bourne, M.C. (1990) Practical texture measurements of cereal foods. In: *Dough Rheology and Baked Product Texture* (eds H. Faridi and J.M. Faubion). Van Nostrand Reinhold, New York, NY.

Calvel, R. (2001) *The Taste Of Bread*. Aspen Publishers, Gaithersburg, MD.

Cauvain, S.P. (1991) Evaluating the texture of baked products. *South African Food Review*, **22**(2), 51, 53.

Cauvain, S.P. (1995) New mixer for variety bread production. *European Food and Drink Review*, Autumn, pp. 51–3.

Cauvain, S.P. (1998a) Dough retarding and freezing. In: *Technology of Breadmaking* (eds S.P. Cauvain and L.S. Young), pp. 149–79. Blackie Academic & Professional, London.

Cauvain, S.P. (1998b) Breadmaking processes. In: *Technology of Breadmaking* (eds S.P. Cauvain and L.S. Young), pp. 18–44. Blackie Academic & Professional, London

Cauvain, S.P. (2001a) Breadmaking. In: *Cereal Processing Technology* (ed. G. Owens), pp. 204–30. Woodhead Publishing, Cambridge.

Cauvain, S.P. (2001b) The production of laminated bakery products. *CCFRA Review No. 25*, CCFRA, Chipping Campden.

Cauvain, S.P. (2003) Breadmaking: an overview. In: *Breadmaking: Improving Quality* (ed. S.P. Cauvain), pp. 8–28. Woodhead Publishing, Cambridge.

Cauvain, S.P. (2004a) Improving the texture of bread. In: *Texture in Food, Volume 2: Solid Foods* (ed. D. Kilcast), pp. 432–50. Woodhead Publishing, Cambridge.

Cauvain, S.P. (2004b) How much more bread research do we need? *Getreidetechnologie*, **56**, 364–66.

Cauvain, S.P. and Chamberlain, N. (1988) The bread improving effect of fungal *alpha*-amylase. *Journal of Cereal Science*, **8**, 239–48.

Cauvain, S.P. and Cyster, J.A. (1996) Sponge cake technology, *CCFRA Review No. 2*, CCFRA, Chipping Campden.

Cauvain, S.P., Whitworth, M.B. and Alava, J.M. (1999) The evolution of bubble structure in bread doughs and its effect on bread structure. In: *Bubbles in Food* (eds G.M. Campbell, C. Webb, S.S. Pandiella and K. Niranjan), pp. 85–8. American Association of Cereal Chemists, St. Paul, MN.

Cauvain, S.P. and Young, L.S. (2000) *Bakery Food Manufacture and Quality: Water Control and Effects*. Blackwell Science, Oxford.

Cauvain, S.P. and Young, L.S. (2001) *Baking Problems Solved*. Woodhead Publishing, Cambridge.

Cauvain, S.P. and Young, L.S. (2006) *The Chorleywood Bread Process*. Woodhead Publishing, Cambridge.

CCFRA (2001) *Bread Advisor*, www.campden.co.uk.

CCFRA (2002) *Cake Expert System*, www.campden.co.uk.

CCFRA (2004) *Baking Technology Toolkit*, www.campden.co.uk.

Chamberlain, N. (1973) Microwave energy in the baking of bread. *Food Trade Review*, **43**(9), 8–12.

Chamberlain, N. (1979) Biscuit research at FMBRA, Chorleywood. *Proceedings of the Technical Conference of The Biscuit & Cracker Manufacturers Association*, London.

Chamberlain, N., Collins, T.H. and Elton, G.A.H. (1965) The Chorleywood bread process – improving effects of fat. *Cereal Science Today*, **10**, 415.

Chamberlain, N. and Collins, T.H. (1979) The Chorleywood Bread Process: the role of oxygen and nitrogen. *Bakers Digest*, **53**, 18–24.

Chin, N.L. and Campbell, G.M. (2005a) Dough aeration and rheology: Part 1. Effects of mixing speed and headspace pressure on mechanical development of bread dough. *Journal of Science of Food and Agriculture*, **85**, 2184–93.

Chin, N.L. and Campbell, G.M. (2005b) Dough aeration and rheology: Part 2. Effects of flour type, mixing speed and total work input on aeration and rheology of bread dough. *Journal of Science of Food and Agriculture*, **85**, 2194–202.

Chinachoti, P. (2003) Preventing bread staling. In: *Breadmaking: Improving Quality* (ed. S.P. Cauvain), pp. 562–74. Woodhead Publishing, Cambridge.

Cluskey, J.E., Taylor, N.W. and Senti, F.R. (1959) Relation of the rigidity of flour, starch and gluten gels to bread staling. *Cereal Chemistry*, **36**, 236–46.

Collins, T.H. (1993) Mixing, moulding and processing of doughs in the UK. *Bread – Breeding to Baking*, Proceedings of an International Conference, 1–16 June, 1993, pp. 77–83. FMBRA, Chorleywood, CCFRA, Chipping Campden.

Devlin, J.J. (1954) Recipe balance. *BBIRA Bulletin No. 39*, 60–4. CCFRA, Chipping Campden.

Farrand, E.A. (1964) Flour properties in relation to the modern bread processes in the United Kingdom, with special reference to *alpha*-amylase and starch damage. *Cereal Chemistry*, **41**, 98–111.

Hajselova, M. and Alldrick, A.J. (2003) Analysing wheat and flour. In: *Breadmaking: Improving Quality* (ed. S.P. Cauvain), pp. 187–89. Woodhead Publishing, Cambridge.

Hodge, D.G. and Cauvain, S.P. (1973) Sponge cake technology: Effect of level of emulsifier when using a planetary mixer. *FMBRA Report No. 58*, CCFRA, Chipping Campden.

ICC (1995) *Standard methods, 5th Supplement*, ICC, Vienna.

Jones, H.P. (1994) Ambient packaged cakes. In: *Shelf Life Evaluation of Foods* (eds C.M.D. Man and A.A. Jones), pp. 179–201. Blackie Academic & Professional, London.

Jones, G., McAughtrie, J. and Cunningham, K. (1997) Sugars. In: *The Technology of Cake Making*, 6th edn (ed. A. Bent), pp. 84–99. Blackie Academic & Professional, London.

Kamel, B.S. and Ponte, J.G. (1993) Emulsifiers in baking. In: *Advances in Baking Technology* (eds B.S. Kamel and C.E. Stauffer), pp. 179–222. Blackie Academic & Professional, London.

Katina, K. (2003) High fibre baking. In: *Breadmaking: Improving Quality* (ed. S.P. Cauvain), pp. 487–99. Woodhead Publishing, Cambridge.

Kilborn, R.H. and Tipples, K.H. (1974) Implications of the mechanical development of bread dough by means of sheeting rolls. *Cereal Chemistry*, **51**, 648–57.

Kilborn, R.H. and Tipples, K.H. (1975) 'Unmixin' – the disorientation of developed doughs by slow speed mixing. *Cereal Chemistry*, **52**, 248–62.

Kilcast, D. (2004) *Texture in Food, Volume 2: Solid Foods*. Woodhead Publishing, Cambridge.

Kulp, K., Lorenz, K. and Brummer, J. (1995) *Frozen & Refrigerated Dough and Batters*. American Association of Cereal Chemists, St. Paul, MN.

Man, C.M.D. and Jones, A.A. (1994) *Shelf Life Evaluation of Foods*. Blackie Academic & Professional, London.

Manley, D. (2000) *Technology of Biscuits, Crackers and Cookies*. Woodhead Publishing, Cambridge.

Marsh, D. (1998) Mixing and dough processing. In: *Technology of Breadmaking* (eds S.P. Cauvain and L.S. Young), pp. 81–119. Blackie Academic & Professional, London.

Marston, P.E. (1983) Moisture content and migration in bread incorporating dried fruit. *Food Technology Australia*, **35**, 463–65.

Millar, S. (2003) Controlling dough development. In: *Breadmaking: Improving Quality* (ed. S.P. Cauvain), pp. 401–23. Woodhead Publishing, Cambridge.

Munsell, A.H. (undated) *Munsell system of colour notation*. Macbeth, Baltimore.

Osborne, T.B. (1924) *The Vegetable Proteins*, 2nd edition. Longmans Green and Co., London.

Pateras, I.M.C. (1998) Bread spoilage and staling. In: *Technology of Breadmaking* (eds S.P. Cauvain and L.S. Young), pp. 240–61. Blackie Academic & Professional, London.

Petryszak, R., Young, L. and Cauvain, S. (1995) Improving cake product quality. In: *Applications and Innovations in Expert Systems III, Proceedings of Expert Systems 95, British Computer Society Specialist Group on Expert Systems* (eds A. Macintosh and C. Cooper), pp. 161–68. SGES Publications, Oxford.

Podmore, J. and Rajah, K.K. (1997) Baking fats. In: *The Technology Of Cake Making*, 6th edn (ed. A. Bent), pp. 25–49. Blackie Academic & Professional, London.

Pomeranz, Y. and Shellenberger, J.A. (1971) *Bread Science and Technology*. The Avi Publishing Company, Westport, CT.

Rask, C. (1989) Thermal properties of dough and bakery products: A review of published data. *Journal of Food Engineering*, **9**(3), 167–93.

Rogers, D.E., Day, D.D. and Olewnik, M.C. (1995) Development of an objective crumb-grain measurement. *Cereal Foods World*, **40**(7), 498–501.

Sahi, S.S. and Guy, R.C.E. (2005) New lipase functionality in bakery products. In: *Using Cereal Science and Technology for the Benefit of Consumers* (eds S.P. Cauvain, S.E. Salmon and L.S. Young), pp. 428–33. Woodhead Publishing, Cambridge.

Schoch, T.J. and French, D. (1947) Studies on bread staling. 1. The role of starch. *Cereal Chemistry*, **24**, 231–49.

Schiffmann, R.F. (1993) Microwave technology in baking. In: *Advances In Baking Technology* (eds B.S. Kamel and C.E. Stauffer), pp. 292–315. Blackie Academic & Professional, London.

Shrewry, P.R. and Miflin, B.J. (1985) Seed storage proteins of economically important cereals. In: *Advances in Cereal Science and Technology* (ed. Y. Pomeranz), Vol. 7, pp. 1–78. American Association of Cereal Chemists, St. Paul, MN.

Stauffer, C.E. (1998) Principles of dough formation. In: *Technology of Breadmaking* (eds S.P. Cauvain and L.S. Young), pp. 262–95. Blackie Academic & Professional, London.

Stauffer, C.E. (1999) *Fats and oils*. Eagan Press Handbook, AACC, St. Paul, MN.

Street, C.A. (1991) *Flour Confectionery Manufacture*. Blackie and Son Ltd., Glasgow.

Sugden, T.D. and Osborne, B.G. (2001) Wheat flour milling. In: *Cereals and cereal products* (eds D.A.V. Dendy and B.J. Dobraszcyk), pp. 140–81. Aspen Publishers, Inc., Gaithersburg, MD.

Taylor S. (1984) The mixing of short paste. *FMBRA Bulletin No. 5*, pp. 200–209. CCFRA, Chipping Campden.

Thacker, D. (1997) Chemical aeration. In: *The Technology of Cake Making*, 6th edn. (ed. A. Bent), pp. 100–106. Blackie Academic & Professional, London.

Thomas Hedley & Co. Ltd. (undated) *Formula Rebalance; New Principles, Up-To-Date Methods*. Thomas Hedley & Co. Ltd Research Bakery Department, Newcastle-upon-Tyne.

Webb, C. and Owens, G.W. (2003) Milling and flour quality. In: *Breadmaking: Improving Quality* (ed. S.P. Cauvain), pp. 200–219. Woodhead Publishing, Cambridge.

Wheelock, T.D. and Lancaster, E.B. (1970) Thermal properties of wheat flour. *Starke*, **22**, 44–8.

Whitworth, M.B., Cauvain, S.P. and Cliffe, D. (2005) Measurement of bread cell structure by image analysis. In: *Using Cereal Science and Technology for the Benefit of Consumers* (eds S.P. Cauvain, S.E. Salmon and L.S. Young), pp. 193–98. Woodhead Publishing, Cambridge.

Wieser, H. (2003) The use of redox agents. In: *Breadmaking: Improving Quality* (ed. S.P. Cauvain), pp. 424–46. Woodhead Publishing, Cambridge.

Wiggins, C. (1998) Proving, baking and cooling. In: *Technology of Breadmaking* (eds S.P. Cauvain and L.S. Young), pp. 120–48. Blackie Academic & Professional, London.

Wilde, P. (2003) Foam formation in dough and bread quality. In: *Breadmaking: Improving Quality* (ed. S.P. Cauvain), pp. 321–51. Woodhead Publishing Ltd., Cambridge.

Wilhoft, E.M.A. (1973) Recent developments on the bread staling problem. *Bakers' Digest*, **47**(6), 14–21.

Williams, T. and Pullen, G. (1998) Functional ingredients. In: *Technology of Breadmaking* (eds S.P. Cauvain and L.S. Young), pp. 45–80. Blackie Academic & Professional, London.

Young, L.S. (1998) Application of knowledge-based systems. In: *Technology of Breadmaking* (eds S.P. Cauvain and L.S. Young), pp. 180–88. Blackie Academic & Professional, London.

Young, L.S. and Cauvain S.P. (1994) Advising the Baker. In: *Applications and Innovations in Expert Systems II, Proceedings of Expert Systems 94* (eds R. Milne and A. Montgomery), pp. 21–33. *British Computer Society Specialist Group on Expert Systems*, SGES Publications, Oxford.

Young, L.S., Davies, P.R. and Cauvain, S.P. (1998) Cakes – getting the right balance. *Applications and Innovations in Expert Systems VI, Proceedings of Expert Systems 98*, pp. 42–55. *British Computer Society Specialist Group on Expert Systems*, Springer–Verlag, London.

Young, L.S., Davies, P.R., Cauvain, S.P. (2001) Rise again, fair knowledge. *Applications and Innovations in Expert Systems IX, Proceedings of Expert Systems 2001*, pp. 89–99. *British Computer Society Specialist Group on Expert Systems*, Springer-Verlag, London.

Further reading

There are many books on baked products, some of which have been referred to at appropriate points in the text. The following list is provided for readers who wish to explore further the extensive literature that has been devoted to baked products. A number of the titles on the list were used in research for the production of this book.

Popular literature

Bailey, A. (1975) *The Blessing Of Bread*. Paddington Ltd., London.

David, E. (1977) *English Bread and Yeast Cookery*. Allen Lane, London.

Davidson, S. (1991) *Loaf, Crust and Crumb*. Michael Joseph Ltd., London.

Ingram, C. (1999) *Breads of the World*. Lorenz Books, New Lorenz Books, New York, NY.

Manufacture of bread and fermented goods

Kamel, B.S. and Stauffer, C.E. (1993) *Advances in Baking Technology*. Blackie Academic & Professional, London.

Cauvain, S.P. and Young, L.S. (1998) *Technology of Breadmaking*. Blackie Academic & Professional, London.

Cauvain, S.P. and Young, L.S. (2001) *Baking Problems Solved*. Woodhead Publishing, Cambridge.

Cauvain, S.P. and Young, L.S. (2006) *The Chorleywood Bread Process*. Woodhead Publishing, Cambridge.

Manufacture of cakes

Street, C.A. (1991) *Flour Confectionery Manufacture*. Blackie and Son Ltd., Glasgow.

Bent, A. (1997) *The Technology Of Cake Making*, 6th edn. Blackie Academic & Professional, London.

Cauvain, S.P. and Young, L.S. (2001) *Baking Problems Solved*. Woodhead Publishing, Cambridge.

Manufacture of pastes

Cauvain, S.P. and Young, L.S. (2001) *Baking Problems Solved*. Woodhead Publishing, Cambridge.

Manufacture of biscuits and cookies

Manley, D. (2000) *Technology of Biscuits, Crackers and Cookies*. Woodhead Publishing, Cambridge.

Ingredients used in baking

Kamel, B.S. and Stauffer, C.E. (1993) *Advances in Baking Technology*. Blackie Academic & Professional, London.

Cauvain, S.P. and Young, L.S. (2000) *Bakery Food Manufacture and Quality: Water Control and Effects*. Blackwell Science, Oxford.

Cauvain, S.P. and Young, L.S. (2001) *Baking Problems Solved*. Woodhead Publishing, Cambridge.

Cereal science and technology

Faridi, H. and Faubion, J.M. (1990) *Dough Rheology and Baked Products Texture*. Van nostrand Reinhold, New York.

Lorenz, K.J and Kulp, K. (1991) *Handbook of Cereal Science and Technology*. Marcel Dekker Inc., New York.

Kent, N.L and Evers, A.D. (1994) *Technology of Cereals*, 4th edn. Elsevier Science, Oxford.

Dendy, D.A.V. and Dobraszcyk, B.J. (2001) *Cereals and Cereal Products*, pp.140–81. Aspen Publishers, Gaithersburg, MD.

Cauvain, S.P., Salmon, S.E. and Young, L.S. (2005) *Using cereal science and technology for the benefit of consumers, Proceedings of the 12th International ICC Cereal and Bread Congress, 23–26 May, 2004, Harrogate, UK*. Woodhead Publishing, Cambridge.

General food technology

Hardman, T.M. (1989) *Water and Food Quality*. Elsevier Applied Science, Barking.

Campbell, G.M., Webb, C., Pandiella, S.S. and Niranjan, K. (1999) *Bubbles in Food*. American Association of Cereal Chemists, St. Paul, MN.

Toussaint-Samat, M. (1992) *History of Food*. Blackwell Publishing, Oxford.

Index